Chapter 1
The Edwardian Navy

As the nineteenth century drew to its close Great Britain had reason to be proud of its navy. Not only was the Royal Navy the strongest in the world by an impressive margin, it was also heir to a hidden reservoir of maritime strength. Ever since the end of the Napoleonic Wars Great Britain had operated a large and effective mercantile marine.

Supporting these two national assets was Britain's massive industrial strength, which enabled British shipbuilders and designers to lead the world. When iron and steel began to replace wood in the 1860s Great Britain became in effect shipbuilder to the world, designing and building the most advanced warships and merchant ships for export. Rivals, particularly France and Russia, did their best to match Britain's strength by innovative design but always the efficiency of British shipyards enabled them to build faster and cheaper than any rival.

Although beset by a number of 'war scares' the Royal Navy had enjoyed decades of virtually unchallenged superiority, and the result was a cycle of slow decline followed by rapid building programmes to catch up. In the mid-1880s, however, the latest Russian war-scare ushered in a new phase. Russia and France were now allies, and their combined fleets were superior to the Royal Navy; not only did the two navies possess more ships but their combined building programmes exceeded that of the Royal Navy.

Britain's riposte was the Naval Defence Act of 1889, which authorized a huge construction programme to put the Royal Navy on a 'Two-Power Standard' – equal to a combination of the next two largest navies.

The Naval Defence Act heralded other reforms. Under the aegis of Sir William White, a leading

PREVIOUS PAGE: *HMS Benbow, with her two single 16.25-inch guns, was one of a dying breed of Victorian battleships, overtaken by rapid progress in guns and armour.*

BELOW: *HMS Hannibal, one of White's aptly named* Majestic *class, which set new standards of fighting power.*

HISTORY OF THE
ROYAL
NAVY
in the 20th century

HISTORY OF THE
ROYAL
NAVY
in the 20th century

Editor: Antony Preston

PRESIDIO

A Bison Book

Published in the United States by
Presidio Press
31 Pamaron Way
Novato, CA 94947

Produced by
Bison Books Corp.
15 Sherwood Place
Greenwich, CT 06830
U.S.A.

ISBN 0-89141-283-2

Printed in Hong Kong

Contributors

Antony Preston Naval historian, writer, editor
and broadcaster. Until recently Naval Editor of
Jane's Defence Weekly, he has written numerous
books, including *Sea Combat off the Falklands*,
Destroyers, *History of the Royal Navy*, *Navies of
World War III* and *Send a Gunboat*, among
others (Introduction, Chapters 1, 4, 6, 10).

David Lyon Research Assistant at the National
Maritime Museum, specialising in ship-design,
naval ordnance and in particular the late
Victorian and Edwardian Navy. He is the author
of the *Sail to Steam* volume of the NMM's
History of the Ship series, and has written many
articles, reviews and monographs (Chapter 2).

Philip Annis Former Deputy Director of the
National Maritime Museum, and world
authority on British naval uniforms, swords and
decorations. He is currently working on the
latest volume of the history of the Royal
Artillery and is the author of numerous articles
and reviews (Chapter 3).

Hugh Lyon An expert on British naval
shipbuilders and the technical history of the
Royal Navy in the 19th and 20th Centuries. He
has written many articles and reviews, and
contributed a chapter to *Technology and Change
in the Royal Navy*. He also conducted the survey
of British Maritime Records (Chapter 5).

Colin G Wood A former civil servant who has
specialized in technical history, particularly the
Royal Navy in the two World Wars. He is
currently working as a consultant and naval
technical writer (Chapter 7).

Desmond Wettern Naval author and former
naval correspondent of the *Daily Telegraph*. He
has written *The Lonely Battle* and *The Decline of
British Seapower*, plus many reviews and articles.
He is an authority on the Royal Navy since the
Second World War, and served in the Royal
Navy and the RNR (Chapter 8).

Anthony J Watts Naval author and editor. He
has been editor of *NAVY International* since
1978 and has written several books, including
The Imperial Japanese Navy (with Brian
Gordon), *The U Boat Hunters* and *Battle for the
Falklands*. (Chapter 9).

Page 1: A British sailor operates an Aldis lamp on
board an RN warship during World War II.
Pages 2-3: A spectacular view of the Type 42
destroyer HMS *Manchester*.
This page: A cross-section of modern NATO
destroyers and anti-submarine escorts, including
HMS *Norfolk* (rear right in the formation).

Contents

Introduction

PREVIOUS PAGE: *One of the great battles of the Second Anglo-Dutch War, the Four Days' Fight of 1666.*

BELOW: *A scene from the English attack on the Spanish Armada. The failure of the Armada dashed Philip II's attempt to invade England and marked the arrival of a British navy on the world scene.*

The history of Great Britain is inextricably linked with the sea. As far back as the days of the Roman occupation the 'Count of the Saxon Shore' was charged with defending the southern coast against marauders from the sea. The later Saxon chronicles record that King Alfred did not inflict serious damage on the Viking invaders until he constructed a fleet of ships. That formidable soldier King Harold might have defeated the Norman invasion had he been able to prevent William the Conqueror from crossing the Channel so easily.

Time and time again the descendants of Alfred and Harold were to pay a heavy price for neglecting their seaward defences, and British history is punctuated with a series of recurring invasion 'scares'. While it is not true to say that enemy forces never again landed on British soil, it is indisputable that no invasion has *succeeded* since 1066. This is, however, usually a reflection on the incompetence or the incapacity of the would-be invaders rather than any continuing commitment to a strong navy.

Even Queen Elizabeth I, who did so much to inspire her subjects during the confrontation with Spain, proved very niggardly when it came to finding money for a permanent fleet of men 'o war. Her father King Henry VIII had left a well-found fleet,

as modern as any in Europe, but by 1588 the Spanish Armada was opposed only by a small number of 'Queen's Ships', reinforced by armed merchantmen. Had the Armada not been ravaged by scurvy and typhus before it met Howard and Drake in the Channel the result might have been very different. However, those few English ships held their own in skirmishes, their skilful use of fireships broke the Armada's tight formation and storms did the rest. The foundations were laid for what was to become a tradition of victory, often against heavy odds. The defeat of the Armada was the first national naval victory. There was as yet no British nation and no Royal Navy, but 1588 marked a very distinct stage in their development.

Queen Elizabeth's navy was soon allowed to decay and King James I brought disaster on his kingdom by a policy of quixotic high-mindedness, reducing the navy to the point where it could not protect shipping against attacks from privateers. His successor, Charles I, sought to remedy the neglect but his ill-judged attempt to levy Ship Money pushed his unruly subjects into revolution.

The English Civil War is usually described as a land war, but in one sense it was decided at sea. The refusal of the navy to join the Royalist cause made it

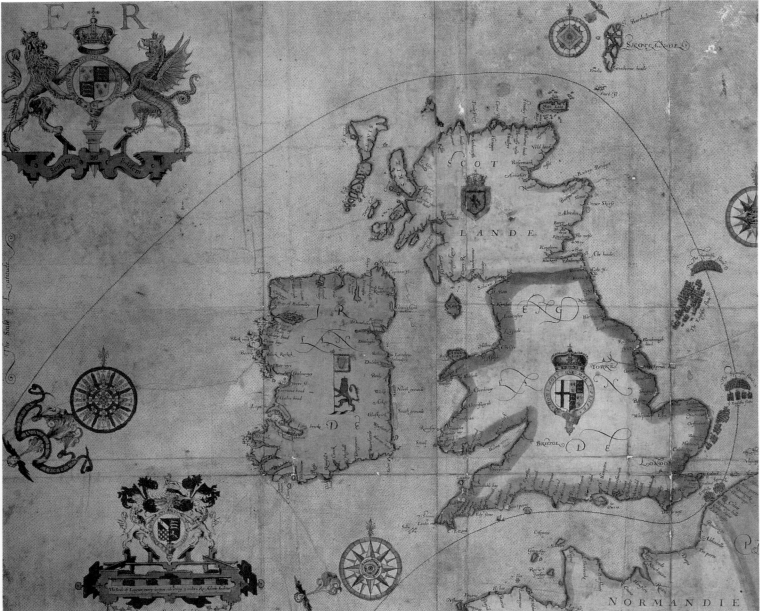

ABOVE: *A contemporary map depicting the route of the Armada around the British Isles.*

impossible for the King's supporters in Europe to intervene. Even when part of the navy subsequently turned against the Parliamentary side, sufficient ships and men remained loyal to deter foreign interference.

Ironically the Parliamentary victory resulted in a far heavier scale of taxation to raise money for new warships. This new Commonwealth Navy was an ideal instrument of policy for the new strong man who emerged, Oliver Cromwell. Like other dictators faced with rising unpopularity at home, Cromwell focused discontent on a convenient foreign enemy, the Dutch.

What distinguished the First Dutch War, which started in 1652, was the appearance of a whole class of soldiers appointed to the navy to make good the loss of Royalist officers. The 'Generals at Sea' were much more successful than anyone expected, and apart from winning battles, they imposed much needed tactical discipline.

The restoration of King Charles II saw the formal creation of the 'Royal' Navy, for behind the mask of profligacy was a shrewd thinker who could see the value of a fleet loyal to the Monarch rather

than Parliament. This was the formal start of the Royal Navy, with its unusual constitutional position, denoted by the prefix 'His Majesty's Ship'.

The King and his now-loyal Parliament were lucky that the Commonwealth had built a powerful fleet, for within a year or two the Second Dutch War broke out. As before the battles were fierce and bloody, for the Dutch were doughty fighters. The war went well, but an amazing act of folly reversed fortunes. To save money the King and his Ministers ordered the Fleet to be laid up in reserve, pending a favourable outcome to the peace negotiations.

Everybody forgot that the Dutch, under their greatest admiral de Ruyter were longing to avenge a particularly destructive raid on their shipping the year before. In June 1667 de Ruyter's forces destroyed several large ships at Chatham and threw the government and the nation into a five-day panic. Peace was signed at Breda a month later on considerably better terms than the Dutch deserved.

Despite this humiliation the Royal Navy and its adminstrative bodies, the Admiralty Board and the Navy Board, were developing on sound lines. The King's younger brother, the Duke of York proved an able administrator, aided by the Clerk of the Acts to the Navy Board, Samuel Pepys. Master and servant transformed the administrative machinery, laying down the foundation for another 200 years of development.

The Royal Navy was to fight yet another war before the Dutch were eliminated as Great Britain's main commercial rival. The next century was devoted to the elimination of two more rivals, France and Spain. It might be expected that the experience of the seventeenth century and the sound principles of administration bequeathed by Pepys would generate a series of brilliant victories. However this was not to be.

The first half of the new century was marred by excessive centralization taking the form of rigid Fighting Instructions and rigid control of ship-design, to say nothing of political directions.

No worse example can be cited than the story of Admiral Byng. His attempt to relieve the island base of Minorca in 1756 was frustrated by a large French force, and rather than disobey the standing instructions not to break the line of battle, he returned to Gibraltar. Minorca fell, and Byng was court-martialled for cowardice and negligence. Although he was acquitted on the major charge, he was found guilty of negligence and sentenced to death (the death sentence had been mandatory since 1749). The King was under political pressure not to reprieve poor Byng, who met his death by firing squad *pour encourager les autres*.

To modern eyes it seems little short of miraculous that the Royal Navy could breed officers and men capable of rising above such a system. Certainly the Seven Years' War showed that the combination of a government with a clear vision of how to use sea power and flag-officers capable of using the loophole of 'Additional Instructions' to evade the strait-jacket of the Fighting Instructions could produce brilliant results.

Although overshadowed by the later Revolutionary and Napoleonic Wars, the Seven Years' War is one of the Royal Navy's greatest periods. Combined operations, known today as amphibious warfare, proved highly successful. Under the strategic direction of William Pitt the Elder, the Royal Navy won a string of victories which laid the foundation of a large colonial empire.

In their conflict with the rebellious American colonies in 1776-83 the British had the misfortune to encounter a revitalized French Navy. The very nature of the conflict, a protracted land campaign at the end of long supply-lines, subjected the British military machine to maximum stress. When France and her allies took up the cause of the American colonists the Royal Navy was hard-pressed to protect shipping and to support the Army in North America. Although the Royal Navy never lost a major battle during this conflict it suffered at the hands of skilled commerce-raiding, and it failed to prevent important French troop reinforcements from reaching America. It also failed in the crucial task of relieving the garrison of Yorktown, which was then forced to surrender.

LEFT: *The three-decker* Royal Prince. *Built in 1670 she was rebuilt in 1694 and renamed* Royal William *after the then monarch of England.*

BELOW LEFT: *Typical gundeck in a large 18th-century man of war. The seamen slung their hammocks and ate their meals between the guns.*

BELOW: *The Battle of Copenhagen, 2 April 1801. The Danes capitulated as soon as Nelson's ships subdued the fire of the shore batteries, for his ships were now free to move within range of the city.*

Although the Battle of the Chesapeake in September 1781 was tactically no more than a draw, it was a strategic defeat, for the surrender of Cornwallis and his starving troops broke the will of the British Government to continue the conflict. The war was not over, but it was no longer winnable.

Having lost one strategic battle the Royal Navy redeemed itself by bringing the war to a close on terms which, if not satisfactory, were less harmful to British interests. The defeat of the main French fleet at the Battle of the Saintes in the West Indies in April 1782 strengthened the hands of the negotiators at the peace conference, allowing them to retain Canada.

Despite the humiliations of the American War the Royal Navy had not done badly, and it put the experience to good use. Its younger captains gained invaluable experience, and its adminstration was thoroughly overhauled. When war broke out against France once more in 1793 the Navy made a rapid transition from its usual run-down state to a reasonable state of efficiency. The economic situation in Britain was also very different from what it had been in 1776, under the influence of the Industrial Revolution whereas France's economic power was stagnating.

As the war dragged on there were disappointments and even very serious problems, notably the mutinies at the Nore and Spithead in 1797. But the spirit of the Navy was strong enough to survive these difficulties, as proved by the performance of the Nore ships against the Dutch at the Battle of Camperdown, shortly after the end of the mutiny. It was the bloodiest battle of the war, and one of the most decisive; it destroyed the Dutch as a first naval

power. The Channel Fleet also returned to its duties cheerfully once its grievances were settled. Although the war gave Nelson his chance, and his three great victories of St Vincent, the Nile and Trafalgar established him as the greatest British sea-captain of all time, there was a whole galaxy of lesser talents. It is said that when the First Lord, Barham, offered Nelson the pick of the Navy's captains for his final campaign against the Franco-Spanish Combined Fleet in 1805, Nelson refused, saying that he would win with whoever he had under his command.

Trafalgar was a brilliant victory, essentially simple in concept but masterly in its subtlety. At the end of the day Nelson was dead but he had destroyed Napoleon Bonaparte's last chance of invading England. The war dragged on another 10 years, but Great Britain was to grow steaily more prosperous, enabling her to subsidise and support the European opponents of France. By 1814 the Royal Navy ruled the seven seas and British military power was brought to bear at any point where it was needed.

It was fortunate that the immense wealth and naval power of Great Britain did not tempt her rulers into establishing themselves as the new overlords of Europe. For this we must thank the new doctrines of Free Trade and a new political philosophy which preached that material progress would eliminate the need for 'bloated armaments'. The Royal Navy would not be abolished, but its mighty three-deckers and two-deckers would slowly reduce in numbers, being replaced by a trickle of smaller warships better suited to protect international (mostly British) maritime trade.

The *Pax Britannica* was a phenomenon which owed much to forces which were never clearly understood at the time, but in practice it meant that the Royal Navy acted as a 'world policeman', putting down slavery, surveying the oceans and generally encouraging trade. It was by no means a totally peaceful role, and British ships often intervened to enforce the rules of Free Trade, but it did not result in large-scale conquests of new territories. As steamships came into wider use a number of coaling stations were acquired, and armed intervention was usually limited to punitive expeditions or retaliatory bombardments.

It goes without saying that very little money was spent on the Fleet, but from 1814 onwards there was slow but sure technical progress. The first steamships were laid down in 1821, iron hulls were introduced in the 1840s and shell guns were quickly copied from the French.

Nelson was mortally wounded on the quarterdeck of his flagship Victory, *but the Battle of Trafalgar was already won. Dighton's painting depicts the moment Nelson was hit by a musket ball from the* Redoubtable's *mizzen top.*

His uniform and many medals made Nelson an obvious target for enemy sharpshooters.

The biggest problem for nineteenth-century naval planners was the lack of practical experience. Tactics were thrown into disarray by the introduction of steam, yet there was no major naval action for nearly 50 years after Trafalgar. Those few actions which did take place gave no clues to future development. In the Crimean War the Navy maintained itself and supported shore operations with commendable efficiency, but never met the Russian Fleet in action.

The Crimean War of 1853-6 accelerated progress remarkably, despite the comparatively minor role of the Navy. It saw the first use of rifled guns and armour, and for the first time large numbers of steamships operated together.

Although the French succeeded in getting ironclad batteries to sea first, the idea came from the Royal Navy, which went a step further, building iron-hulled batteries. For the first time 'floating factories' or support ships appeared. Even more significant was the fact that the health of the Navy's men remained better than the Army's, even when warships were used to transport sick troops from Balaclava to Scutari. In the Baltic the Navy encountered Russian mines for the first time, and devised ways to sweep them.

After the war the main rival was now France, clearly trying to challenge British naval superiority with a fleet of ironclads. The Admiralty's response was crushing; two very powerful iron-hulled ships were built at great speed, superior in protection, gunpower and speed. One of this pair, HMS *Warrior* survives, and has recently been restored to its original condition.

The country's industrial resources were harnessed to create a new ironclad fleet to match the French. Within a short time the pre-Crimean Navy had been replaced by a new fleet of ships, many of them experimental, but in sufficiently large numbers to preserve the Navy's pre-eminent position. It was the heyday of 'gunboat diplomacy', when small warships were often the only British presence on foreign stations, under the command of the most junior officers.

Such a period of effortless supremacy carried with it an inevitable conceit. Generations of naval officers (and to some extent the nation as well) came

to believe that the Royal Navy was destined to be the World's Policeman by divine right. During the 1870s and 1880s it became obvious that few senior officers had any grasp of strategy, or anything more than an elementary grasp of tactics. It therefore came as a shock to find in the 1880s that other nations were beginning to catch up in the art of ship-design, and reforms were instituted.

The reforms of the 1880s were far-reaching. The old Surveyor's Department was replaced by a new Director of Naval Construction's Department. The Navy won back control of gun-design and manufacture from the Army, and a Naval Intelligence Department was established for the first time.

Even more important was the revival of public interest in the Navy. In 1884 the *Pall Mall Gazette* ran a series of articles called 'The Truth about the

BELOW: *New methods of building-up guns enabled gunmakers to build much larger guns from the 1860s onwards.*

BREECH-LOADING WINS

Breech coil

Trunnion

Cascable

'C' coil

'B' tube

'C' tube

ABOVE: *One of the frigate battles of the War of 1812: the US ship* Constitution *overpowers the smaller HMS* Java *after an epic sea fight.*

RIGHT: *HMS* Bouncer, *one of many gunboats which enforced the Pax Britannica in the 19th century.*

Navy', to challenge official complacency. A year later it was revealed that there had been endless delays in mobilizing the Fleet during a war-scare.

By the mid-1880s the science of warship design had advanced beyond the stage of a 'Fleet of Samples', and it was possible for the Navy to embark on a new policy of series production of various classes. All that was missing was public will, but the nation was swept by a new enthusiasm for empire. The public support for Imperialist policies could be matched by industrial capacity.

The Naval Defence Act of 1889 marked a turning point. The Royal Dockyards had been modernized to enable them to cope with an accelerated building programme, and Parliament was prepared to vote money to build 70 new warships over a period of five years. These ships, eight 1st Class battleships, two 2nd Class battleships, nine 1st Class cruisers, 29 2nd Class cruisers, four 3rd class cruisers and 18 torpedo gunboats were to be the main strength of the Navy at the turn of the century.

What nobody knew was that the Victorian Age and the British Empire had already reached its zenith. Despite the rise of jingoism and the 'Scramble for Africa' the Empire was threatened. Commercial rivals were attacking Britain's markets, and a dangerous new rival, Germany, was laying the foundations for its own naval expansion.

The high noon of the Victorian Navy was Queen Victoria's Diamond Jubilee in 1897. Anchored in four lines were more than 25 miles of ships, covering an area of some five square miles. This fleet of some 150 warships including 22 battleships, over 40 cruisers and 20 torpedo boats, and yet not a single unit had been withdrawn from any of the foreign stations. If the Victorian Navy was overbearing it had good reason, for this mighty assembly included the most powerful ships in the world.

RIGHT: *Admiral Sir John Fisher, who spearheaded the drive to modernise the Victorian Navy.*

naval designer who was recalled from private industry, the Royal Dockyards were overhauled and modernized to make them more efficient than private shipyards. Under White's guidance the Royal Corps of Naval Constructors produced a new generation of battleships and cruisers without equal. In place of the hotchpotch of experimental designs, the 'fleet of samples' built since the Crimean War, White produced large classes of homogeneous ships, cheaper to build and cheaper to maintain. In the early 1890s two Royal Dockyards, Chatham and Portsmouth, established record building-times for battleships.

Industrial progress had much to do with the new confidence in warship design. Steelworks and gun factories produced better armour plate and more powerful guns, while chemists played their part in producing better propellants. Marine engineering made rapid advances, with new boilers and lighter machinery driving ships at higher speeds.

The gun still dominated naval warfare but other contenders were coming to the fore. The automotive 'fish' torpedo had been developed by the Royal Navy in the early 1860s but various constraints prevented the weapon from realizing its potential for another 20 years. By the late 1880s the Royal Navy found itself hoist by its own petard; having pioneered the steam-powered torpedo boat, it was in turn threatened by large numbers of French torpedo boats.

After a few false starts the answer was found, the torpedo boat destroyer (soon shortened to the now-familar destroyer). Characteristically the Admiralty gave two leading torpedo boat builders a broad specification, out of which came two successful prototypes, and a spate of orders from a wide range of builders. The destroyer was so successful that within a decade it had replaced the torpedo boat.

Another challenger of the big ship was the mine, which had been tried in various forms for as long as gunpowder had been available. By the end of the century it had become reliable enough to be a standard feature in modern navies' armouries, although little thought was given to methods of countering it.

The submarine was still in its infancy, waiting only for improvements in propulsion to transform it from an amusing toy into a serious weapon of war. Typically the Royal Navy had watched French, Russian, American, Swedish and even Spanish experiments, without showing much enthusiasm; several primitive submersibles had even been built in British yards for foreign navies. As with the shell-gun and the ironclad, it made sense to let others carry out risky experiments, and wait until a successful design emerged.

The late Victorian Navy was technically innovative, whatever later critics may suggest, but tactical thought had not kept pace. Without doubt the Royal Navy reflected the vices as well as the virtues of contemporary British society. The unchallenged supremacy of the nineteenth century had made the Navy insular, snobbish and suspicious of social change. The education of officers was narrow and the whole officer corps was drawn from too narrow a

social group for its own good. And yet, it must be said that the Royal Navy was undoubtedly better-placed than its rivals to meet the challenge of the twentieth century.

Many harsh things have been said about the Victorian Navy, suggesting that it was a gin- and snobbery-ridden exclusive yacht club, whose officers preferred to throw shells overboard rather than let gunnery practice damage the paintwork. Much of this lurid criticism comes from over-zealous propagandists in the Edwardian period, anxious to present themselves as naval reformers. According to them the Dark Ages ended in 1904, when Admiral Sir John Fisher became First Sea Lord.

While Fisher deserves his reputation as a reformer and modernizer, his achievements must not be distorted. He inherited a Victorian Navy which had confidence and experience, as well as superb industrial support. However, the period 1900-14 was to be characterized by a pace of technical change which was even faster than the period 1885 1900. At the same time, a new and more dangerous rival emerged, complicating the Royal Navy's political and strategic problems.

Fisher had been the Navy's most fervent technocrat 30 years earlier, and he made no secret of his determination to shake the Navy to its foundations, to meet the German threat. On taking office in 1904 his first act was to set up a Committee on Designs to consider new warship designs, larger and more powerful than anything seen before.

The first fruit of Fisher's Committee was the battleship *Dreadnought*, which gave her name to a whole era of warship design. Although she was no more than the culmination of a number of trends, by bringing them together in one hull and ensuring that she was built in the record time of 14 months, Fisher caught the imagination of the public. Once that was assured, political support for his reforms was much easier to achieve.

The secret of the *Dreadnought* was the adoption of steam turbine machinery; the weight saved could be devoted to a massive armament of 10 12-inch guns (as against four in previous battleships), and speed went up from 18 to 21 knots. The 250 per cent increase in gunpower had more to it than mere bombast: a bigger broadside of 12-inch shells made it easier to correct gunfire at long range.

As late as 1903 the battle range was still 3000-4000 yards, not, as some supposed, because Victorian admirals were too conservative to think otherwise, but because the older fast-burning gunpowders made it difficult to predict the fall of shot at anything beyond this range. Only when new slow-burning nitrocellulose propellants were perfected, and new optical rangefinders were available, could gunnery officers hope to hit targets up to 10 miles away. Even with these aids the only way to correct shooting was by observing the giant splashes made by large shells falling around the target.

Fisher's committee next created a more lightly protected but faster big-gun ship. Intended to replace the large armoured cruisers built at the turn of the century, the new ship was first designated a *Dreadnought*-type armoured cruiser, but some years later the even more ambiguous term 'battlecruiser' was bestowed on her. She was a hybrid, with two 12-inch guns fewer than the *Dreadnought* but with the unheard-of speed of 25 ½ knots.

To Fisher the *Invincible* and her two sisters seemed much more potent fighting ships than the *Dreadnought*, but their armour belts were five inches thinner. To convince himself Fisher coined the phrase 'armour is speed', suggesting that the battlecruiser would be able to avoid punishment from a battleship by using her margin of speed to stay out of range. Time was to show that the *Invincible* and her successors were a magnificent technical achievement, but they were, however, flawed by a fatal misconception about naval warfare. As hybrids the battlecruisers had no clear-cut role, and came to be treated as fast battleships. The term 'capital ship' used to cover both battlecruiser and battleships did nothing to help.

Fisher used his formidable influence to improve destroyer design by introducing oil fuel, but the first examples were flimsy and short-lived. The problem lay in Fisher's impatience; the specialist firms were given no time to prepare detailed proposals and little evaluation was done. The ships of the resulting Tribal Class were hardly a major addition to the Navy's strength, for their tactical weaknesses outweighed their nominal advantage in speed. Succeeding designs were forced to revert to the previous well-tried formula of modest speed and robust, weatherly hulls.

Cruiser design suffered less if only because Fisher despised the cruiser as a ship 'too weak to fight, and too slow to run away'. He was convinced that future naval warfare required only the battlecruiser and the super-destroyer.

The Royal Navy finally made up its mind about submarines in 1901, when the successful Holland design was bought from the United States. Although Fisher was enthusiastic about them, he envisaged their main role as coastal and harbour

LEFT: *HMS* Indomitable, *one of the first 'Dreadnought armoured cruisers', later upgraded to battlecruisers.*

ABOVE: *The* Dreadnought's *uncompromising profile marked a complete break with the elegance and balance of the White era.*

RIGHT: *HMS* Terrible *and her sister* Powerful *were huge protected cruisers, contemporaries of the* Majestic *class battleships.*

defence, seeing little use for them in the offensive role. Curiously, for a man who had made his name as an expert in mine warfare 35 years earlier, he used submarines as an excuse to get rid of the harbour-defence mining organization. Although the Royal Navy quickly became the world's major submarine operator, the submarines were all small boats of modest capability.

Where Fisher's reforms showed to much greater effect was in the field of education and training. He and his disciples recognized that education in civilian life was raising the expectations of sailors. Opportunity for promotion and specialist training did much to improve the Navy as a career for the long-serving man on the lower deck, and a start was made in promoting exceptionally gifted senior ratings to officers.

Although many of the attitudes of the Edwardian Navy seem archaic and repressive to us today, they must always be compared with contemporary attitudes ashore. What cannot be denied is that the lower deck regarded Fisher as their champion, and by 1914 many minor iniquities and injustices had been swept away. Pay and conditions were not good but to both officers and men the 'Andrew' offered security and a sense of belonging which kept morale high. When put to the supreme test of war Royal Navy morale did not collapse, whereas in 1917 the

German Navy experienced the first of a series of mutinies culminating in the events of November 1918. An organization of such complexity could hardly be expected to have no pockets of poor performance or disaffection but taken overall the morale and loyalty of the Edwardian Navy was remarkably high, as countless contemporary accounts testify.

The Arms Race

The German Navy, under its equally dynamic chief, Grossadmiral Alfred von Tirpitz, had thrown down the gauntlet by the passage of a series of Navy Laws. What Tirpitz had wanted was a commitment by the Reichstag to a long-term building programme, but it had the effect of alarming British opinion. The building of the *Dreadnought* brought the rivalry to a new pitch; by making the enormous preponderance of the pre-dreadnought battleships out-of-date, she caused Anglo-German naval rivalry to be reduced to a simple totting-up of dreadnoughts. This in turn led to artificial devices such as upgrading British battlecruisers to 'capital ships', and projected German armoured cruisers being classed as battlecruisers.

With her vast shipbuilding industry, it was a race that Great Britain could hardly lose but the cost would be enormous. At a time when the Liberal

ABOVE: *This view of a stokehold gives no impression of the terrible heat in the boiler rooms of a large coal-fired warship.*

ABOVE: *The battleship* Swiftsure *and a sister were bought from Chile in 1904 to prevent them falling into Russian hands.*

Government was dedicated to a long-overdue programme of social reform the Opposition and the Navy League could chant 'We Want Eight and We Won't Wait'. No matter that the rumours of secret dreadnought-building in Germany turned out to be untrue. The *Dreadnought* did not start Anglo-German rivalry but her name became part of the language of war-fever and jingoism.

A further unfortunate side-effect was to stampede the Royal Navy into a hurried building programme, before the *Dreadnought* and the *Invincible* designs could be properly evaluated. Six more battleships, only slight improvements over the prototype, were laid down and three more battlecruisers with all the faults of the *Invincible*, nor were the following designs much better; but such was Fisher's pride in his creations that nobody dared utter public criticism. To make matters worse, Fisher's love of publicity led him to leak false information to the press, crediting his battlecruisers with considerably more fighting power than they possessed.

The Fisher Age came to an end in 1910 when the old man retired. His virtual embargo on cruisers was lifted, for it was widely recognized that the long shipping routes of the Empire needed modern cruisers, and the Fleet needed fast scouting ships. Fisher's super-destroyer, HMS *Swift* proved far too

flimsy even for destroyer duties and quite useless for scouting; more to the point she was extremely expensive.

Time was running out but there was still time to rebuild a balanced navy. The design of battleships began to show signs of improvement and in 1911 the new First Lord of the Admiralty recognized the weakness of the battlecruiser, admitting that the future lay in faster battleships. Out of this new thinking came the magnificent *Queen Elizabeth* Class battleships, armed with 15-inch guns and using oil fuel instead of coal. Before them, the adoption of the 13.5-inch gun had given the Royal Navy a lead over the Germans, but the 1912 decision to go for 15-inch guns secured a commanding lead, just in time.

Cruiser building started again, and a series of sturdy 6-inch gunned ships was built, suitable for protecting commerce and fleet-scouting duties with the Fleet. A new class of fast, lightly armoured cruisers was then begun in 1912. Both types were to prove their worth in wartime.

After the shaky start with the 'Tribal' Class, destroyer design settled down again and by 1914 destroyers had an enviable reputation for seaworthiness and fighting power. As with the cruisers, the soundness of the design was reflected in the fact that very few improvements had to be made when standard wartime production started.

Submarine design had languished in the dol-drums as a result of the monopoly exercised by Vickers. Dissatisfaction with modest performance led the Submarine Service to break the monopoly and to invite foreign firms to tender. This bold step came to nothing as the French and Italian pro-totypes were delivered too late; the eve of war was not the right time to start an elaborate trials pro-gramme; these 'oddballs' were given to Italy in 1915.

However, this abortive effort did not hold up indigenous submarine design. The diesel engine had been adopted as early as 1906 (well ahead of the German Navy) and by 1914 efficient boats capable of offensive operations were in service. Other ideas were under development, notably steam propulsion for higher surface speed to allow boats to accom-pany the battlefleet.

Mine warfare still suffered from neglect, and the only mine in the inventory was a commercial type bought from Italy. The Admiralty had, however, finally tackled the problem of mine countermea-sures. Old torpedo gunboats were converted to minesweepers and the nucleus of a wartime pool of fishing trawlers was created. Lord Charles Beres-ford had initiated the first moves as early as 1907 in response to the experience of the Russo-Japanese War of 1904-5, but a large-scale scheme for regis-tration of trawlers and crews had to wait until 1911.

RIGHT: *A Holland-type submarine is hoisted into the water.*

BELOW: *The limited size of early submarines is clearly shown in this fine pre-WWI photograph.*

One of the worst problems faced by the Edwardian Navy was the very pace of technical progress, which led most planners and thinkers into believing that all previous experience was irrelevant. It was held that the experience of the Russo-Japanese War was irrelevant. The battleships were pre-dreadnoughts, and far outclassed by the latest British and German dreadnoughts and, therefore, the argument went, their battle experience held no lessons. Even the tactical lessons were regarded with some scepticism – except when they supported the enthusiasm for battlecruisers.

In fact, the lessons, particularly from the Battle of Tsushima, were very relevant. The use of radio, the value of mines, the dangers of ammunition fires and the difficulties in controlling underwater damage were all experienced and noted by the Japanese after Tsushima, as well as the limitations of long-range gunnery.

The Edwardian Navy's worst weakness was the lack of a central Staff. It was controlled by the Board of Admiralty, in essence four Sea Lords (naval officers) ruled by the First Lord (a politician). What made it unusual as an administrative instrument was the fact that the Admiralty was bound to act together as a Board. The First Lord acting on behalf of the ruling party and ultimately the House of Commons had full authority and responsibility for running the Navy but he could not act alone. This gave the Sea Lords considerable power, for if they disagreed fundamentally with the First Lord they could and did threaten to resign as a body.

Despite its obvious drawbacks the system worked well. First Lords tended to be men of ability, skilled in presenting the naval case to Parliament and endowed with sufficient common sense to accept the professional advice of the admirals. However, the Agadir Crisis in 1911 revealed an alarming lack of correlation between the war plans proposed by the Navy and those of the Army. Briefly the Army had arranged in strict secrecy over some years to send troops to France in the event of war with Germany. In contrast the Navy had vague intentions to use the Army as 'the largest projectile which can be fired from a naval gun' – that is in amphibious operations against Germany. Unfortunately for the Navy, Fisher had developed a habit of discussing his so-called 'Baltic Plan' in broad terms, without committing any details to paper. In 1910 his successor as First Sea Lord, Sir Arthur Wilson, inherited the doctrine without Fisher's flair for presentation, with the result that the Agadir Crisis left the Cabinet with a well-founded suspicion that the Royal Navy had no strategic plans at all.

The upshot was the appointment of the young political maverick, Winston Churchill, to the post of First Lord of the Admiralty, charged with the duty of creating a Naval Staff and generally improving the Navy's readiness for war. It was to be a stormy period; Churchill got rid of two First Sea Lords before he found one with whom he could work. Prince Louis of Battenberg guided the zeal and enthusiasms of Churchill (whose critics regarded them as dangerous crazes) and by his tact reduced the impact of Churchill's abrasive manner. Sadly Battenberg was a victim of growing anti-German feeling, initially within the Service but by 1914 among the public at large. His royal connections meant that blood ties with the Hohenzollerns were unavoidable, but whereas the press and the public could reconcile themselves to ties between King George V and his Prussian cousins, Prince Louis would be blamed for any wartime disaster.

Despite Churchill's efforts to create a Naval Staff organization the three years before the outbreak of war was not long enough in which to do it. The system remained obstinately over-centralized, resulting in a colossal strain on the First Sea Lord and his close advisers. It also meant that important matters were often given a lower priority and thereby consigned to limbo. For example in 1910 firing trials against the old ironclad *Edinburgh* had shown that the large armour-piercing shell had poor penetration when it struck armour at an oblique angle. The fault was noted but as soon as the Controller, Rear Admiral Jellicoe, was promoted to another post the matter was forgotten.

Other serious omissions were the failure to study long-range gunnery, the logistics of amphibious warfare and convoy escort. It has been claimed that Fisher had a 'genius for war' whatever that may be – but the briefest examination of Admiralty papers for the period 1900-14 show little interest in the vital subject of what the Navy was to *do* in wartime. Whereas the Army had a clear objective – to

get six divisions to France – the Navy merely insisted that it wanted to fight 'somewhere else'. While the Army assigned pre-war staff officers to the humdrum tasks of compiling railway timetables and had established links with French Army logistics experts, the Navy had devoted little or no time to detailed plans for landing troops on a hostile shore.

Fisher's most obvious strategic reform, the one for which he is most widely remembered, had been to end the world-wide distribution of British warships. He saw the scattered gunboats, sloops and small cruisers as an anachronism left over from the days of 'gunboat diplomacy', and rightly claimed that in time of war these weak ships would be either useless or vulnerable to enemy warships of superior fighting power. There was truth in this view, for the habit had grown up over the years of maintaining solitary warships on distant stations merely to provide a local consul with a semblance of military power. As a concept the role of 'world policeman' had been useful up to the 1880s, but it had become outdated. As the other European powers became more interested in acquiring colonies; they had also taken to sending out powerful cruisers and even small battleships to remote parts of the world. Fisher had likened these foreign ships to armadillos, which would lap up isolated 'ants' with ludicrous ease. There was also the problem of cost and manpower. To maintain minor war vessels on foreign stations required large numbers of men and the ships needed to be repaired and maintained. Fisher had argued that the new fleet which he planned to build was only affordable if the costly 'police navy' was wound up.

As always there was more to it than that. The 'Two-Power Standard' was becoming harder to sustain as not only the European powers, but also the United States and Japan, started to reap the benefits of large-scale industrialization. The only way in which Great Britain could spare resources to contain the challenge from Germany was to reduce the number of potential enemies. Differences with France were smoothed out, a major diplomatic triumph which also helped to achieve an understanding with Russia. Another major achievement was an alliance with Japan, eliminating the need to maintain powerful forces in the Far East. Of course, there was a price to pay. The elimination of large numbers of cruising ships of all sizes created a shortage of suitable ships for the protection of commerce and a few years later a new cruiser-building programme had to be started. Although the 1904 edict to scrap everything 'too weak to fight and too slow to run away' made good reading in the newspapers many of the ships listed as scrapped were later reinstated to fulfil humble but essential secondary roles as minelayers, repair ships and so on.

Despite these problems, Fisher's policy had achieved a shake-up in strategic thinking. By removing the dominant role of Imperial policeman, he had forced the Royal Navy to concentrate its thoughts on a war-fighting role in European waters. To aid this process he had overhauled the Victorian system of maintaining the Reserve Fleet.

There had always been a Reserve Fleet, traditionally laid-up 'in Ordinary'. During the Annual Manoeuvres reservists marched abroad and readied the ship for a short commission. It was wasteful, and if the ships were ancient or in particularly poor condition they frequently failed to get to sea at all, or were in such poor state that they could play only a nominal part in the exercises.

To overcome these problems Fisher organized the Navy into three fleets, the First comprised the most modern ships, the Second was an operational reserve manned by half-crews and kept at a high state of readiness, while the Third was made up of the oldest and least effective ships. Although pooh-poohed by Fisher's critics, the new fleet organization finally proved its worth in July 1914, when the great Trial Mobilization put virtually the entire Royal Navy on a wartime footing before the outbreak of war with no serious hitch.

LEFT: *A portent of the future: Cdr Sampson's Short 'hydro-aeroplane' is prepared for takeoff from the battleship* Africa *in 1912.*

BELOW LEFT: *By 1913 a standard British destroyer was beginning to emerge.* HMS Shark *was armed with three 4-inch guns and two 21-inch torpedo-tubes.*

RIGHT: *The after twin 13.5-inch guns of the battlecruiser* Queen Mary. *Failure of flash-protection was to lead to her catastrophic loss in 1916.*

The dominant naval weapon was still the big gun, and gunnery tactics dominated tactical thinking. The Navy's leading gunnery expert, Captain Percy Scott was given ample scope to develop his ideas on training, and under his leadership gunnery made huge strides. Despite his abrasive and strident style, shortly before the outbreak of war he persuaded the Gunnery Branch to adopt his principle of Director Control, an up-to-date version of centralized gunnery control tried in the 1880s.

The impression sometimes given by writers about World War I is that the Royal Navy went to war untrained and dangerously ill-equipped. Nothing could be further from the truth. Pre-war memoirs harp on the incessant training and exercises at sea; much of it may have been misdirected, but by the summer of 1914 the Royal Navy knew full well who its enemy would be and spent most of its time preparing for *Der Tag*.

Naval Aviation

In one respect above all others, the Royal Navy showed considerable foresight. Although not the first navy to embrace aviation, the Senior Service showed as much enthusiasm as the Army when powered aircraft became practicable. After a shaky start in 1907, when the Wright brothers were turned down by the Admiralty with the curt dismissal that aircraft were 'of no practical use to the Naval Service', a naval member was appointed to the government's influential Advisory Committee on Aero.nautics. Early in 1909 the energetic and talented Captain Murray F. Sueter was appointed the first Inspecting Captain of Airships. Despite a disaster in 1911 when the first naval airship the *Mayfly* was destroyed in an accident and the Airships Section was disbanded, the Admiralty gave permission for five officers to start flying instruction.

The first waterborne take-off was made by

Commander Oliver Schwann in November 1911, and only a fortnight later Lieutenant Longmore succeeded in landing on water for the first time. In January 1912 Lieutenant Samson flew his 'hydro-aeroplane' off a platform built over the forecastle of the battleship HMS *Africa*.

In May 1912 the committee of Imperial Defence presented a White Paper on naval aviation to Parliament, in which it called for the establishment of a new military aviation service, known as the Royal Flying Corps but divided into army and navy wings. Although this sounds like a separate third service there was no unified command and in 1914 the Admiralty stamped the naval wing of the RFC clearly as part of the Royal Navy by renaming it the Royal Naval Air Service.

Before the end of 1912 a momentous decision was taken, to convert the old light cruiser *Hermes* into a 'Parent ship' for naval aircraft. She was fitted with two platforms, one over her bows for launching

floating-planes, and one aft for stowing them. The new enthusiasm owed much to the support of Winston Churchill who insisted that the clumsy word 'hydro-aeroplane' should be replaced by the term 'seaplane'.

The *Hermes* took part in the annual manoeuvres in 1913, but her performance was marred by a 'security leak' – one of her seaplanes ran out of fuel and had to be rescued by a German ship. However, she was such a success in her new role that plans were soon approved to buy a suitable mercantile hull for conversion to a seaplane carrier capable of operating as many as 10 aircraft.

The Edwardian Navy underwent one of the most remarkable transformations that any large military organization has ever experienced in peace-time. The picturesque and tradition-laden Victorian Navy was swept away in a remarkably short time by Fisher and his fellow-reformers, but in spite of the hectic pace of change a surprising number of

Fleet reviews were part of the Victorian and Edwardian naval scene. This was the 1911 Spithead Review, with destroyers in the foreground and cruisers and battleships behind.

ships were still in existence in 1914 facing weapons that had not been envisaged 20 years earlier.

On balance the changes were for the better, and Fisher's Royal Navy was infinitely better-prepared to face the High Seas Fleet of the Kaiser. Mistakes had been made, and old inefficiencies had been replaced by newer ones in too many cases, but the Royal Navy's morale remained undiminished.

Although it had been planned for months the Test Mobilization in July 1914 coincided opportunely with the assassination of the Archduke Franz Ferdinand at Sarajevo. The first steps had been taken as early as 12 July, and only five days later the last ships from the two reserve fleets left their home ports for Spithead.

The Fleet Review held in Spithead to celebrate the Test Mobilization was a fitting end to the Edwardian summer. It was the largest and most powerful fleet ever seen: 24 dreadnought battleships and battlecruisers, 35 pre-dreadnoughts and 123 cruisers, destroyers and lesser craft. With only three battlecruisers, two old battleships and a few armoured cruisers away on foreign stations, it was virtually the entire might of the Royal Navy which sailed past the Royal Yacht *Victoria and Albert* on 20 July as they put to sea on exercises.

All ships were to disperse to give leave, to take on coal, or to return to the reserve, but by noon on Sunday 26 July the international situation was so alarming that the First Lord returned to London. There he found that his First Sea Lord had anticipated his wishes by cancelling orders for the First Fleet to leave Portland.

When Churchill reached the Admiralty that evening he found that the first orders had gone out cancelling leave, and the First Fleet was taking on coal. As he was later to admit, his nightmare of a surprise attack on the Fleet had been averted. Whatever the future might hold in store the ships and men of the Royal Navy were prepared.

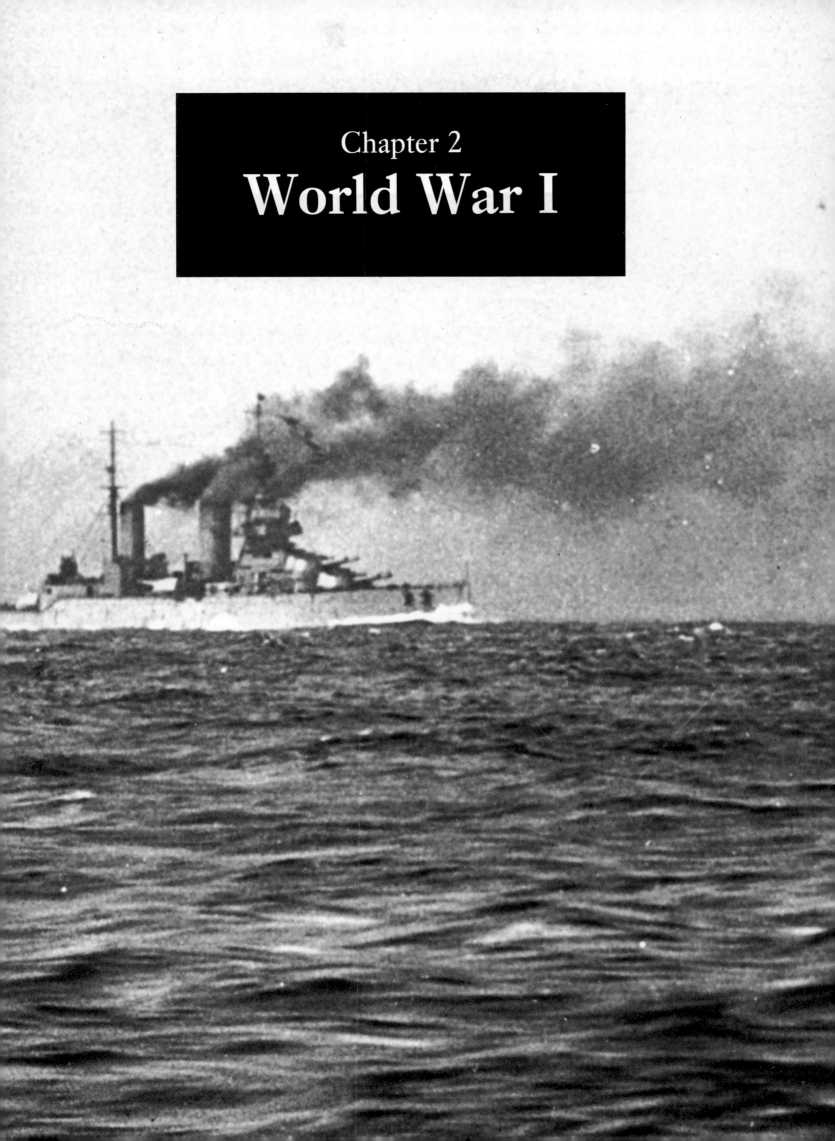

Chapter 2
World War I

In 1914 the Royal Navy could look back on 200 years of being the most powerful force of its kind in the world. For 100 years that supremacy had not been seriously tested in battle. Now a new enemy had arisen on the other side of the North Sea and was threatening just such a test. Rapid advances in technology had apparently totally changed the basic conditions of the naval warfare, while there had been insufficient practical testing of these developments or of the doctrines that had grown up around them for there to be any clear indications of their relative worth. Given these circumstances how well did the Royal Navy perform in the war fought with the Central Powers between 1914 and 1918? Did it maintain its reputation and position? Above all how did its performance compare with that of its new rival, the Imperial German Navy, its chief antagonist?

It is often forgotten that the Royal Navy did not fight the war at sea by itself. The French Navy, though handicapped by a decade of neglect and muddle and possessing few modern vessels, was a far from negligible or inefficient force. It played a major part in the Mediterranean in particular. Both the Russian and Japanese navies, which had fought each other at Tsushima a decade before, were on the Allied side in 1914. The Japanese fleet relieved the Royal Navy of many responsibilities in East Asiatic waters, and provided destroyers for escort duties in the Mediterranean from 1917. The Russian fleet, though bottled up at the eastern end of the Baltic, was an efficient force which caused the Germans a number of problems until taken out of the war by the revolution of 1917. The addition of

the Italian fleet was not generally held to have added much to the strength of the Allies when that country joined the war in 1915. British and French ships had to assist in containing the small but efficient Austro-Hungarian Navy in the Adriatic – but since they would have had this task anyway had Italy remained neutral this was hardly a justified complaint. At the time Russia was removed from the Allied side the United States joined, and its large, modern and efficient fleet became a most effective addition to Allied naval strength. Not only were flotillas of destroyers used in the anti-submarine role, but enough powerful battleships were added to the Grand Fleet to form an extra battle squadron. The smooth integration of this American force with the British fleet must count as one of the most effective examples of cooperation between Allies on record. However, the basic fact remains that the Royal Navy was by far the most important and active Allied navy – and the force which ensured Allied naval superiority against Germany.

There can be no doubt that in matters of seamanship, the practice of squadron manoeuvres and the like the Royal Navy was supreme. Despite all the problems of fighting a four-year war in all seasons, weathers and seas, the number of vessels lost by wreck, collision or stress of weather was very low.

Despite bad living conditions and what would now appear to be extreme social discrimination the crews of British ships maintained high morale until the end. Although still rooted in the class differences of the time the British officer/seaman relationship was notably better than that in the German

PREVIOUS PAGE: *The 'Splendid Cats', the battlecruisers* Tiger *and* Lion *at sea.*

BELOW: *The battlecruisers* Invincible *and* Inflexible *took a terrible revenge on Spee's squadron at the Battle of the Falklands, avenging Cradock's defeat at Coronel.*

ALLIED STATES
ALLIED POSSESSIONS
CENTRAL POWERS
AND OCCUPIED TERRITORIES
NEUTRAL STATES
— · — · — 1914 BOUNDARIES
ALLIED BLOCKADES AND
BARRAGES, WITH DATES

0 NAUTICAL MILES 400

Blockade of Denmark Strait (between
Greenland and Iceland)

ICELAND

*Norwegian
Sea*

1915-18

1915-18

North Sea Mine
Barrage: 1918
Inset ①

NORWAY
KRISTIANIA
(Oslo, 1924)

SWEDEN
STOCKHOLM

*North
Sea*

Baltic Sea

UNITED KINGDOM

Inset ②

*ATLANTIC
OCEAN*

1914

LONDON
THE HAGUE
NETHS.
BRUSSELS
BELG.
LUX.

BERLIN

GERMANY

Vistula

RUSSIA

PARIS

Rhine

FRANCE

SWITZ.
BERNE

Danube

VIENNA

AUSTRIA-HUNGARY

Dnieper

PORTUGAL
LISBON

MADRID

SPAIN

GIBRALTAR
(Brit.)

CORSICA

BALEARIC
IS.

FRENCH

ITALY*

Adriatic

ROME

SARDINIA

ITALIAN

*ITALIAN
Sea*

BELGRADE
MONTE-
NEGRO
SERBIA
ALBANIA

RUMANIA
BUCHAREST

SOFIA
BULGARIA

Black Sea

CONSTANTINOPLE

OTTOMAN EMPIRE

Tigris

Euphrates

1915

SPANISH
MOROCCO

BRITISH

FEZ

MOROCCO
(French)

Allied patrol zones
in the Mediterranean,
1914-16

ALGIERS

Mediterranean

TUNIS

SICILY

MALTA
(Brit.)

GREECE
ATHENS

BRITISH

FRENCH

CRETE

To Italy

CYPRUS
(Brit.)

FRENCH

ALGERIA
(French)

TUNISIA
(French)

TRIPOLI

ITALIAN
Gulf of Sirte

Sea

BRITISH

LIBYA
(Ital.)

EGYPT
(Brit.)

CAIRO

*Suez
Canal*

Nile

ARABIA

*ITALY NEUTRAL UNTIL DECLARING WAR ON CENTRAL POWERS IN MAY 1915

© Richard Natkiel, 1985

Inset ①:
SHETLAND IS. LERWICK
Area C BERGEN
FAIR ISLE Area A
ORKNEY IS.
Area B
Scapa Flow
NORWAY
STAVANGER
Minelaying begun:
B: 3 Mar 1918
A, C: 8 June 1918
Completed in August
0 N MILES 100

Inset ②:
MINE BARRAGES, WITH DATES
EXPLOSIVE NET MINES, 1916
DEEP MINES, 1916-18
SANDBANKS

May 1918
Strait of Dover
abandoned by U-boats

RAMSGATE
ENGLAND DOVER
FOLKESTONE
1914-15
Strait of Dover
1917-18
Cap Griz Nez
CALAIS
OSTEND
BELGIUM
FRANCE
0 N MILES 25

ABOVE: *The North Sea and the Mediterranean were to be the decisive theatres of the naval war, and the Allies succeeded largely in confining the Central Powers to those areas.*

Navy. It is probably the difference that does most to explain the mutinies in the German fleet in 1917-18.

The ships of the Royal Navy were generally at least as good and often better than those in the other navies. The latest cruisers and destroyers were more powerful and effective than their German equivalents. With battleships there was little to choose between the two navies – the British had heavier guns while the Germans had thicker armour, factors which balance one another neatly. Faulty doctrine caused the design of the British battlecruisers to emphasize speed and armament at the expense of protection. Their German equivalents were better-balanced ships and were the one example of German superiority in ship design.

However, the British had handicapped themselves by deficiencies in some aspects of their weaponry. This was especially true of the inferior propellant and arrangements for its safety which proved so fatal at Jutland, and of the totally inadequate mines which had to be replaced by a direct copy of German design. Inadequate armour-piercing shells were to be another problem. In favourable conditions the Germans had more effective rangefinders; on the other hand the British rangefinders relied less on highly trained operators with perfect eyesight and their performance was likely to deteriorate in the stress of battle. The British were also well ahead of the Germans in adopting director firing, although they neglected the most effective system available.

It is important to remember that many of these developments – such as wireless telegraphy, long-range firing, dreadnoughts, practical submarines and aircraft – were all developments of the previous 20 years, some, indeed, of the last decade before the war. None of them had been adequately tested in combat. This should be borne in mind when considering what the naval leaders of the time did with these weapons – they had had their training decades earlier, when weaponry and ships were much less complicated.

In both British and German navies there were signs of a certain deficiency in aggressive leadership, at least during the early stages of the war – particularly surprising in the Royal Navy, with its tradition of attack. The rapid development of technology encouraged a certain caution, but it is also worth remembering that the Admirals commanding the greatly expanded fleets of 1914-18 were drawn either from the comparatively small pool of those who had joined the financially starved Royal Navy at the period known as the 'dark ages' of the Victorian Navy, or from the very small though growing German Navy of the period. By 1914 it seems that there were probably too many commands for the available talent to go round. Also the rigidity of peacetime navies, the lack of education for higher command, 'Admiral worship' and perhaps even over-emphasis on a very narrow view of what was important technically (specifically, the great importance given to the Gunnery Branch) all played their part in the muddles, mistakes and disasters which marred both sides' conduct of the war at sea. The Royal Navy was particularly handicapped by the unfortunate tendency of most of its senior officers to over-centralize the system of command, and the late and half-hearted adoption of a naval staff system. On the other hand the Germans had such a muddled and divided system of higher command – mainly because of the Kaiser's influence – that it is surprising that they achieved as much as they did against the incomparably more effective British Admiralty system.

The Royal Navy also had the advantage of a world-wide network of bases and coaling stations, and the support of the British shipbuilding industry then at its zenith (see Chapter 5). The volume of new tonnage, the speed of repairs of action damage, the development of new designs – all despite the great weakening of the workforce by army recruiting – indicated the quality of this great industry, which was unmatched in Germany or even the United States.

The long and successful history of the Royal Navy, its position of primacy and international respect, led to a natural expectation that the Royal Navy would win, hence the other side always felt it was likely to lose. Despite the obvious dangers of complacency on the British side, on balance this seems to have been a source of strength.

This was the situation when war broke out in 1914, with the Grand Fleet already at its war station, thanks to a convenient practice mobilization. In numerical terms the Royal Navy had only a small

lead in dreadnought battleships, although this would steadily grow as those ships still under construction came into service. Two battleships completed for Turkey and one for Chile were taken over to add to this margin. Argument has raged over the Turkish ships and the role their seizure played in pushing the Turks on to the German side, but recent research apparently shows that the Turks were seriously considering passing these ships on to the Germans after taking delivery so it is difficult to deny that the Admiralty took the right action. In all other types of ships, including both older battleships and submarines the Royal Navy had a clear numerical lead over Germany. Furthermore, the vast majority of German warships were in home waters and therefore blocked in the North Sea by British naval forces. Right from the start the naval war assumed the character of a distant blockade, much to the confusion of the Germans who had expected the British to attempt to keep forces close off their coast and therefore lay them open to attack by torpedo boats and mine warfare. This was a major error of judgment, as great as the constant but completely unjustifed British fear of a German invasion or major amphibious raid. In both cases these moves would have been too obviously playing into the enemy's hands for anyone to consider them seriously. The Germans never managed to break the Royal Navy's control over the exits from the North Sea except by evading it through submarine operations or sneaking a few disguised raiders through the British patrols. So the story of the naval war can be neatly divided between the struggle for naval

RIGHT: *The sole survivor of Spee's Pacific Squadron, SMS* Dresden *was trapped in Chilean waters by British forces.*

BELOW: *Sturdee's squadron getting under way from Port Stanley in the opening stages of the Battle of the Falklands. The cruiser* Kent, *battlecruiser* Inflexible *and cruiser* Glasgow, *seen from the maintop of HMS* Invincible.

supremacy in the North Sea, and what went on in the other waters of the world. We shall consider the latter first.

The opening months of the war saw the elimination or containment of all German ships at large in the oceans of the world. The most powerful of these was the battlecruiser *Goeben* which, with the light cruiser *Breslau*, was in the Western Mediterranean when war approached. The *Goeben* managed to outsteam two British battlecruisers who were trailing her a few hours before war was declared, and made for Turkey. Admiral Troubridge with another British force of armoured cruisers and destroyers could have intercepted her with some possibility of success although probably at heavy cost. He decided not to do so – a decision which was much regretted when the *Goeben* was 'donated' to the Turks in place of the ships constructed and requisitioned in Britain. Thus the world was treated to the curious spectacle of a British admiral choosing the path of caution in such a situation. Perhaps he was too conscious of a disparity in gunpower and too little of the advantages of numbers and of torpedo attack.

The other major German overseas force was the superbly trained 'East Asiatic Squadron' of Admiral Graf von Spee. With two armoured cruisers and accompanying light cruisers he disappeared into the wastes of the Pacific on the outbreak of war. The uncertainty about his position tied up a large number of Allied warships in defensive dispositions and

this was the period when the support of the Japanese fleet really paid off. Finally he emerged on the Chilean coast where he annihilated Cradock's smaller cruiser squadron of older and less efficient ships at the battle of Coronel. After Troubridge's failure to intercept the *Goeben* and the resulting outcry it is difficult to see what alternative Cradock had to his gallant but fatal attack on the German squadron. Though he failed to inflict any damage he forced Spee to use up ammunition which was irreplacable and set in motion the operations which would lead to the destruction of the German squadron in a similary one-sided battle with two British battlecruisers and supporting cruisers off the Falkland Islands. Only one German cruiser, the *Dresden*, escaped from this second massacre – but she was tracked down and destroyed soon afterwards.

Arguably this was the one time that battlecruisers were used in the right way – to run down and destroy lesser ships. It is therefore appropriate to remember that the architect of the victory was Fisher, who was directly responsible for their development in the nick of time to achieve this undeniable success. It was perhaps an ominous portent for future clashes involving this type of ship that the expenditure of ammunition to achieve fatal damage to the German ships was much higher than had been expected. Also a portent was the fact that the German ships fought to the end, with few survivors. Naval warfare in the twentieth century was not to see

the surrenders in the face of the superior force, or the capture of prizes after hard-fought actions which had characterized the age of sail. Steam, steel, armour-piercing shells and torpedoes heralded a grimmer fate for those defeated in a sea battle.

The same fate of ultimate destruction overtook the few other German warships at large on the oceans of the world when war broke out. SMS *Emden* did a great deal of damage to trade in the Indian Ocean before being destroyed by HMAS *Sydney*, and the destruction of the *Königsberg* after she was trapped in the Rufiji River in East Africa took a specially mounted operation with monitors and seaplanes. The armed merchant cruiser *Cap Trafalgar* was destroyed in an epic single-ship action (one of the very few examples of this in the twentieth century) by a British equivalent, the *Carmania*. However, these ships were only marginal nuisances to the Allies and the same applies to the later surface raiders which broke out of the North Sea – even the very successful *Möwe* and *Seeadler*.

The Navy played an important part in gathering in Germany's overseas colonies, which had always been hostages to British seapower. It also played a vital role in the Mesopotamian campaign in what is now Iraq but was then part of the Turkish Empire. This was second only to the river campaigns of the American Civil War as an example of river fighting,

LEFT: *The Battle of the Dogger Bank in January 1915 was the first clash of modern capital ships, but proved indecisive.*

BELOW: *The naval assault on the Dardanelles in March 1915 was a failure, and led to the bloody land campaign on the Gallipoli Peninsula.*

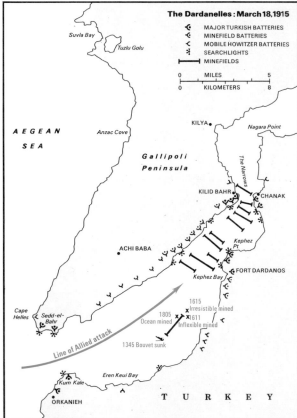

LEFT: *The Anglo-French fleet at the entrance to the Dardanelles. Most of the ships, even the destroyers, were coal-burners.*

RIGHT: *The periscope of the submarine E.11, hit by a Turkish shell.*

and an entire fleet of gunboats, supply vessels and other support craft was built by British shipyards for use here. They played a vital part in the ultimate capture of Baghdad, while naval gunfire helped to repel Turkish forces from the Suez Canal and supported Allenby's initial attack in Palestine. In one of the most complicated minor operations of the war two small gunboats were transported across Africa to Lake Tanganyika, where they reversed the balance of power by sinking the improvised German gunboat which had dominated the lake. This was the episode which inspired Forester's *The African Queen*, together with an unsuccessful but gallant attempt by the Germans to sink the gunboat *Dwarf* which was playing a very active part in the subjugation of their colony of the Cameroons.

The Dardanelles campaign, like Jutland, is one of the great 'what ifs?' of history. The sequence of missed opportunities is still infuriating to read today. Whether the initial purely naval attack on the Narrows could have broken through to Constantinople, and whether the presence of Allied battleships off that city would have driven the Turks out of the war, are still subjects of controversy. It does seem likely that success would have been achieved had troop landings been combined with bolder handling of the obsolete Allied battleships. As it was, effective use of mobile howitzers and a well-laid minefield stopped the naval attack. When troops were finally landed Turkish reinforcements had arrived and losses were heavy. A secondary landing petered out because of the failure to press ahead, and despite constant naval gunfire support Gallipoli became a stalemate. The most successful part of the whole operation were the two final evacuations. Had more time been devoted to preparation and amphibious warfare thought about earlier, the evacuations

might not have been necessary. As it was, the Navy's greatest success in the campaign involved the new weapons of aircraft and submarines. Besides using aircraft for artillery spotting, a seaplane made the first successful aerial torpedo attack. In operations of great skill and bravery British submarines penetrated the Narrows and caused havoc among Turkish supply ships in the Sea of Marmora. They also fought a very successful campaign in the Baltic operating from Russian bases. Until the Russian Revolution brought their activities to an end these submarines caused considerable losses among the ships carrying iron ore from Sweden to Germany.

In general the activities of the Navy away from the North Sea and the Western Approaches to the British Isles were unglamorous, tedious and necessary. They took large numbers of ships – mostly old or small – and of men; but only outright failure could affect the course of the war. As might be expected, there was no major failure, except that of failing for some time to contain the German and Austrian submarine offensive in the Mediterranean. This was part of the U-boat problem in general, to which we will return later.

The North Sea presented problems to the British and offered opportunities to the Germans, but the basic facts of geography were very much in favour of the British, who could contain the German High Seas Fleet by blocking the exits at the Straits of Dover and between Scotland and Norway. Close blockade of the German North Sea bases had been ruled out some time before the war. It would have imposed great strains on the ships concerned and exposed them to the full perils of mine and torpedo boat attack, arms in which the Germans had invested very heavily. The Germans continued to expect that the Royal Navy would play into their hands in this way and found that their small torpedo boats were far less suited to operations in the northern part of the North Sea than the larger and more powerful British destroyers. However, at the start of the war the Germans had a number of opportunities of which they failed to take advantage.

In the opening months of the war the numerical balance of dreadnought battleships was at its least unfavourable to the Germans. After a while the balance would tilt increasingly in Britain's favour as ships under construction came into commission. The British fleet was further handicapped by the lack of any suitable North Sea base until Scapa Flow was fully defended. The main alternative, Rosyth, was not ready for use by the full fleet until close to the end of the war. While waiting for Scapa to be readied for it the Grand Fleet suffered an unexpected and unnecessary loss, the mining of the new battleship *Audacious* – which revealed grave deficiencies in damage control. Timorous and inefficient leadership prevented any German attempt to take advantage of this opportunity. The same applied to their complete failure to interfere with the transport of the British Expeditationary Force to France. Indeed, the supply of the growing British Army in France, arguably the chief agent in the final defeat of the German Army, was never interrupted.

LEFT: *The congested scene at 'V' Beach after the landings from the* River Clyde. *The troops relied on the Navy for everything, from ammunition down to drinking water.*

LEFT: *The fatal hit on the battlecruiser* Queen Mary, *as seen by a German artist.*

BELOW LEFT: *The four* Queen Elizabeth *class battleships of the 5th Battle Squadron open fire on Hipper's First Scouting Group at the start of the Battle of Jutland.*

RIGHT: *Another artist's impression of the loss of the* Queen Mary, *with the* Tiger *and* New Zealand *pulling clear to avoid the stricken ship.*

BELOW RIGHT: *The armoured cruiser* Black Prince *was destroyed by German gunfire at short range during the night action at Jutland.*

Once the Germans had occupied most of the Belgian coast the conditions were favourable for the localized struggle which raged for the rest of the war. The British built up a force of bombardment ships, based on a new type of vessel, the monitor (despite taking its name from the earlier American monitors there was litte resemblance) designed and built at great speed after the war had begun. Considerable technical ingenuity was expended on fire control, sound ranging and the like, in what amounted to a private war against the shore batteries, which replied with devices which included remotely controlled explosive motor boats. Night raids by German destroyers on the 'Dover Patrol' scored some successes, but also defeats of which the most celebrated was by the two British destroyers *Swift* and *Broke* – one of the few surface actions in which ramming and hand-to-hand fighting took place. The British made considerable use of another new type of craft, the 'coastal motor boat', the precursor of the motor torpedo boat. It was an occasionally dramatic struggle of great technical interest, but not one of significance to the outcome of the war. It is probably as well that a proposed landing on the Belgian coast (which would have included tanks) never took place. Conversely landings on the English coast – either as raids or as a full-scale invasion – though much feared by the British, who tied up large numbers of troops for home defence, were never even considered by the Germans. This was sensible, for any possible short-term gains would have been overshadowed by the inevitability of defeat.

Soon after the beginning of the war in the North Sea the British had learned from hard experience that the forecast of dangers from mines and from submarine topedoes had not been exaggerated. The most spectacular demonstration of this was the sinking of three old cruisers in an hour by one U-boat, a loss which removed any lingering temptation there

RIGHT: *Sir David Beatty led the Battle Cruiser Force at the Dogger Bank and Jutland, and then took over from Jellicoe as C-in-C.*

LEFT: *HMS* Lord Clive, *one of two monitors to receive an 18-inch gun for shore bombardment. These makeshift gun-platforms performed valuable work on the Belgian coast and in the Mediterranean.*

RIGHT: *Sir John Jellicoe commanded the Grand Fleet from 1914 but was replaced by Beatty in 1917.*

might have been to attempt a close blockade. However raids on German home waters were another matter. Despite a monumental failure in planning and communications which might well have led to catastrophe, a raid into the Heligoland Bight by British cruisers and destroyers, supported by Beatty's battlecruisers led to the sinking of several German ships with little loss on the British side. This defeat in waters close to their main base did little to help the morale of German Navy.

By the end of 1914 Britain had a great and hidden advantage that remained unknown to her opponent for the rest of the war. By accident she acquired all three of the main German naval codes. One was recovered by the Russians from a wrecked cruiser and generously handed over, another was trawled up from a sunken vessel, and the third captured by the Australians. An excellent team of cryptographers was assembled, and for the rest of the war the Navy had the inestimable advantage of being able to read much of the German wireless and cable traffic. This was not as decisive an advantage as it should have been; the lack of an adequate organization prevented full use being made of this invaluable intelligence. Interpretation and transmission of the information also was inadequate – the lessons of this were fortunately learned in time for World War II, but altogether too many priceless opportunities were fumbled in 1914-18 because of the shortcomings of the Admiralty staff system. The Battle of Jutland was made possible by intercepted signals, but the trap was not fully sprung because the right information was not sent to Jellicoe. However the decoding of the Zimmerman telegram, which provided evidence that the Germans were stirring up Mexico against the United States, began a magnificently handled intelligence operation which speeded America's entry into the war.

Radio was a new and unprecedented source of intelligence and the conditions for its effective use were still imperfectly understood so teething troubles were inevitable. By the end of the war Admirality intelligence under the formidable Admiral 'Blinker' Hall was by far the most effective organization of its kind, and had an incomparably better record than its German equivalent. Besides intercepting enemy messages the efficient Admiralty wireless organization also obtained valuable intelligence by radio direction-finding.

On Christmas Day 1914 the Royal Navy demonstrated that in another respect it led the world in innovation. The first carrier strike ever launched attempted to attack the Cuxhaven Zeppelin base. The fact that the few seaplanes which managed to take off after being hoisted out from converted cross-channel ferries caused no damage was much less important than the fact that such a daring innovation had been attempted. It also led to the first air/sea action by German Zeppelins and seaplanes, which retaliated with an equal lack of results. Later in the war more successful carrier strikes would be launched against Zeppelin sheds. By the end of the war not only were most larger Royal Navy vessels fitted to carry aircraft, but the true aircraft carrier had

become a practical proposition. The Navy had taken the lead in the development of the weapon which was to dominate the sea by the end of World War II. This development might have been hastened had World War I gone on into 1919, as a full-scale torpedo plane attack on the High Seas Fleet in its bases had been planned. There is no reason to doubt that this would have proved as dramatically successful as the attack on Taranto two decades later.

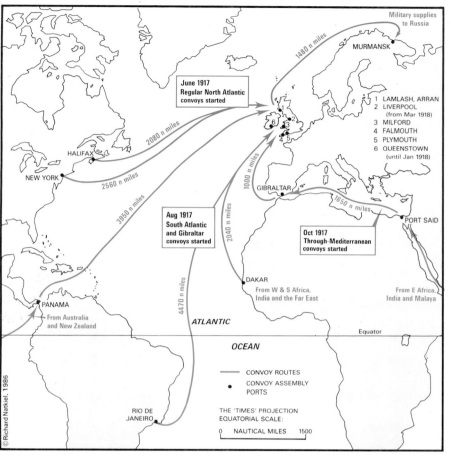

June 1917
Regular North Atlantic
convoys started

1 LAMLASH, ARRAN
2 LIVERPOOL
  (from Mar 1918)
3 MILFORD
4 FALMOUTH
5 PLYMOUTH
6 QUEENSTOWN
  (until Jan 1918)

Military supplies
to Russia

MURMANSK

1480 n miles

HALIFAX

2080 n miles

NEW YORK

2560 n miles

3950 n miles

GIBRALTAR

1000 n miles

1650 n miles

PORT SAID

2040 n miles

Aug 1917
South Atlantic
and Gibraltar
convoys started

Oct 1917
Through-Mediterranean
convoys started

DAKAR
From W & S Africa,
India and the Far East

From E Africa,
India and Malaya

4470 n miles

PANAMA

From Australia
and New Zealand

ATLANTIC

Equator

OCEAN

RIO DE
JANEIRO

© Richard Natkiel. 1986

CONVOY ROUTES
CONVOY ASSEMBLY
PORTS

THE 'TIMES' PROJECTION
EQUATORIAL SCALE:

0   NAUTICAL MILES   1500

LEFT: *Long lines of communication were the weak point of British sea power. Only when these were secured in 1917 could the Royal Navy and its allies begin to win the war.*

BELOW: *A German 'U-cruiser' at sea in 1918. Despite their imposing armament they were less effective than the medium-sized U-Boats.*

ABOVE: *In 1916-17 U-Boats were able to sink large numbers of ships by gunfire. The convoy system brought this to an end.*

RIGHT: *K/Lt Otto Weddigen's U.9 sank four large cruisers in the first two months of the war, the* Hawke, Aboukir, Cressy *and* Hogue.

LEFT: *The light battlecruiser* Furious *returned to service in 1918 with a landing deck in place of her after 18-inch gun.*

RIGHT: *Despite her modifications* Furious *was not successful as an aircraft carrier but operated small 'blimps' in the closing months of the war.*

BELOW LEFT: *Commander Dunning's first attempt at landing a Sopwith Pup on the flying-off deck of the Furious was a success, but he was killed trying to repeat the feat.*

BELOW RIGHT: *Dunning's Pup was caught by a gust of wind and fell in to the water, drowning him.*

The Royal Naval Air Service (RNAS) was probably the best and most innovative service of its kind in the world until cut short by the decision of April Fool's Day 1918 to form the Royal Air Force. The Royal Navy had much greater experience of technical contracting than the Army and combined with the high quality of its personnel this resulted in consistently better types of aircraft (such as the Sopwith 1½ Strutter, Handley Page 0/400 and Sopwith Triplane) than were supplied to the Royal Flying Corps. It was the RNAS that developed armoured car warfare, invented strategic bombing (and saw the vital importance of accurate navigation for this task), the torpedo-bomber and the aircraft carrier.

In late 1914 the German battlecruisers began a series of raids on British east coast ports. These caused little real damage, but were of great propaganda value; the Royal Navy apparently could not protect its own homeland. In fact, with the main British force based at the extreme northern end of the British coast, the east coast was bound to be exposed to such raids, unless intelligence gave adequate warning of a German attack. The second time the Germans came out there was some warning from decoded signals, but it was not appreciated that the main German fleet had come out in support of its battlecruisers. The British had only sent a detachment of the Grand Fleet, so it was fortunate that in a series of blind gropings and occasional contacts between the scouting forces on each side the Germans failed to realize what was happening. They missed the best chance they were ever given to overwhelm a part of the British fleet with their main force.

Shortly afterwards the Germans planned an attack on British fishing vessels on the Dogger Bank. The British detected this move and sent the more numerous battlecruiser force to intercept their German equivalents. They did this successfully, but the Battle of the Dogger Bank was less of a triumph than it should have been. The Germans fled, losing the weakly armed *Blücher* (overwhelmed by the combined gunfire of the British force when she fell behind). A combination of signalling errors and damage to the British flagship *Lion* meant that the pursuit of the already heavily hit German battlecruisers was abandoned just when it might have led to their destruction. The Germans were lucky that they escaped so lightly, especially as their flagship, *Seydlitz*, nearly blew up after being heavily damaged.

The near-catastrophe demonstrated to the Germans the need for greater anti-flash protection in turrets, a lesson the British were not to learn until the grim losses at Jutland. German battlecruiser gunnery was also on the whole more accurate than the British. The British battlecruiser base at Rosyth was a far from suitable area for gunnery practice, so the marked inferiority of their gunnery standards as compared to those of Jellicoe's battleships is understandable, and cannot be totally blamed on Beatty. However, it is difficult not to blame him for his failure to do something about the deplorable nature of his signalling arrangements which were to cause problems again at Jutland.

By the time of the Dogger Bank the British had perfected the mechanism of distant blockade which was slowly to strangle Germany. The unsuitable old cruisers which had taken the initial burden of patrolling the approaches to the North Sea and the Channel had been replaced by the much more suitable armed liners which were to carry on that boring but important task for the rest of the war. The tricky but essential job of stopping and inspecting neutral vessels for contraband went on in all seasons and weather. The memory of the American War of 1812, caused by just such interference with neutral trade, helped to restrain both sides in a potentially very dangerous argument between the Allies and the USA, the most powerful neutral. Fortunately the growing U-boat campaign against merchant shipping was much more hurtful and tactlessly conducted. There was obviously gaps in the blockade; neutral countries such as Holland, Denmark and Switzerland had common boundaries with Germany, while Sweden and Norway were only a short sea voyage away. Some control had to be exerted over the commerce of these countries without arousing as much hostility. In the long run the combined Allied naval and diplomatic efforts were reasonably successful in cutting down German supplies through these countries. The whole effort of the blockade, hitting a Germany weakened by the diversion of most of her manpower to the Front, was enough to cause widespread misery leading to revolt. It led finally to the collapse of both the regime and the war effort when combined with military defeat. At first only obvious war materials had been intercepted but the logic of total war soon expanded the definition to include foodstuffs. The Allies imposed a maritime siege on Germany and she tried to do the same with her U-boats against Britain. The Allied siege won, with consequent suffering to the defeated population.

By the late spring of 1916 all expectations of a short war had long since vanished. The Grand Fleet, trained to perfection in manoeuvre and well practised in gunnery seemed doomed to wait out the war at Scapa Flow, making the occasional fruitless sweep. Then came the opportunity for decisive battle. In the Battle of Jutland, the only fleet action of the war, the basic moves are clear. The two battlecruiser forces came into contact and Beatty began to chase Hipper southwards. Superior German gunnery and inferior British propellant and protection cost two British battlecruisers, but Beatty continued to pursue until the High Seas Fleet was sighted. Then it was his turn to lure the enemy onto the guns of his own battleships by withdrawing in the direction of the Grand Fleet. Despite the deplorable failure of many of his subordinates to pass on information about the course and position of the German fleet, Jellicoe deployed his ships brilliantly – and the German fleet found itself with its 'T' being crossed, at a grave tactical and numerical disadvantage. Though the British lost another battlecruiser and two armoured cruisers the balance of the battle went definitely in their favour. The German fleet commander Admiral Scheer, reversed course under cover

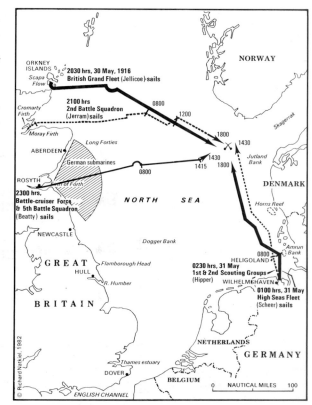

LEFT: *The Battle of Jutland, 31 May 1916, showing the tracks of the main fleets.*

BELOW: *A shell hole in the roof plate of one of HMS Tiger's 13.5-inch gun turrets.*

ABOVE: *The battleship*
Warspite *lying in Scapa
Flow. Note the triangular
baffles fitted to masts and
funnels, an attempt to fool
German rangefinders.*

of a torpedo attack and achieved a temporary escape
only to have to repeat the process when he blun-
dered into the devastating fire of the Grand Fleet
again. At this stage darkness fell, with the British
between the German fleet and its bases. During the
night the opportunity to close the trap faded away as
the Germans managed to batter their way through
the screen of light forces behind the main British
force. Communications failed and the Admiralty
did not inform Jellicoe of the vital information they
possessed from decodes about the German destina-
tion. The British destroyer flotillas launched gallant
but uncoordinated attacks without thinking to tell
Jellicoe where the enemy was. Had Jellicoe known
what was happening there is little doubt that the next
morning would have seen an overwhelming German
defeat by the scarcely blooded Grand Fleet, though
no doubt with some further British losses.

As it was, the balance of losses was clearly in
favour of the Germans, who had only lost one battlecruiser and one obsolete battleship, with another
battlecruiser so heavily damaged as to be sinking
when she reached harbour. However, the German
fleet was well aware that it had been lucky to escape
a massive defeat, if not outright destruction. The
experience of seeing the whole northern horizon
lighting up with gun flashes as it steamed into the
fire of the Grand Fleet was a powerful incentive to

caution. The allegation that the High Seas Fleet
never ventured forth from its bases after Jutland is
not true, but its subsequent sorties into the North
Sea were of little significance. As an American
newspaper aptly put it: 'The German fleet has
assaulted its jailor but is still behind bars'.

The battle itself will no doubt continue to be a
subject of controversy, particularly on the British
side where there were so many missed opportunities. It certainly exposed a number of major weaknesses, the most obvious being those that led to the
massive explosions in which three battlecruisers
were lost and another was nearly blown up. Lack of
anti-flash precautions and propellant far more liable
to explode than that in German ships formed a fatal
combination. Beatty's battlecruisers with their
inferior gunnery and poor signal organization had
clearly suffered a defeat at the hands of their German opposite numbers. The quite appalling failure
from nearly all the commanders of the British scouting forces to keep their commander in chief
informed of what was going on nearly prevented the
Grand Fleet of intervening effectively. The fact that
it did deploy in exactly the right way to catch the
Germans at the maximum disadvantage is due
almost entirely to Jellicoe's brilliance as a tactician.
Jellicoe can also take the credit for its excellent gunnery, although poor shell quality diminished the

RIGHT: *The destroyer* Badger *picking up the handful of survivors from the wreck of HMS* Invincible, *during the Battle of Jutland.*

BELOW: *The full might of the Grand Fleet at sea in 1917;* Iron Duke *class ships seen from the flagship* Queen Elizabeth.

effect of the hits on the leading ships of the German line. Considering what was known at the time it is also difficult to blame Jellicoe for his decision to turn away from rather than turn towards torpedo attack; it caused him to lose touch with the Germans just as maximum damage was being inflicted. He was probably rather too sensitive to the idea that he was 'the only man who could lose the war in an afternoon' if too many of his ships were sunk. With the Allied margin of superiority in warships this would have been very unlikely though not quite impossible. It is also difficult to see the Germans taking full advantage of a temporary superiority in numbers because of their difficult strategic position and their cautious leadership.

Jutland did demonstrate the superiority of British destroyers over German torpedo boats – the former were much more successful in breaking through their opponents to get into a position to launch their torpedos, although they carried too few of them for full effectiveness. The aftermath of the battle also demonstrated again the predominance of the British shipbuilding industry – damage was repaired much faster than anything the Germans

could manage. There was great dissatisfaction with the outcome of the battle in the Royal Navy – and in the long run this was perhaps its most important result. Better shells and anti-flash precautions were quickly introduced. The careful study of what went wrong in the battle, from communications to gunnery, from training to searchlights, became a powerful engine of change in the Royal Navy. Its excellent performance during World War II owes much to the shock when the 'second Trafalgar' that was expected at Jutland turned out to be a muddled and indecisive mess. The very losses themselves paid a handsome dividend in providing a great deal of useful information on how to avoid such catastrophes in future.

After Jutland the war in the North Sea lapsed into anti-climax. The Germans made a couple of successful cruiser raids on Norwegian convoys, but heavy ships were not to clash with each other again. Gradually the social pressures within the German fleet rose to a level which produced lower deck unrest in 1917, and finally the mutiny of 1918. The High Sea Fleet would sail North again, but only to be escorted to internment at Scapa Flow. Here it

BELOW: *The battlecruiser* Indomitable *at full speed during the approach to* Jutland.

would scuttle itself, a spectacular suicide which was a temporary embarrassment to Britain, but proved a blessing in disguise, as it solved the problem of distributing the ships among the squabbling Allies.

Long before this the German fleet had ceased to be the chief menace to the Allies at sea. Jutland had made fairly clear that there was little chance of significantly weakening British naval predominance. Tirpitz's 'Risk Fleet' had not been a success. It had been counter-productive in its basic purpose of blackmailing Britain into giving Germany a free hand. Instead the threat had driven Britain to form the *Entente* with her old enemies France and Russia. It can also be argued that the diversion of so much manufacturing capacity and manpower into building up a fleet prevented Germany from winning the struggle on land which was so much more vital to her. In any case her last chance of success at sea now appeared to be the exploitation of the submarine offensive.

Germany was late in starting the building up of a submarine arm, and had very few U-boats at the outbreak of war. Initial success against British warships caused a spate of new orders. The use of submarines to attack merchant shipping gave Germany her only chance to combat the Allied blockade and here only serious chance to knock Britain out of the war. Not only was the island nation totally dependant on sea communications for supporting her war effort, she would also starve if denied food imports. The great decline of British agriculture since the 1870s and over-reliance on meat and grain from the Americas and the Antipodes had given a major hostage to fortune. Understandably the Germans found irksome the restrictions on commerce raiding imposed by International Law, which dated from the time before the submarine was a practical proposition, and were eventually to ignore them. Considering that the result of the Allied blockade was equally inhuman, if not so obvious, it is difficult to condemn the Germans as unthinkingly as people did at the time.

Although the U-boat offensive was Germany's best chance of obtaining outright victory against her most dangerous enemy it also proved to be her greatest mistake. Other factors, from high-handed behaviour in occupied Belgium to ill-considered encouragement of Mexican anti-Americanism played their part, but above all it was the inhumanity in sinking merchant ships that drove the USA into finally declaring war. The other Allies could not have survived until victory came without that moral boost let alone the practical support that came across the Atlantic.

The success of the U-boat offensives was due, in part, to a confusion of tactical thought within the Admiralty. Somehow the belief had grown up in the late nineteenth century that the traditional methods of protecting commerce, hinging on the use of convoy, had been outdated by the development of the steamship. The naval history fashionable at the time had been written in terms of fleet actions, and the advance of technology had apparently swept away all the old certainties. The

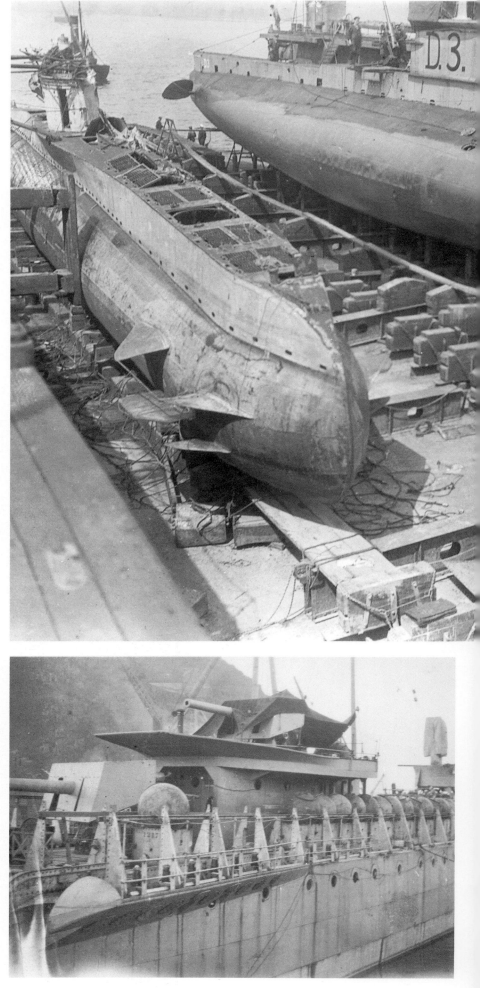

LEFT: *The salvaged minelaying U-boat* UC.2 *lying in a floating dock at Harwich alongside* HMS/m D.5.

BOTTOM LEFT: *The new minelaying destroyer* Vehement *in 1917. As improved mines became available the offensive against the U-boat bases was stepped up.*

BELOW: *Despite the lack of anti-submarine weapons and sensors, U-boats were sunk from time to time.* U.8 *was sunk in March 1915 by the destroyer HMS* Maori *and others, using explosive sweeps.*

lack of a Naval Staff until just before the war, and the lack of proper training in Staff duties or appreciation of the analytical and logistical task a Staff should do, all played their part in allowing an untested dogma to cripple any effective countermeasures to the U-boat sinkings until almost too late. One of the oddest features of the whole business is that escorts were given to the battle fleets from the very start of the war, and convoy was organized on certain routes to Norway and for troop transports going to France. The psychological reason behind the failure to adopt convoy was that it was seen as defensive. Even in 1942, despite this World War I experience and the evidence of the Battle of the Atlantic, the US Navy still fought against the adoption of convoy on the American East Coast routes. Jellicoe's Admiralty, grappling with an entirely untested technology, at least had more excuse for its failure to act promptly.

The first German submarine offensive came in 1915. This was premature, as there were far too few U-boats to succeed, and they merely succeeded in arousing a great deal of unfavourable reaction in the USA, especially by sinking the liner *Lusitania*. This reaction forced the Germans to abandon their campaign. However the stalemate of 1916 led to the gamble that a renewed offensive with more submarines would succeed before America could make any effective intervention in Europe. If the higher command of the Royal Navy had had their way it

probably would have done. An overtired Jellicoe, now transferred to the post of First Sea Lord, persisted in the belief that nothing could be done which had not been tried already. 'Offensive' anti-submarine patrols and disguised decoy ships had achieved far too few sinkings of U-boats to make any serious difference to the rising total of lost merchantmen. His insistence that it was vital to capture the German submarine bases in Belgium (although most of the mercantile losses were actually caused by submarines based in Germany) drove the British Army into the muddy hell of the Passchendaele offensive. By the middle of 1917 defeat was a very real prospect unless an answer was found to the U-boats and the Admiralty had no suggestions. Fortunately some junior naval officers urged convoy, and David Lloyd George, the Prime Minister, listened to them and to the American Admiral Sims. The sums that had been used to show that there were far too many sailings to provide convoy for were shown to be false. Escorts were found from the useless patrols and from the swollen flotillas of the Grand Fleet.

Once they were instituted convoys proved a great success in reducing although not ending the sinkings. An unexpected consequence was that the U-boats found it far more difficult to find targets. Instead of a constant stream of independently sailing ships crossing their sights, the sea was now empty of traffic. When a convoy did appear there were far too many targets to cope with, even ignoring the fact that any attack would expose the U-boat to retaliation by the escorts. Equally the vicinity of the convoy proved to be far the best place for a warship to find a submarine, rather than occupying its time in useless patrols or hunting submarines in the trackless wastes of the sea. In the absence of an effective device for detecting submerged submarines (hydrophones of various kinds were tried but without much success) the best use of an escort vessel was by its very presence to keep a submarine submerged and thereby less effective. The most efficient way to protect merchant ships was to accompany numbers of them in a convoy. Even if the submarine courted detection by attacking the convoy it would do so submerged, thereby using up its limited supply of torpedoes rather than achieving easy sinkings by using its gun or boarding parties and scuttling charges. The firing of a torpedo provided a reasonable mark for the newly invented depth charge and therefore helped solve the submarine detection problem. Once convoy was instituted it brought many such uncovenanted benefits. Although the organization of convoys and the task of making merchant ships steam in formation caused some problems, they were not the insurmountable difficulties that had been feared. It is probable that if practical experiments had been made earlier to test the assertion that convoy was impractical, the war could have ended sooner with much less loss to the Allies.

Other measures besides convoy were also instituted. Shipyards which had concentrated on warship-building for most of the war were switched over to mass-producing standardized merchant

ships to replace the tonnage lost. An offensive mining programme of increasing technical complexity resulted in the sinking of many more U-boats. Development of hydrophones for detection and depth charges for attack had already posed an increasing threat to the submerged submarine, although the experiments which led to the development of ASDIC (Sonar) only came to fruition after the war had ended. Aircraft and airships were used with increasing success to deny the surface to submarines and thereby reduce their range and effectiveness, though actual sinkings by this method were very few. Defensive mine barriers across the Straits of Dover and Otranto proved to be of some value, although the enormous effort the Americans put into a barrier across the top of the North Sea seems to have been wasted. By 1918 the U-boat menace had not been defeated outright but it had been reduced to manageable proportions and no longer offered the Germans a chance of easy victory. Of course geography was very much against the Germans and Austrians, restricted to bases on the North Sea and Adriatic. Their success with such a new weapon owed at least as much to the errors made by their enemies as to the skill with which they used it.

The most spectacular, but not the most successful, anti-submarine operation was the raid on the U-boat base at Zeebrugge on Saint George's Day 1918. With considerable technical ingenuity and great bravery blockships were sunk and the long harbour mole assaulted. There were heavy losses to the powerful defences, but the blockships were only partially successful, and in any case the number of U-boats based there was not large. However, the raid was a great propaganda success, and gave a great lift to the morale of a navy which did not feel it

ABOVE: *The convoy, previously rejected as too defensive, proved to be the only way to combat the U-Boat.*

ABOVE RIGHT: *The combination of Churchill (left) as First Lord and Fisher as First Sea Lord was dynamic but erratic and ultimately proved unstable.*

BELOW: *A typical scene in Scapa Flow, with battleships, tenders and a 'G' class submarine.*

was doing enough to balance the sacrifices of the Army. Shortly afterwards another simple blockship attack achieved a similarly limited success at Ostend. These examples of action and aggression for their own sake were characteristic of their leader, Roger Keyes. On balance their moral effect probably justified their launch, despite their limited practical effect against the U-boats.

The need of anti-submarine and minesweeping craft, with all the other multifarious demands for manpower demanded a great expansion of the Navy. Much of the additional manpower came from the reserve of men who had previously served in it, while a valuable core of professional seamen came in from those merchant seamen who had joined the Royal Naval Reserve. Many fishermen were called up to man the trawlers and drifters requisitioned for minesweeping and patrol. These expedients were not, however, enough. It was now that the recently founded Royal Naval Volunteer Reserve (RNVR) came into its own. Tragically it was not those keen pre-war volunteers who had given up spare time to train to work in the fleet who got the benefit of this. They were swept up into Churchill's brainchild, the Royal Naval Division, and spent the war fighting on land. This misuse of a trained force resulted in peacetime yachtsmen and others reaping the rewards of serving at sea, eventually commanding motor launches and other small craft. In any case the experiment of using others besides professional seamen proved a success, making the navy less of a society apart than it had ever been before, and providing the necessary experience for the much greater expansion of the peacetime Royal Navy in 1939.

The British shipbuilding industry had risen triumphantly to the challenge of the war, as had British ship designers. Brand new types like the monitors and aircraft carriers have already been mentioned. There were also specialist anti-submarine craft (the 'P' boats), minesweepers (twin-screw

'Hunt Class'), new classes of cruiser (the 'D' and 'E' classes) which maintained the British lead in this type of ship, the superb 'V & W' Class destroyers which set the pattern for destroyer design for the next 20 years, and many other classes designed and built in large numbers during the war. Perhaps the most sensible and successful type of general-purpose small warships ever built were the excellent group of classes known as the 'Flowers', designed to make use of mercantile yards and expertise. It was unfortunate that so many of the later ships of this type and other types as well were handicapped by being made to look like merchantmen, one of the more pernicious results of the early success of

'Q'-Ships against U-boats. There were also some very interesting developments in submarines. The bizarre steam 'K' Class and the 'M' Class with their 12-inch guns were bright ideas but failures. The 'R' Class, designed as anti-submarine submarines were a promising line of development, but probably in advance of contemporary technology. The 'L' Class, the most modern conventional type available at the end of the war, was well designed and among the best submarines in the world at the time. With the worst defects revealed at Jutland rectified, better shells, improved propellant, adequate flash protection and updated fire control British battleships were much more formidable.

Having made a very bad start with defective mines, the Navy became much better at mine warfare as the war went on. A magnetic mine was in service in 1918, and specialized anti-submarine mine were in service. Specialized minelaying flotillas of destroyers were laying their deadly cargoes in the channels leading to German submarine bases at night, using specially designed taut-wire measuring gear for accurate navigation. Submarine minelaying gear had initially been copied from a salvaged German submarine, but the original had been improved on.

Minesweeping techniques had advanced considerably since the beginning of the war. Improved sweeps and increasingly skilled crews had in the main coped well with the long-drawn out task of clearing German minefields, a job which was not complete until well after the end of the war. The invention of the paravane had provided a device which enabled ships to steam at speed with resonable protection against being struck by a mine.

The Royal Navy made a very real if by later standards imperfect attempt to utilize scientists in this war. The ultimately successful project to develop ASDIC is one example, the development of a magnetic mine another. A Board of Invention and Research was set up. Though only partially successful, it was a step in the right direction. The use of civilian scholars in the famous and highly successful Room 40 decrypting organization was another. The Admiralty had always been, and had to be, a technically minded body and despite popular legend one that looked favourably on technical and scientific innovation.

The Admiralty itself had a somewhat patchy record during the war. The energetic and occasionally brilliant combination of Churchill as First Lord and Fisher as First Sea Lord achieved much in a rather uncoordinated way. It was, however, a basically unstable combination and it collapsed in political scandal and military failure in the Dardanelles. The successors of these larger-than-life characters were less spectacular. Jellicoe's period as First Sea Lord was a disappointment to his admirers, but hardly surprising considering his over-centralizing nature and his exhaustion after years of high command. It is probable that the best First Sea Lord of the war years was the one who held that office at the end of the war, Sir Rosslyn Wemyss, in a very effective combination with the engineer-businessman

ABOVE: *Admiral Sturdee, the victor at the Falklands, seen earlier on the quarterdeck of the battleship* Hercules.

Geddes, imported to the Admiralty from railway management. 'Rosy' Wemyss was a good all-round seaman. He was popular but had not been considered one of the 'brains' of the Navy. These 'brains' – mostly inventive gunnery officers – had not done very well in high command during the war. Jellicoe was probably the best of them but others such as the difficult Bacon of the Dover Patrol or the self-satisfied and intolerant Sturdee indicated what the defects of such specialists were – and the limitations of what the pre-war Navy considered to be intelligence. The successful officers of the war – Tyrwhitt the very professional commander of the Harwich Force, Goodenough the only cruiser admiral at Jutland who did his job properly, or Gough-Calthorpe who culminated his successful Mediterranean command by making a superb job of the preliminary peace negotiations with Turkey – were all rounders, practical seamen of good intelligence. They were also superb leaders, as was Beatty who replaced Jellicoe in command of the Grand Fleet – where his main contribution was to maintain high morale despite the failure to obtain a decisive result at Jutland. As the war progressed it slowly produced a better class of leader in the Royal Navy, and one of its lessons was to ensure the quality was to be kept up for the much greater trial of World War II.

The Royal Navy emerged from the war disappointed but by no means unsuccessful. It had failed to achieve what it had considered to be its main job of destroying the enemy fleet in battle, but it had achieved its end by out-staying that fleet. Despite its near-catastrophic failure to appreciate the U-boat threat until nearly too late it had in the end defeated the U-boat menace – which was just as much its real job. It had given the Allies the priceless advantage of naval superiority. Its role in final victory was passive but none the less vital. The Imperial German Navy had proved a worthy enemy, but in the end the combination of numbers and a more enduring morale had told. Despite a near-crushing weight of tradition and of bad, or at least misunderstood, history, the Navy had proved it was able to adapt to the challenges of twentieth-century sea warfare. It proved to be at least as technically innovative as its chief rival – and rather more flexible in such matters as the use of new forms of intelligence. There were even signs as the war was coming to an end that it was at last adapting itself to the proper use of a naval staff. The war had been 'no end of a lesson' and most of the lessons were learned. In a most encouraging, imaginative and significant move, just after the war had ended, a large number of junior officers were sent to study at universities for a year.

The war itself, however, had been won at a cost. Though the chief European rival Germany was temporarily destitute and exhausted, the underlying trend of Britain's relative economic decline had been accelerated. The USA was now potentially the world's most powerful nation. Germany and Russia could and would advance from their temporarily prostrate condition and Japan had gained in power. The basis for the Royal Navy's unchallengeable superiority was no longer there. Despite the complaints at the time the 1921 Washington Conference on naval limitation was a great British diplomatic success. It restrained the USA from taking immediate advantage of her economic strength to build a navy that Britain could not match. The writing was already on the wall – it would only be a matter of time before the Royal Navy lost its position of being the most powerful navy in the world, though it took World War II to make that fully apparent.

World War I did none-the-less play a major part in ensuring that the Royal Navy remained a world leader in efficiency, skill and morale. It administered a salutary shock to an organization which had long suffered from complacency and rigidity. It also showed that many of the old lessons learned in the struggle to supremacy in previous centuries were still valid, and the Royal Navy still had many of its old strengths, though sometimes hidden under the accretion of many years of peace and unthinking superiority. Above all the lessons of 1914-18 were invaluable in the struggle for survival in the next great conflict.

BELOW: *The light cruiser* Cardiff *leading the German High Seas Fleet to surrender in November 1918.*

Chapter 3
Naval Uniforms

A system of uniform dress for naval officers was introduced into the Royal Navy in the middle of the eighteenth century. Warrant Officers received their uniforms half a century or so later and ratings achieved recognition as military servants of their monarch about 50 years after that. By the end of the nineteenth century detailed and remarkably comprehensive regulations existed to cover all the functions which seamen and their officers were expected to discharge.

In early days uniforms demonstrated nothing more than calling and status, and status was simply a matter of gentility, real or assumed, even though officers' ranks were differentiated as far back as 1748. The increasing complexity of the Royal Navy in the nineteenth century was reflected, from time to time, in a corresponding increase in the varieties of uniform and the badges it bore. The twentieth century has seen this carried further, with the new complexities of more complicated machinery, submarines, aircraft and the introduction of women.

Changes in uniform stem from the changing tasks and duties, and involve complete articles of dress and the badges worn, and the influence of civilian fashions and thought. Not to be forgotten is the individual sailor's own ability, regardless of rank, to alter his dress to his own way of thinking.

What we are looking at is not simply a matter of the width of a piece of gold lace, the size and design of a button or the length of the slings of a sword belt. We are looking at the way in which the Royal Navy regards itself. From the start of the eighteenth century an officer's uniform was required to demonstrate that the wearer was a gentleman and a military servant of the king. When he was joined by professional, specially trained men – Masters, Surgeons and Pursers to begin with – he was able to accept them completely in professional terms but only partially in social ones. This divide continued into the twentieth century and reflected contemporary attitudes ashore. These were far more rigid than those at sea; the classes and sections of society could to a great extent ignore each other on land and where they could not, a generally accepted master-servant relationship could be safely employed. None of this was possible in a ship. Uniform reflected these attitudes to the extent that the executive officer was distinguished from his specialized col-

ABOVE LEFT: *A Warrant Officer in 1902, this Gunner under ten years' seniority would be wearing a gold stripe above the three buttons on his cuff. He wears the undress sword belt and black-gripped sword of his rank.*

ABOVE: *This Captain wears the standard full dress uniform, including a sword belt with three gold stripes. His aiguillettes indicate he is an Aide de Camp.*

PREVIOUS PAGE: *Lieutenant H J Bray of the Royal Naval Reserve in 1916, in undress uniform. Note his cuff stripes.*

ABOVE: *Vice Admiral Lord Charles Beresford in 1903 wears the oak leaf and acorn cuff in force from 1901 to 1904, with the gold laced white slash and its three buttons. He wears the white-handled sword of an officer with a flag officer's belt and scabbard, and flag officer's trousers with a broad gold stripe.*

ABOVE RIGHT: *A Rear Admiral in the full dress uniform of 1904. The broad stripe on his cuff has replaced the oak leaf decoration of 1901, a return to the pattern of 1856. The laced white slash has given way to one embroidered overall with oak leaves and acorns.*

leagues by details of uniform.

The regulations in force in 1900 were primarily those introduced in October 1891. These were comprehensive and well illustrated and for the first time included detailed instructions as to the occasions on which each type of uniform should be worn. The nineteenth century had seen a dramatic increase in the range of variety of duties of naval officers which led, naturally, into a degree of proliferation of dress. At the same time, largely following civilian fashion, there was a move towards simplification. The results were a large number of individual 'dresses' or classes of uniform and a marked reduction in the varieties of design.

At the turn of the century the primary colour of uniform was dark blue. White was the only alternative and was largely restricted to use in hot climates. The method of distinguishing an officer's rank was by the application of gold stripes to his cuff, a practice introduced in the eighteenth century and continued to this day, albeit in a different form.

The executive branch officer wore a curl of gold lace on his uppermost stripe whereas specialist officers of the civil branches did not, a feature intro-

duced in the middle of the previous century. Specialist officers wore coloured cloth between their stripes to indicate the branch of the service to which they belonged. Surgeons, for example, wore red cloth while Paymasters wore white. These basic indications of rank and branch of service were applied to all types of uniform dress. The principal types of dress were as follows:

Full dress: An eighteenth-century tail coat worn buttoned across in double-breasted form and bearing lace in amounts graduated in accordance with rank. Trousers bore a gold stripe down their outer seams and the thickness of this varied with rank. Epaulettes and a laced sword-belt were also worn with a black beaver cocked hat with loop, gold tassels and lace for senior officers. This form of dress began the century with white cuff slashes – the last vestige of the eighteenth century 'mariner's cuff' – but in 1901 flag officers received, in place of their broad lowest stripe, a band of oak leaf and acorn embroidery. This lasted until 1904 when the cuff slash for flag officers was altered to one covered with oak leaf and acorn embroidery and the broad stripe was reintroduced. Apart from minor details this

uniform remained the same until it effectively disappeared in 1939, seeing only a brief revival for a few officers at the Coronation in 1953 and on a small number of other official occasions.

Frock coat: This plain blue, double-breasted, knee-length coat was widely used for ceremonial occasions and could be worn with or without epaulettes and sword. The trousers worn with it were plain navy blue.

Undress coat: Better known as the 'monkey jacket', this differed only slightly from the double-breasted 'reefer' pattern jacket worn today and was the most widely worn form of dress.

Ball dress: A plain blue double-breasted tail coat worn unbuttoned over a white waistcoat, with full dress trousers and epaulettes. This form of dress remained in partial service until 1939.

Mess dress: Not unlike ball dress but without the tails to form a round jacket not worn with epaulettes. A gold-laced waistcoat was worn for a time but the lacing was abolished in 1903. In hotter climates a white mess jacket was also worn fitted with shoulder straps to carry the badges of rank whereas the blue mess jacket had cuff stripes in the usual way.

White undress: this consisted of a white tunic worn with shoulder straps, white trousers and shoes and a tropical helmet.

Headgear consisted of the cocked hat already mentioned, which was rarely worn and only with epaulettes. There was also a cap with a smaller crown and peak than is worn today, and finally the tropical helmet, the general shape of which was changed to the Wolseley pattern in 1906.

Only minor changes took place until 1914 when the Royal Naval Air Service was formed. This event would eventually lead to a variety of new items of dress but from the start officers wore a gilt representation of an eagle above their cuff stripes. Instead of

the crown and foul anchor badge pilots and observers wore a crown over a gilt eagle and their buttons were similarly decorated. It is of interest to note that in 1913, when there were very few naval officers trained to fly and there was no RNAS, 'aeroplane pilots' wore gilt eagle's wings on their left breasts – some sections of the Admiralty were air-minded from an early stage. In March 1914 Lieutenants who had served for eight years in the ranks were renamed Lieutenant-Commanders; they were already wearing a stripe of half the normal thickness on their cuffs mid way between the existing two stripes.

World War I saw further changes as the Royal Navy adapted to new circumstances. Engineering officers gained a greater recognition when their uniform was brought into line with that of the executive branch, although they continued to wear their purple distinction cloth between their stripes.

The early formation of the Royal Naval Division (63rd Infantry Division) led to the appearance, for practice purposes, of khaki uniform. This was formally recognized by the Admiralty in October 1916, but a variation of the Army uniform had been already widely adopted. At first gold stripes were applied to the cuffs but as this was regarded by the wearers as both expensive and impracticable, lighter colour khaki stripes were substituted and khaki cap covers also appeared. Many RNAS officers followed suit: although the 'maternity jacket' of the Royal Flying Corps does not seem to have been adopted, khaki tunics were. In 1916 full dress, frock coats, ball dress and mess dress were placed in abeyance for the duration of the war. In the same year watch coats were approved for wear at sea instead of the less practical great coats.

Khaki clothing was generally restricted to those employed on land overseas although regulations for the RNAS in 1917 – employed in home defence against aerial attack – called for blue breeches and grey shirts to be worn in the air and when employed on airfields. It is likely that some form of this dress was already being worn and that the Admiralty was simply recognizing the fact. The still-new concept of service to the Royal Navy in the air was further recognized by the short-lived requirement for some officers to wear stars over their stripes to indicate rank and responsibility when flying and observer officers wore a gilt letter 'O' with wings instead of the eagle on each sleeve.

The end of the war saw the granting of executive branch titles to all other branches, together with the addition of the curl to the top cuff stripe though the various coloured cloth distinction stripes were retained. This order appeared in October 1918 and is of considerable interest as it reveals the breaking down of the barrier between executive and civil branch officers. Experience had made it abundantly clear that they were fighting the same enemy.

Regulations for officers of the two reserves, the Royal Naval Reserve (RNR) and the Royal Naval Volunteer Reserve (RNVR), broadly followed those of the regular service. Their badges, buttons and cuff stripes differed in design and the variety of uniforms they wore was more restricted. Officers of the RNR were almost invariably officers of the merchant navy and, in the major companies, especially in their passenger vessels, merchant uniform was similar to that of the Royal Navy apart from badges, buttons and cuff stripes. It was during World War I that the general merchant navy uniform appeared which involved cuff stripes, and a cap badge common to all officers.

In 1918 Warrant Officers received further recognition as their status improved. They lost their three-button cuffs, something they shared with Midshipmen and Chief Petty Officers, and adopted a cuff stripe of lace a quarter of an inch wide. They also received a full dress coat modelled on that worn by commissioned officers but with thinner lace. Since the eighteenth century the status of the wearer played an important part in changing dress regulations for wholly understandable reasons. Warrant Officers bore great and increasing responsibilities and their uniforms demonstrated this. The rank was abolished in 1949.

In 1919 further changes followed which demonstrated the influence of altered attitudes ashore. The undress tail coat became optional wear for all officers below the rank of Captain, ball dress was virtually ousted by mess dress and the wearing of full dress was restricted to levées at home. The frock coat, worn with epaulettes, was now considered adequate for all other important occasions. Full dress coats now appeared in only three varieties – one for flag officers, one for all other officers and one for Warrant Officers – the only other distinction of rank being the cuff stripes. Laced trousers were similarly dealt with, the widths of lace being restricted to two. Laced trousers, dating from 1833, with widths of lace varying with the rank, formed the oldest item of uniform dress pattern still in service. They changed only in details of cut and only disappeared in 1939

save for occasional reappearances after World War II when restricted to flag officers. The Royal Canadian Navy also continued their use until the introduction of the tri-service uniform. The year 1919 also saw an increase in the size of the diameter of the top of the officer's cap, and at the same time the round jacket finally disappeared as the uniform of the Naval Cadet although it continued elsewhere.

Further gradual changes followed. In 1921 the two reserve services lost their distinctive buttons and adopted those of the Royal Navy. In 1925 officers of the Fleet Air Arm attached to the Royal Air Force were ordered to wear a cuff badge consisting of a foul anchor superimposed on the wings of an albatross. In common with styles in civilian life soft-fronted shirts, albeit with stiffened cuffs, were approved for war with mess undress and similarly, soft cuffs might be worn with monkey jackets, the everyday undress uniform, by 1928. Further small changes occurred in the period before World War II. In general these made matters easier for the wearers of uniform and further integrated all branches of the service. For example in 1936 Pay-

Admiral of the Fleet.

Admiral.

Vice-Admiral.

Rear-Admiral.

Commodore 2nd Class & Captain over 3 years' seniority.

Captain under 3 years Seniority.

Commander.

Lieutenant over 8 years' Seniority.

Lieutenant under 8yrs. Seniority. Sub-Lieutenant, Chief Gunner & Chief Boatswain.

Staff Commander.

Inspector-General of Hospitals & Fleets.

Secretary to an Admiral of the Fleet.

Inspector of Machinery under 8 years' Service as such.

Fleet Surgeon.

Naval Instructor of 8 years Service.

Chief Carpenter.

ABOVE: *Epaulettes and their devices, illustrated in the 1891 Regulations. Officers of the executive branch wore silver devices and had a silver edge to the epaulettes; civil branch officers wore gold. The St Edward's crown was used then, and reintroduced in 1953; the Tudor Crown with its round top was used from 1901 to 1953.*

LEFT: *This Naval Cadet of 1909 wears the round jacket, waistcoat and collar badges of his rank. His cuff was the same as a Midshipman and a Warrant Officer.*

RIGHT: *A naval beach party in the Mediterranean in 1943, wearing Army equipment.*

BELOW: *A Lieutenant Commander RNVR examining beach obstacles with a Major, Royal Engineers, on a Normandy beach in 1944.*

master Midshipmen and Paymaster Cadets wore the uniform of Midshipmen of the executive branch but retained the white cuff stripe of their branch. Although known and recognized for nearly a century it was not until 1938 that tropical dress was introduced in the form of a white shirt, worn with shoulder straps, white shorts and white or blue stockings. Previously, warm-weather clothing had been largely concerned with more formal orders of dress.

As in 1916, the more elaborate forms of dress went into abeyance in 1939, some of them never to reappear. White cap covers disappeared in home waters and khaki uniform reappeared quite extensively, especially with early commando forces. Beach-communication parties were also permitted to wear khaki battledress but the wearing of the same article of clothing dyed navy blue was forbidden. In practice it went on being worn and in 1943 blue battledress was officially permitted.

Also borrowed from the Army was the beret. The Admiralty seems to have ignored it until May 1945 when it was ordered for air crews for wear with working dress. In practice both battledress and beret being simple, hard wearing and protective had been popular for some time, not least with the flight-deck crews on aircraft carriers. Another wartime feature was the spread of protective clothing. Boiler suits and anti-flash wear had been known for some time. The submariner's heavy white wool sweater had appeared before World War I and battledress appeared during World War II. Flying clothing began with the appearance of aircraft and then developed to take into account the changing demands which affected the air branch of the service. Not all of these can satisfactorily be described as uniform though all came to be of a uniform pattern.

On the whole the end of the war did not lead to the mass reappearance of pre-war styles. Indeed, on 25 March 1949, the wearing of full dress coats, laced trousers, epaulettes and cocked hats was placed in abeyance and frock coats, tropical helmets, wellington boots and white gloves were abolished. White caps and white cap covers did reappear in 1946 and cuff stripes were ordered to be run right round the cuff in the following year (they had run only half way round since 1941). New Chaplains were ordered to wear naval uniform instead of the 'yachting dress' formerly deemed appropriate but the wearers remained firmly outside the naval rank structure unlike their brethren in the Army and Royal Air Force. Dark blue shorts were ordered into tropical working dress in 1949 and the watch coat was abolished. In the same year it was accepted that for 'state occasions' the undress coat or monkey jacket, the double-breasted jacket with its eight buttons, could be worn as ceremonial dress with medals and swords. The same rule was applied to the white tunic worn in the Tropics.

The reserves came in for further attention in 1951 when all officers lost their distinctive waved or interwoven stripes and adopted the straight ones of the Royal Navy itself being distinguished by the insertion of the letter 'R' inside the curl of the top stripe. The 'R' was to be omitted when the officer was mobilized. Officers of the Air Branch were to wear the letter 'A' instead. The distinctive buttons abolished in 1921 returned, bearing the appropriate letters RNR or RNVR. In November 1958 the reserves were unified as the Royal Naval Reserve and the standard Royal Navy button was readopted.

With the virtual disappearance of full dress and consequent reliance on the monkey jacket, itself strictly an undress uniform, it was eventually realized that there was still a need for some form of ceremonial uniform and a ceremonial day dress for flag officers was introduced in 1959. This was a simplified version of the former full dress coat, being a double-breasted tail coat with a white collar edged with gold lace and the usual cuff stripes depending on rank. It is worn with laced trousers and a black belt ornamented by three horizontal gold lines of the form previously worn by Captains. Instead of epaulettes, shoulder straps are worn as is the sole pattern of cap. Admirals of the Fleet wear the same coat but with eight buttons instead of six in each of the two rows and they also wear the original full dress flag officer's belt decorated with gold embroidery of acorns and oakleaves.

Ball dress returned in modified form some years after the war but its use has been limited as has that of laced trousers. Officers may wear this form of dress if they wish. Mess dress, though plainer and simpler than before, is widely used on appropriate occasions.

A further sign of the times was another borrowing from the Army. Just as the watch coat was based on the 'British Warm' and working dress on battledress so the Army's pullover, in navy blue instead of khaki, appeared first at sea and then on land as well in the 1970s. Like its military predecessor, and

unlike contemporary civilian copies, the shoulders are not only strengthened but are equipped to carry badges with shoulder straps of rank. The 'wooly pully' had already achieved the status of undress uniform, being worn with navy blue trousers, white shirt, black tie and shoes and the usual cap. Comfort and practicality had again played their part in uniform design.

We have looked so far at the cut and primary design of uniforms but not at the distinctive badges signifying rank and specialization. Rank badges have changed little since they appeared in modern form for officers of the executive branch in 1856.

ABOVE: *The rating behind Admiral of the Fleet Sir John Fisher wears the sennet hat and three Good Conduct Badges. The sennet was abolished in 1921.*

LEFT: *Semaphore signalling aboard a trawler-minesweeper. Apart from the cap and tally, working dress remained largely civilian in trawlers taken up for naval service.*

RIGHT: *A Leading Seaman in tropical dress in 1926, wearing three Good Conduct Badges, and on his right sleeve the device of a Leading Torpedoman. The Wolseley Pattern and white duck uniform are typical of the period.*

BELOW: *These 6-inch gun turret crewmen in HMS* Orion *during World War II are wearing anti-flash gear and working overalls.*

Steps in rank have been and are indicated by half-inch gold lace stripes (though these used to be five-eighths of an inch wide) ranging from a single stripe for a Sub-Lieutenant, two for a Lieutenant, two and a half for a Lieutenant over eight years in the rank, retitled Lieutenant-Commander in 1914, three for a Commander and four for a Captain. Flag Officers have traditionally worn a broad strip of gold lace as a part of their cuffs and this has been retained with the addition above it of a single stripe for Rear-Admirals, two for Vice-Admirals and three for Admirals. Admirals of the Fleet have four and Commodores wear only the broad stripe with a curl. Officers of civil branches did not receive the curl in 1856. They had previously worn and continued to wear single- rather than double-breasted coats and coloured cloth to distinguish their branch specialization. The first branches to receive these in 1863 were Navigating (light blue), Medical (scarlet), Accountant (white) and Engineer (purple). The Navigating Branch kept its distinctive cloth for only four years but as time went on and the number of branches increased more colours appeared. In 1918 Shipwrights wore silver grey, Wardmaster maroon, Electrical Officers dark green, Armoured and Ordnance Officers dark blue, and Dentists orange.

At the same time, all officers of all branches were granted the curl; navigators and engineers already had it but the coloured cloth remained the mark of the civil branches for some considerable time. Ordnance Officers switched to purple from navy blue in 1950 as they became Ordnance Engineering Officers and in 1951 Wardmasters changed to salmon pink and Electrical and Special Branch Officers to a lighter shade of green. Most of these distinction colours were abolished in 1955 save for Medical, Dental and Wardmaster Officers who complied with the Hague Convention on the prominent wearing of some item of uniform to indicate medical training or skills. Two groups of civilians who may be required to wear uniform still retain their coloured cloth – officers of the Royal Corps of Naval Constructors retain the silver grey of 1884 and some civilian electrical officers retain their light green. These last two are relatively uncommon as civilian dress is worn much of the time.

Midshipmen have retained the patch of white either side of their throats which they were first given in 1748, originally the silk lining of the thrown-back collar of their coats. In the 1750s this changed to a patch of white cloth with a strip of white lace secured by a button and so, apart from varying in size, it has remained.

Reserve officers wore different lace until 1951. The first uniform regulations for the Royal Naval Reserve appeared in 1864 and, what concerns us here, is that their rank was indicated by two narrow stripes of braid so arranged as to be waved and to cross each other. The same form was also to be used for the loop of the cocked hat where the regular executive branch wore bullion loops and the civil branches flat gold lace. The letters RNR and the full title of the organization were employed on badges, buttons and buckles. The Royal Naval Volunteer

Reserve was created in 1903 as a supplement to the RNR. In this case, although ranks followed ordinary naval practice the cuff stripes were to be of a waved three-eighths of an inch gold lace. A variant of the curl was adopted for executive branch officers of both reserves and civil branch officers followed the practices of their regular counterparts.

An interesting feature of recent times has been the introduction of the gilt dolphin's badge of the submariner. Officers and ratings wear it on the left breast. With the Fleet Air Arm's winged badge it is the only such distinct branch badge left apart from the different arrangements made for Chaplains.

Although ratings of the Royal Navy had no formal uniform until 1857 there was, inevitably, a fair degree of uniformity produced by the 'slop' system of issuing clothing to seamen. Such clothing was provided to Admiralty order and was purchased in bulk, and seamen adopted a form of clothing which offered some protection both from the elements and from the materials with which they worked so this uniformity was hardly surprising. The uniform adopted in 1857 represented a formalization of what seamen were wearing already; neither for the first time nor the last the Admiralty showed common sense based on experience in recognizing the suitability of what was already worn. Change has been very gradual ever since.

At the start of the twentieth century ratings had a well-established system of uniform where the main distinction lay between those of the rank of Petty Officer [the equivalent of an army sergeant) and above and those of Leading Rate and below. Some features of the nineteenth century such as the seaman's round jacket soon disappeared – the sailor was no longer strictly a 'bluejacket' from 1891 and the 'frock', a jumper with cuffs and gold badges which was worn tucked into the trousers, disappeared in 1906. Trousers were bell-bottomed and made of serge rather than the former cloth. The jumper, not tucked in the trousers, was worn over a square-necked white flannel shirt trimmed with blue cloth edging. The flannel shirt was replaced by cotton in 1938. A blue cloth collar, bordered by three white tape stripes and a black silk handkerchief worn under the large rear flap of the collar and secured below the 'V' of the front of the jumper together with a white lanyard completed the dress. A cap, rather larger and floppier than that worn today, or a broad-brimmed hat of woven sennet or straw was also worn. Black shoes were provided but a preference for going bare-foot existed among some seamen into the twentieth century. White working dress of similar cut was also worn. In time boiler suits replaced this and white tropical clothing was introduced. This uniform, and its later derivatives, was the normal dress of men 'dressed as seamen'.

For Petty Officers and higher ranks, as well as for certain lower rates a form of dress related to that of officers was worn. This 'fore and aft' version involved ordinary blue trousers, blue double-breasted jacket, white shirt and black tie. The uniform was worn with a peaked cap, similar to that of an officer but with a different badge. White cap

covers were worn when ordered and as with officers the white part of the cap eventually become permanent and is made of plastic today. Badges were of gold wire for important occasions and of woven red wool at other times. In white uniform woven blue badges were eventually replaced by blue printed ones. The wearing of a cap ribbon bearing the name of the wearer's ship appeared early in the nineteenth century. The practice gradually became formalized and painted letters were replaced by woven.

In 1975 modifications to seamen's dress appeared. Bell-bottomed trousers disappeared to be replaced by somewhat flared trousers creased in the twentieth-century style down front and back rather than at the sides. The black silk has gone to be replaced by a simple facing to the zip-fastened jumper, so that ribbons are no longer needed to tie it down, and the lanyard has been abolished. Fore and aft rig has been gradually modified following civilian practice, in much the same way as the officer's monkey jacket.

ABOVE: *On the flight deck of HMS* Hermes *Captain Middleton is wearing flying overalls and the crewmen are wearing distinctive 'bonedomes' and ear-protectors. Fleet Air Arm equipment owes much to American influence.*

Ratings of the reserves have generally followed the practices of their regular counterparts with only changes of detail to indicate their service. Both types of seaman can be found in every branch but there has never been a need for coloured distinction cloth as the badges worn on their right sleeves, indicating specialization and degrees of skill and qualification have been sufficent.

Although changes in uniform have not been anything like as extensive as those for officers and although, until fairly recently, uniform has been issued centrally rather than being made up for each individual by a tailor, the same individualism referred to above has surfaced and will no doubt continue to do so. The submariner's white sweater, worn instead of the jumper when at sea, did not receive immediate sanction and variations in detail can still be found.

A major innovation seen by the twentieth-

BELOW: *A 1977 combined view of (left) the serge dress for WRNS ratings in 1917, and (right) a Leading Wren in the Women's Royal Naval Reserve.*

century Royal Navy is, of course, the recruitment of women to the service. Queen Alexandra's Royal Naval Nursing Service was established in 1902. Though strictly civilian this organization is worthy of mention as, although its members wore a nursing uniform not unlike that worn by civilian counterparts, the emphasis was and is on providing a service to the Royal Navy. Their badge consists of the monogram of Queen Alexandra superimposed on a foul anchor. There is the usual crown above and the red (Geneva) cross below.

In 1917, in response to the cry 'Release a man for sea service' the Women's Royal Naval Service was established. Ratings were issued with a long navy blue serge dress equipped with a small collar not unlike that worn by seamen. A shapeless, more-or-less circular hat with a stiffened brim was added and working overalls were also provided. Officers were given a feminine version of the uniforms worn by naval officers though the monkey jacket buttoned right over left and skirts were almost of ankle length. Officers wore a velour tricorne hat of considerable size and greatcoats were also issued. Badges were of light blue throughout. Officers wore light blue cuff stripes and those more senior wore a diamond in place of the naval officer's curl. Ratings were given a navy serge dress and a floppy hat. The uniform was not popular and it is hardly surprising that yet again the wearers undertook modifications including deepening the 'V' neck of the serge dress and inserting a version of the seaman's 'flannel'. Some ratings wore men's 'sailors' collars' instead of their own smaller ones. Black stockings and black shoes or boots were worn by all ranks.

The WRNS was disbanded in 1919 and speedily re-established 20 years later. Officers' uniforms were similar to those previously worn but were extensively remodelled in accordance with contemporary civilian styles. The tricorn hat also reappeared though in far smaller format and its use was later extended to Chief Petty Officers and Petty Officers. Ratings' uniforms were quite unlike those of 1919 being of the fore and aft pattern and not unlike those worn by officers though the buttons were black instead of gilt. White shirts and black ties were normally worn. An unpopular headdress was ordered but this was replaced in 1942 by a variant of the seaman's cap which proved successful. Bell-bottomed trousers were also worn in wartime. A wide variety of specialist clothing was also available.

The service became a permanent part of the Royal Navy in 1949. In 1951 mess dress was introduced for the first time. More suitable trousers were designed for working dress and a better working shirt was brought into use. In 1952 the Women's Royal Naval Reserve was established and a letter 'R' was set within the diamond above the cuff stripes which all WRNS officers had worn since 1939.

The third category of women in naval service concerns those who are medical and dental officers of the Royal Navy itself. As naval officers, their uniforms resemble WRNS patterns but they wear gold cuff stripes with coloured cloth distinction stripes and the cap badge of the Royal Navy.

Chapter 4
The Inter-War Years

As life returned to normal after the terrible trauma of the Great War the Royal Navy found itself beset by many problems. First priority was to deal with the loose ends of the war; the so-called 'Intervention War' against the forces of Russian Bolshevism resulted in a series of small, expensive and politically unpopular campaigns in the White Sea, the Baltic, the Black Sea and even the Far East. By 1920 these commitments disappeared, but not without a number of clashes with the Russians and some casualties in men and ships.

A pressing problem was the hugely swollen number of ships and men, far exceeding any peacetime needs. The 'hostilities only' officers and ratings could be discharged easily but the regular Navy could not be maintained at its 1914 level and providing a reasonable pay and promotion structure for all was to prove a major headache for the Admiralty for many years. In 1922 the notorious 'Geddes Axe' pruned the Navy List drastically, eliminating a number of junior officer-posts.

An enormous number of obsolete warships were sold for scrapping, and a considerable number of incomplete hulls were also broken up to clear slipways. What could not be tackled so easily was the problem of block obsolescence among comparatively modern ships. The 12-inch gunned dreadnoughts, for example, were now outclassed by 14-inch and 16-inch gunned ships in the Japanese and United States' navies. Even the 15-inch gunned *Queen Elizabeth* and *Royal Sovereign* Class ships were outclassed by the latest foreign battleships, and the Director of Naval Construction had minuted in 1918 that the new 41,000-ton battlecruiser *Hood* ought not to be completed. Many of the light cruisers and destroyers were worn out by war service, and were fit only for the reserve.

ABOVE: *The four* Iron Duke-*class vessels were a major element of the battle fleet until the end of the 1920s.*

LEFT: *HMS Iron Duke firing at Bolshevik positions near Kaffa Bay in the Black Sea, while covering the withdrawal of 'White' forces in 1919.*

PREVIOUS PAGE: *The battlecruiser* Repulse *and other capital ships dressed overall at King George V's Jubilee Review at Spithead.*

On the credit side, there were sufficient numbers of robust and well-armed destroyers and submarines built late in the war, and these would provide the backbone of the Fleet for some years to come. The cruiser squadrons were not so well served as a result of pre-war vacillations of policy. The standard wartime 'North Sea' type of light scout was not suitable for work on overseas stations and so the older coal-burning cruisers were kept for that purpose while more modern ships went into reserve.

Although the Navy had expanded and extended the capabilities of the Royal Naval Air Service (RNAS) enormously during the war, the post-war situation was unsatisfactory. As a panic reaction to air raids on London the RNAS and Royal Flying Corps (RFC) had been combined to form the Royal Air Force in April 1918. The fledgling independent service fought successfully against post-war plans to revert to the original system with the result that the Royal Navy was left with the responsibility for aircraft carriers but no control over aircraft and pilots.

Space does not permit a detailed account of the long struggle by the Admiralty to win back control of naval aviation, but let it suffice to say that it was a bad time for the Navy to lose control. The Japanese and the Americans were developing doctrines of carrier warfare and advanced types of aircraft to match while the Royal Navy, stripped of most of its air-minded officers, was not permitted to investigate such novel ideas as dive-bombing. The bulk of its flying personnel had volunteered to transfer to the RAF in 1918, understandably anxious to further their careers as aviators, and this factor was to become more harmful as the years passed.

The Admiralty and Royal Navy were not to be left in peace to resolve these problems. Rivalry be-

RIGHT: *The* Royal Oak *and others of the* Revenge *class were modernised in the 1930s, but were still unsuitable for front-line duties*

BELOW: *The 'Mighty Hood' ranked high in public esteem but her protection was pre-Jutland in standard. The DNC's 1938 prediction of disaster was fulfilled three years later.*

INSET: *One of HMS Hood's 4-inch anti-aircraft guns.*

tween Japan and the United States had led both navies to embark on large ship-building programmes in the middle of the war. It was these giant battleships and battlecruisers, all armed with 16-inch guns, which outclassed every capital ship in the Royal Navy. To make matters worse there were strong bodies of opinion in Washington and Tokyo which regarded Britain as a potential enemy and the Admiralty had to face the unpalatable fact that the new American and Japanese fleets were intended to fight the Royal Navy as well as each other.

Faced with such a threat there were only two choices – to start a new arms race or to negotiate. The Admiralty chose a careful compromise, by announcing a programme of new construction, and at the same offering to negotiate. It was a shrewd move because neither the United States nor the Japanese governments were prepared to spend huge sums of money to complete their bloated war programmes; political support was not there and neither was the money. The Americans, in particular, were looking for a way to avoid a confrontation with Japan.

The upshot was the Naval and Disarmament Conference held in Washington in 1921-2. For the Royal Navy it meant a formal end to the Two-Power Standard, and acceptance of parity with the United States' Navy in capital ships and limits on tonnage for lesser warships. It was bitterly denounced by naval opinion in Britain but from a vantage point 60 years later the Washington Treaty can be seen to be merely formal recognition of a state of affairs created by the Great War. The British Empire had over-extended itself to support a ruinous war and the industrial and economic strength which underpinned the Royal Navy was now diminished to the point where it could no longer afford the Two-Power Standard.

What the Royal Navy did achieve at Washington was the right to build two new battleships, displacing 35,000 tons and armed with 16-inch guns whereas the USA and Japan were forced to scrap some of their new construction to get down to the agreed numbers. It gave British designers a chance to implement wartime lessons, which were to prove invaluable when the time came to rearm in the next decade. It also secured the Royal Navy two new aircraft carriers, to be converted from light battlecruisers of little fighting value. An over-optimistic attempt to ban the submarine failed, but taken overall the Treaty put a useful brake on naval expansion and by killing off a breed of super-battleships forced designers to look at new ways of saving weight.

In the 1920s the routine of the Royal Navy seemed little different to what it had been before the war. The Atlantic Fleet operated in home waters, and was principally concerned with training, while the Mediterranean Fleet operated the most modern ships. British interests were still world-wide and a large volume of seaborne trade passed through the Mediterranean to the Far East through the Suez Canal. Smaller squadrons were stationed in China and the East Indies to maintain and safeguard trade-routes to the Far East.

The post-war world was unsettled and British warships were constantly involved in 'police work' evacuating Greek refugees from Smyrna, White Russians from the Black Sea, or fugitives from the

BELOW: *HMS* Malaya *in 1922, largely unchanged from the war years, before two funnels were trunked into one.*

Spanish Civil War. As the power of central government in China crumbled, the ambitions of local warlords brought their troops into frequent confrontations with British naval units. The great rivers of China became the last outpost of 'gunboat diplomacy', with standing patrols on the Yangtse and West Rivers.

The battlefleet came to be the visible instrument of foreign policy, in some ways more than it had in pre-war days. To conceal the lack of finance the diplomatic value of the battlefleet was elevated to the level of a fetish; battleships were denied urgent modernization because they 'could not be spared'. At a time when the Americans, French, Italians and Japanese brought all their battleships up to modern standards the Admiralty and the Foreign Office connived at the fiction that the withdrawal of a pair of battleships would encourage international aggression. The last victim of this strange delusion was the battlecruiser *Hood*; her known defects could not be rectified because a three-year refit would alter the balance of power in Europe!

German naval rivalry had been officially buried at Versailles, but in 1929 the *Reichsmarine* launched the *Deutschland*, first of three new 'armoured ships'. In spite of all the efforts of the statesmen to prevent Germany from building commerce-raiding cruisers the ingenuity of German ship-designers had outwitted them. The *Deutschland* was officially within the 10,000-ton limit for cruisers, but had the 11-inch (28-cm) guns allowed for coast-defence ships. She was another Fisher-type 'armadillo', capable in theory of sinking any 8-inch gunned cruiser with impunity and fast enough to outrun any battleship.

According to all the naval pundits the so-called 'pocket battleship' could only be dealt with by the British battlecruisers *Hood*, *Renown* and *Repulse* and the Japanese *Kongo* Class.

Here was the beginning of another naval race, which the hard-pressed Admiralty had laboured to avoid. Like the Germans and Italians the Japanese were prepared to cheat on the international treaty conditions, frequently quoting tonnage 30 per cent below the real figure. Despite this, these treaty limitations acted as a brake on numbers and for that reason the Admiralty acquiesced in Foreign Office initiatives to extend the international naval treaties.

The London Naval Conference in 1930 extended the 'holiday' in battleship construction until 1936, and extended the principle of numerical ratios to cruisers and destroyers. This affected the Royal Navy particularly badly as it possessed a larger number of over-age cruisers than anyone else. Japan was permitted for the first time to have the same number of submarines as Britain and the USA.

Heavily in debt to the United States, Great Britain was dragged down with other debtor-nations by the Wall Street Crash and the ensuing Depression. Financial orthodoxy suggested massive deflation in the form of wage-cuts, but whereas other bodies of public servants such as the police were able to deflect the most severe pay-cuts by the threat of strikes, the Armed Forces were seen as soft targets. By inept handling of the news, the Admiralty triggered off the Invergordon Mutiny of 1929, when a substantial part of the Atlantic Fleet refused to go to sea. In truth the 'mutiny' was more of a sit-down strike, and even the sporadic acts of minor violence

HMS Centurion *and her sisters* King George V *and* Ajax *were deleted in 1927 to comply with the Washington Treaty.*

were perpetrated by sailors unaffected by pay-cuts of any sort. It was none the less a bitter moment for the Royal Navy, and the effect on world opinion was equivalent to the declaration of a republic in Great Britain. An international loan was being negotiated by the government to get it through the financial crisis, but news of Invergordon helped cause the international banks to withdraw the offer and was a contributory factor in Britain abandoning the Gold Standard.

As history relates, going off the Gold Standard proved to be a blessing in disguise, and the Invergordon Mutiny was soon settled without bloodshed. Rigorous enquiries failed to uncover any proof of Bolshevist subversion, and a chastened Admiralty took a long, hard look at pay and conditions of the lower deck. A substantial improvement in relations between officers and men was noticeable thereafter, and that can almost certainly be listed as the most important consequence of the mutiny.

More serious was the parlous financial state of the nation. The public was largely apathetic or pacifist in outlook, and its political leaders lacked the will to tell the truth to the electorate. Only gradually did the public begin to perceive the threat to world peace posed by the Dictators. Hitler's abrogation of the Treaty of Versailles and his creation of a new *Kriegsmarine* passed apparently unnoticed by the man in the street.

Recognizing that pressure from international opinion could not halt German rearmament, the Admiralty collaborated with the Foreign Office to negotiate an Anglo-German naval agreement in 1935. Under its terms the *Kriegsmarine* was to be permitted to expand to a figure representing 35 per cent of the Royal Navy and to possess submarines once more, equal to the Royal Navy's strength.

As can be imagined the agreement was denounced by naval opinion and by those few people who saw the dangers of Fascism but it made a great deal of sense. For one thing German rearmament was a fact; it could not be stopped. Eight U-boats were already under construction and plans were afoot to build new capital ships. What the Anglo-German Naval Agreement achieved was a politically backed limitation of German naval expansion. Its total tonnage limitations put the *Kriegsmarine* on the horns of a dilemma, whether to emphasize U-boats or big surface ships; any decisions to build very large ships in one category would automatically reduce

ABOVE: *HMCS* Fraser, *formerly HMS* Crescent. *In 1930 the 'C' class of destroyers was halved as a gesture of disarmament.*

ABOVE: *The Royal Australian Navy's battlecruiser HMAS* Australia *was ceremonially scuttled off Sydney Heads in April 1924.*

RIGHT: *The submarine* Odin *passing the carrier* Eagle *in Malta.*

power's expansion, a right that the Royal Navy was to exercise in 1938-40 to counter German and Japanese moves.

By acting through the League of Nations, Britain and France had one chance to stop the rise of the Dictators. When Italy attacked Abyssinia in 1936 the League of Nations called for sanctions against Italy and the Royal Navy was mobilized to enforce them. It was more than a match for the Italian Navy but the nations of Europe refused to back the call for sanctions after Mussolini had made it clear that war would follow if the sanctions were extended to include oil. After a brief show of force by the Royal Navy at Alexandria and in the Red Sea Mussolini and his 'forests of bayonets' were left alone to complete the conquest of Abyssinia. The League of Nations was clearly no protector of peace.

The mobilization showed how far efficiency had been eroded by neglect. To provide Mediterranean and Red Sea ships with sufficient escorts the Home Fleet (formerly the Atlantic Fleet) had to be stripped

the tonnage available in other categories. Taken in conjunction with Hitler's intention to keep Great Britain neutral until he had overrun Europe, this was sufficient restraint on the German Navy in the short term.

The political climate of the time can be gauged from British public reaction to the Anglo-German Naval Agreement. Many Labour politicians and even some Tories hailed it as a victory for disarmament. It was also the time of the Oxford Union debate which resolved not to fight for 'King and Country'.

Few people had anything good to say about the second London Naval Treaty of 1936. It reduced the calibre of battleship guns to 14 inches and cut cruiser displacement to 8000 tons, but when the Japanese gave notice that they would not be bound by its limitations any hope of restraining naval expansion vanished. The treaty contained 'escalator clauses' to permit any signatory to match another

of virtually all its destroyers until replacements could be brought forward from reserve. Most of the smaller destroyers were fit only for scrap, and it would be necessary to keep the rest running long after their normal lifespan had been exceeded.

Infinitely more serious was a security failure which went undetected. Ships in the Red Sea sent numerous radio messages to Alexandria and Malta and these were monitored by Italian cryptographers. The messages were in cipher but the large volume of traffic provided the Italian cipher experts with what they needed and the first crucial 'break-in' was achieved. This vital information, soon in German hands, was to hamper the Royal Navy during World War II. However, the Abyssinian Crisis gave the Royal Navy timely warning of many other weaknesses, although a war with Italy would doubtless have been a victory, for the Italian Navy was, in the words of an American historian, more hot air than hardware.

ABOVE: 'H' class
submarines in 1931 still
made up a large part of the
strength.

LEFT: H.51 and her sisters
were developed from an
American design of 1915.

The nightmare of a war on two fronts haunted the Admiralty throughout the 1930s. The reborn German Navy was still small enough to be handled by the Royal Navy, and any threat from Italy could be neutralized with the aid of the French Navy. But the considerable British interests in the Far East could not be defended at the same time. All hopes rested on the big base at Singapore which had been a central point of Jellicoe's 1919 plans to defend the Empire. Year after year money was voted to complete the base or work stopped as a result of changing government priorities. What nobody chose to recall was Jellicoe's emphatic opinion that the only reason for fortifying Singapore was to provide a base for a major fleet. Without the base a fleet could not be stationed in the Far East, but the base without a fleet was useless.

The Admiralty's assessment was correct as things turned out. Naval Intelligence was also prescient about the timing of the next war. In a policy document on battleship design drafted as early as 1936 it was stated that the first pair of a new class of battleships had to be ready in the spring of 1940 'by which time we shall be at war with Germany'. It was

proposed to station all the new and most powerful capital ships in home waters, leaving the older ships to watch the Japanese in the Far East.

After the 1936 London Naval Treaty the British Government finally recognized what the Admiralty had been trying to tell them for some years, that a new construction programme must be started without further delay. Sadly the magnificent industrial support enjoyed up to the end of the previous war no longer existed. The 'locust years' of the 1920s and early 1930s had caused many of the armament and shipbuilding firms to close and those firms still in business had lost many of their experienced staff. This industrial weakness was to prove the biggest handicap of all in the struggle to rebuild British military strength.

So bad was the state of the shipbuilding industry that a secret Admiralty committee was formed. The Supply Board had no fewer than 13 sub-committees, all charged with creating contingency plans for war-production, including mass-produced merchant ships. The board was chaired by Admiral of the Fleet Lord Chatfield, the Minister responsible for Co-ordination of Defence.

The major items in the 1936 rearmament programme were two 35,000-ton battleships, the *King
George* and *Prince of Wales*, and two 23,000-ton aircraft carriers, the *Illustrious* and *Victorious*. The
battleships were armed with 14-inch guns to conform to the latest treaty but were heavily armoured
while the carriers incorporated a unique armoured
hangar, to improve their resistance to battle damage.
A year later three more battleships and two carriers
were ordered but the British steel industry was so
overloaded that flight-deck armour for one of the
carriers had to be ordered from Czechoslovakia (*see*
Chapter 5).

The once-powerful armaments industry could
now only produce heavy gun mountings at a very
slow rate. When in 1938 an additional battleship was
proposed to strengthen the forces in the Far East,
the Director of Naval Ordnance told the Controller
that no new gun turrets could be delivered until
1944.

The Admiralty had fought unsuccessfully since
1918 to regain control of naval aviation, but a new
generation of air-minded senior naval officers
renewed the fight with greater success and in the
summer of 1937 the government announced that the
Royal Navy would be given responsibility for all
naval aviation except maritime patrol aircraft. By a
fortunate coincidence an expanding RAF was
obsessed with strategic bombing and found the
requirements of naval aviation a tiresome distrac-
tion. However, as in 1918, a large number of pilots
and maintainers were taken back, leaving the new
Fleet Air Arm in a parlous state.

As with ships and weapons, naval aviation suffered from the weak state of industry. For years the
Navy had flown slow torpedo bombers and reconnaissance aircraft, and there were no naval aircraft
capable of matching the performance of land-based
fighters. The latest aircraft was a combined torpedo
bomber and reconnaissance biplane; the Swordfish
was to win immortality, but it was a poor reflection
on the pre-war aircraft procurement policy to have a
naval aircraft capable of only 138 mph.

New aircraft were ordered but the aircraft
industry was fully occupied with producing new
high-performance aircraft for the RAF and a series
of very disappointing fighters and bombers were all
the Navy could get.

The danger to the Fleet from air attack had been
recognized surprisingly early. In 1921 the Admiralty
had issued a requirement for heavy multiple anti-
aircraft guns but as with everything else parsimony
ruled the day. The intention was to provide each
capital ship with four of the multiple pom-poms, but
only two per ship could be achieved. To make matters worse this well-engineered mounting used
inefficient ammunition because the Treasury
refused to write off a million and a half pom-pom
shells left over from the previous war.

Anti-aircraft guns needed fire control, but lack
of money prevented the ineffective High-Angle
Control System from being replaced. Although an
efficient twin 4-inch anti-aircraft gun mounting was
developed, it was only intended to serve as a second-

RIGHT: *The M.2 was
converted from a 12-inch
gunned submarine to
operate a small floatplane.*

BELOW: *The diminutive
Parnall Peto leaves M.2's
catapult. It was recovered by
the crane over the hangar.*

ary weapon in cruisers. The lack of a dual-purpose gun suitable for destroyers and escorts was admitted, but no money was available for developing a new gun mounting.

There were one or two rays of light in the gloom. At the end of the previous war the Admiralty's scientists had succeeded in producing the first underwater sensor capable of detecting the range and bearing of a submarine. Known as ASDIC, it was perfected and fitted to fleet destroyers. Here at last was a countermeasure against the submarine, and anti-submarine tactics were practised assiduously.

The properties of ASDIC became rather exaggerated in the cosy atmosphere of peacetime exercises but the Admiralty was fully aware of its potential and in the late 1930s plans were laid to put the latest model into mass-production. When in 1938 it was decided to build a cheap escort based on a whalecatcher design, the new 'Flower' Class corvettes would have the same ASDIC as the fleet destroyers.

Another shrewd move was the development of a new series of magnetic influence mines. The Royal Navy had developed the world's first magnetic mine in 1918, but it had not been very reliable and much work went on between the wars to refine the concept. A spin-off from this work led to a magnetic influence pistol for torpedoes, intended to detonate the torpedo beneath the target's keel.

What is surprising is the success of the Royal Navy in keeping both developments secret. The Germans suspected that ASDIC existed but had not hard intelligence about its technology until mid-1940. Despite the fact that information about the 1918 magnetic mine had been published in 1931, the German Navy continued to think of its own magnetic mine as a 'secret weapon', unaware that the same type of mine was being used against them.

After a period of comparatively unsuccessful experiment, submarine design had settled down in the early 1930s, out of which emerged three classes which would be adopted for mass-production in wartime. The earlier boats suffered from being too unwieldy and had external fuel tanks which leaked oil. Later designs had welded hulls and internal fuel tanks eliminated the leaks, but above all the later submarines could all dive fast. The design philosophy assumed that British submarines would generally be operating under hostile airspace, so rapid diving was essential for survival.

British torpedoes had always been rugged and reliable but work in the 1920s was to produce an outstanding weapon for surface ships and submarines. An engine driven by oxygen-enriched air was produced, but the liquid oxygen proved dangerous to handle and it was abandoned (the Japanese were to use oxygen successfully for their Long Lance torpedo). A new Brotherhood compressed air engine offered nearly as much efficiency and it was chosen for the new Mark 8 torpedo, which sank many Axis ships in World War II and survived to sink the *General Belgrano* in 1982. Very few modern weapons in any navy can claim to have been in front-line service for nearly half a century.

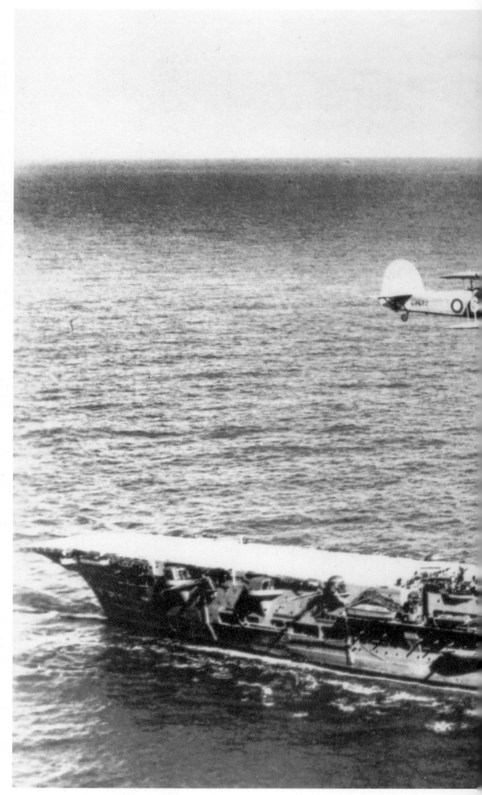

None of the new warships would be in service before the end of 1939, so from 1936 onwards a number of old light cruisers and destroyers were refitted. The most urgent need was for air defence, particularly for convoys, and as the older ships were not suited to the rigours of front-line service they were a natural choice. The small light cruisers built for the North Sea had little fighting value in a modern war, but they could be rearmed with high-angle 4-inch guns, and support convoys or small naval formations.

Another urgent requirement was for escorts to

ABOVE: *Swordfish torpedo-bombers flying over the new carrier* Ark Royal. *Ingenious ship-design was to prove no substitute for good aircraft.*

convoy shipping on the east coast, where they would be vulnerable to air and surface attack. A new class of small destroyers was on order but to fill the gap a number of old destroyers were taken in hand for rearming with modern anti-aircraft guns.

The deficiencies of the battle fleet had been tackled after many delays. In 1937 the battleship *Warspite*, veteran of Jutland, re-emerged after the three-year reconstruction which totally altered her appearance. With new armour and machinery, and her 15-inch guns given higher elevation to increase the range, she showed what could be done to extend

the life of old warhorses. It was hoped to bring her four sisters up to the same standard, but as things turned out only two more were fully modernized, the *Queen Elizabeth* and the *Valiant*, and both ships were still in the dockyard when war broke out.

When Fisher returned to office in October 1914 he had persuaded the Cabinet to let him build two new battlecruisers, the *Repulse* and *Renown*. The former was given a partial modernization but it was admitted that she and her sister were too lightly protected to fight modern capital ships. A better use for them was to work with aircraft carriers, providing a deterrent to hostile surface forces and at the same time improving the carrier's air defences. The *Renown* was therefore given a major reconstruction, strengthening her anti-aircraft armament and renewing her machinery. She rejoined the Fleet in 1939 and was to prove a good investment.

The development of land radar (still known as Radio Direction Finding) was primarily to defend the country against air attack but its applications to naval warfare were obvious and in 1936 the first primitive air search set was installed in a minesweeper. By the outbreak of the war search sets had been installed in the battleship *Rodney* and the cruisers *Sheffield* and *Curlew*.

The Royal Navy was, despite all it vicissitudes, still the largest in the world. With the Dominion navies it mustered a formidable array of ships. On the outbreak of war in September 1939 it numbered over 400 major warships:

Battleships
2 *Nelson* Class
5 *Queen Elizabeth* Class (1 modernized, 2 completing modernization)
5 *Royal Sovereign* Class
+ 5 *King George V* Class + 4 *Lion* Class under construction
Battlecruisers
1 *Hood*
2 *Renown* Class (1 modernized)
Aircraft carriers
1 *Ark Royal*
2 *Courageous* Class
1 *Furious* (modernized)
1 *Eagle*
1 *Hermes*
1 *Argus*
+ 4 *Illustrious* Class + 2 *Implacable* Class under construction
Heavy cruisers
2 *Exeter* and *York*
13 'County' type (including two Australian ships)
Light cruisers
2 *Edinburgh* Class
8 *Southampton* Class
4 *Arethusa* Class
3 *Amphion* Class (Royal Australian Navy)
5 *Leander* Class (2 with New Zealand Division)
2 *Emerald* Class
3 *Effingham* Class
8 *Despatch* Class
2 *Capetown* Class
3 *Caledon* Class
Anti-aircraft cruisers
6 'C' Class
+ 11 *Dido* Class + 5 *Bellona* Class under construction
Cruiser-minelayers
1 *Adventure*
+ 4 *Abdiel* Class under construction
Destroyers
113 modern types
+ 24 under construction
68 old vessels
+ 11 under conversion to escort vessels

Submarines
47 modern types
+ 12 under construction
12 old types
Escorts
54 various types (including 4 Australian + 2 Indian)
+ 80 under construction
Fleet minesweepers
42 various types
+ 10 new construction + requisitioned trawlers
Monitors
2 *Erebus* Class
Netlayers
2 *Guardian* Class

Although the Royal Navy had built successful motor torpedo boats in the Great War and had used them against the Bolshevik fleet at Kronstadt in 1919 interest had lapsed after the war. Persistent lobbying by the smaller shipyards had forced the Admiralty to invest in a few prototypes but no money had been invested in developing high-performance engines, equivalent to those of the German *Schnellboot*.

The Admiralty has been bitterly criticized for its shortcomings between the two world wars. It has been charged with failure to anticipate the pattern of naval warfare, in particular the threat from aircraft and submarines. It is also held to have overvalued the battleship at the expense of aircraft carriers.

Contemporary policy documents do not support the charges of neglecting air defence and anti-submarine warfare. As already noted, the funds were never available for improving anti-aircraft weapons after the sound start made in 1921. What little money there was went into the development of ASDIC, without which the navy would have been defeated by the U-boats, so that charge can be dismissed. The 1938 plans to build large numbers of corvettes show that future needs were anticipated.

It is true that the Royal Navy devoted more of its resources to rebuilding the battle fleet than it did to building up a modern carrier force. On the other hand the poor quality of all foreseeable naval aircraft, and for that matter the lack of any counterbalancing anti-ship capability of the RAF, meant that for at least the next few years enemy battleships at sea could only be sunk by other battleships.

The reasons for the parlous state of naval aviation have been outlined but there were other causes. The RAF, in its constant efforts to emphasize its need to exist separately from the Army and the Navy, harped on its ability to sink warships. It also remained obsessed by the appeal of strategic bombing, ignored such innovations as dive-bombing and left torpedo-attacks largely to the Navy. As a result combined air and sea exercises gave the Royal Navy little idea of the developing scale of the air threat. Any question of the Navy acquiring high-performance strike aircraft was always opposed by the RAF, so another avenue leading to improved techniques was blocked. By the time the Navy regained control of flying it was too late.

'Too little and too late' was nearly the epitaph of the Royal Navy. Fortunately Hitler's *Kriegsmarine* had problems of its own.

ABOVE: *The carrier* Eagle, *seen here at Hong Kong in 1931, was converted from the hull of a Chilean battleship.*

RIGHT: *The smaller* Hermes *was the first carrier built from the keel up. She proved too small to be fully effective, but provided useful experience.*

Chapter 5
The Admiralty and Shipyards

Chains to be hung when not in use

Partnership

Navies have always been expensive. Not only do they require large numbers of skilled men, they also need complicated equipment and maintenance facilities – at least by contemporary standards. For the past 300 years the Royal Navy has been more expensive than most, because of its world-wide commitments and potential enemies, and it was very natural that the large-scale use of the costly new technologies based on steam and iron in the mid-nineteenth century should result in a search for partners to share the burden of providing the new equipment. The Admiralty, therefore, turned to engineering firms and shipyards that already had some experience in the new technologies to help design and build the new ships and equipment. This laid the groundwork for a partnership between the Admiralty and industry that enabled the Admiralty to cope with the massive expansion of the Royal Navy in the last decade of the nineteenth century and enabled the British shipbuilding industry to provide warships for the world.

The partnership has never had an official existence. Instead it has survived on shared needs and interests and as a result has been flexible enough to cope with the successive changes in fortune both of the Royal Navy and of the shipbuilding industry. Part of the reason for this flexibility has been that it has never been a single, simple relationship, but a series of partnerships between different parts of the Admiralty and the industry that have varied in scope and scale at different times. These different relationships divide into two areas – technical and industrial.

Technical

The technical partnership has been concerned with the design and development of the various elements of the warship. At different times it has related to different parts of the ship and the only constant factor has been that the Admiralty has always maintained its right to extract the best solution from the work of an individual firm and then to allow the whole industry to benefit from it.

RIGHT: *Installing boilers in the hull of the* Chester, *a light cruiser laid down at Birkenhead for Greece.*

BELOW RIGHT: *Workmen repairing damage to the battleship* Warspite *after the Battle of Jutland.*

PREVIOUS PAGE: *One of HMS* Rodney's *16-inch Mk I guns arriving at Cammell Laird's Birkenhead shipyard.*

BELOW: *Work progressing on hull* No. 811 *at Birkenhead, a ship which became HMS* Chester. *Modified versions of Admiralty designs were often sold abroad.*

With hulls for example, the Admiralty has generally been the senior partner in this field thanks to the lead given to the Royal Navy by the inspired decision taken in 1870 to fund the research of William Froude. He created what became the basis of the Admiralty Experiment Works (AEW). Froude's work on hull design, continued by his son Edmund, gave the Admiralty a headstart, not only over the private shipyards, but also over the rest of the world. Despite the establishment of testing tanks and research establishments in individual yards such as John Brown's and an industry-wide facility at Teddington in 1910 the AEW has maintained its supremacy throughout this century. However, in specific cases – particularly with high-speed vessels – the Admiralty was always prepared to allow industry to take the risks and come up with its own solutions. This also occurred in wartime, when the instant demand for new types of ship and shortages of design staff led to a greater reliance on the expertise of the shipyards.

In the case of the other elements of a warship – engines, guns, armour, auxiliary machinery, and (from the 1940s) electronics – the relationship was often very different. Most of the basic research and development in these fields has been done by industry leading to a much more equal distribution of power and responsibility. The situation has often been the exact opposite of that in hull design, with the Admiralty very much the junior partner, though it has always retained ultimate control.

Industrial

The industrial partnership has been a much simpler one although it also changed with time. In general, the Admiralty provided the outline design and then divided the work up between the competing firms and (when applicable) its own dockyards. This relationship started out with the Admiralty and the major firms talking to each other as not-quite-equals, and ended with the shipyards (as opposed to the manufacturers building engines, electronics and other parts) becoming entirely dependent on the orders from the Admiralty.

For the Admiralty there were two benefits from the partnership. First it needed to build and maintain the peacetime navy as economically as possible. It could never afford to keep abreast of all the latest developments in ship and weapon design simultaneously. However, throughout this century it has been expected to provide a navy whose ships, on average, are second to none in combat worthiness and seakeeping ability. The Admiralty's solution to this problem was to concentrate on such areas as hull design, basic research and service evaluation. In other areas industry was encouraged to find the answers by research contracts, development orders, or even by the mere knowledge that the Admiralty was likely to place an order after the firm had proved the equipment was workable. When the technology had matured sufficiently for the equipment to be reliable the Admiralty was then able to buy at a reduced cost and without having to maintain its own design teams.

The second benefit was that it enabled the Admiralty to keep a sufficient reserve of shipbuilding capacity and repair expertise available in the event of a major war. It was for this reason that the Admiralty allowed the yards to make almost unlimited use of its designs for foreign orders – at least in the first part of this century. The availability of trained administrators, engineers and design staff well versed in the requirements of the Royal Navy was also useful, as was the fact that at the start of a war the Royal Navy had access to suitable vessels completing for export to other countries in British yards.

The wartime partnership has always been very different from the peacetime one. The need to build and repair as much as possible in the shortest time has resulted twice this century in a temporary lowering of the many barriers between the Admiralty and industry. Although the shipbuilding industry retained its separate identity on both occasions the need to juggle trained men and scarce resources meant that industry was treated much more like a sub-department of the Admiralty for the duration of the war. Firms' activities were strictly controlled and the design departments of the major companies took over many of the functions of the hard-pressed Admiralty design staff.

The shipbuilding industry has also had many reasons to welcome the partnership. Had the Admiralty been able to design and build most or all of its own ships and equipment much of the shipbuilding industry would have found if difficult to survive. The Royal Navy is a demanding customer but the profits have always been good and its custom has brought many advantages.

Until the 1940s British industry was associated with the most powerful navy in the world which set standards that other navies copied. The Royal Navy is still in the forefront of technical developments, and the MoD normally allows industry to make full use of all but the most secret designs. In many cases the attitude has been that if a development is known about then there is no point in keeping the details secret. From about 1910 the Admiralty maintained a stricter control over what may be provided to foreign navies but it is only in recent years that this has seriously hampered foreign sales.

In many cases industry has been able to provide foreign navies with vessels that are all-but identical to Royal Naval designs. However, many foreign navies – while preferring designs similar to those of the Royal Navy – have their own requirements that change the nature of the vessels considerably. In the Royal Navy, with a few well-known exceptions such as the early battlecruisers, the emphasis in major warships has always been on a balance of qualities. Smaller navies, without world-wide commitments, have been able to emphasise some qualities at the expense of others. Thus the battleships taken over at the start of the World War I, which had been originally designed by private industry for Brazil (the *Agincourt*), Chile (the *Canada*) and Turkey (the *Erin*), all made use of the Royal Naval standards and design techniques, but all departed to a greater or lesser extent from its design philosophy in range, guns or armour. From the viewpoint of the shipbuilding industry, it was the use of Royal Navy standards and design techniques that made their job easier.

There are many other ways in which industry had benefited. Where the Admiralty ordered ships or equipment designed by individual firms, such as Yarrow or Thornycroft destroyers, Parsons turbines, or Marconi radar, this has been an important selling point. Development contracts have enabled firms to perfect equipment that would not otherwise have been put into production. The employment of ex-Admiralty staff with specialist skills has given companies access to technologies and markets at a much smaller cost than doing it all themselves.

It has been very rare for the Admiralty not to lay down the basic design standards and provide the overall design of their own warships and it has also always kept tight control over small details. Items such as watertight doors, davits and other small fittings have been standardized (and occasionally updated) since the 1870s. Until recently shipyards did their own detailed design within the Admiralty framework, using standard Admiralty fittings.

For some ships, such as the Scout cruisers of the early 1900s, the Admiralty simply provided an outline specification and the shipyards created the complete designs using standard fittings. In peacetime shipyard designs have been used to cope with particular requirements. In the case of the early torpedo boat destroyers, the Admiralty was saved the expense of developing lightweight high-speed designs until it became clear which areas of research gave the best results. In the case of the 1960s Type 21 frigates, a slightly modified commercial design was used because there was an urgent requirement for several general-purpose frigates at a time when the Frigate Section of the naval design staff was fully occupied with the preliminary studies for what became the Type 22s.

In wartime this overburdening of the naval design staff and the urgent need to provide quick solutions becomes more critical. Examples are the World War I 'Z-Whalers' and the World War II 'Flower' class corvettes, both of which answered an immediate need for anti-submarine escorts. Sometimes private industry can come up with a better solution than the naval staff. The best example of this occurred in World War II when Thornycroft's reworking of the escort destroyer requirement resulted in the excellent 'Hunt' Type IV, whose design pointed the way to post-war developments.

Throughout this century, the Admiralty (more recently known as MoD Navy) has been under the ultimate control of the various Lords of the Admiralty. Important decisions about the type and number of ships required are normally made by the Sea

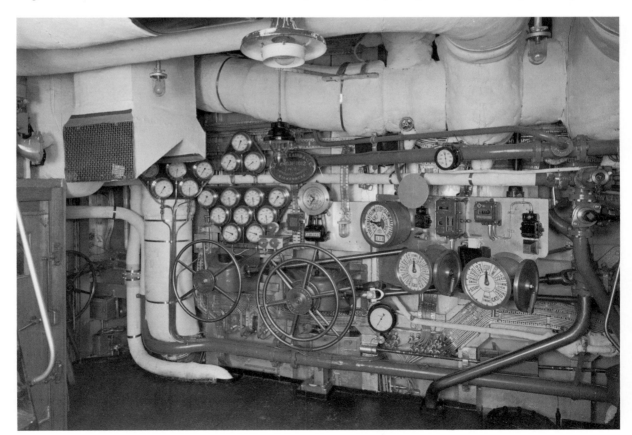

RIGHT: *The new carrier* Ark Royal's *main machinery controls. She and the* Illustrious *class had an unusual three-shaft installation.*

Lords, and the ships are designed and built under the overall control of the Third Sea Lord (now known as the Controller). The Third Sea Lord delegated the design and supervision of the construction to the Director of Naval Construction or DNC (later to become Director-General Ships), who in turn consulted the Engineer in Chief (EinC), the Director of Naval Ordnance (DNO) and any other relevant head of department about details of the design. The DNC's department coordinated the design and supervised the construction of the hull and assembly of the ship, while the specialist departments also supervised construction of the armament, engines and other parts of the vessel. The Admiralty exercised supervision and control of standards through officers of the various Admiralty departments (DNC, DNO, EinC etc) who watched the work being carried out at the various works and carried out regular tests to ensure that materials, etc, came up to specification.

At the start of this century ship contracts were entirely under the control of the Third Sea Lord's department and the Contracts Department had very limited powers and was mainly concerned with buildings, coal, food, clothing and other related items. In 1912 it was thoroughly overhauled, and after that it gradually took a greater control over contracts for ships. Their Lordships decided who should get large contracts on the advice of the Third Sea Lord's Department but it was the Third Sea Lord, the DNC and the other officers in the Department who made all but the most crucial decisions. Proper cost accounting methods are very recent indeed, and not until half-way through World War I did the Admiralty take the first faltering steps in this direction.

To help it make the correct decisions, the Admiralty created a formidable array of research facilities. The first was the AEW, and by 1900 HMS *Vernon* and HMS *Excellent* had done considerable work on underwater weapons and guns respectively. The Admiralty Engineering Laboratory was created in 1917, and the Naval Construction Research Establishment was only one of several facilities created in the interwar period. Subsequent growth has been rapid. However, in the early years of the century the only department within the Admiralty which could act as much more than well-informed critic of other people's designs was the ship design department run by the DNC (thanks mainly to the work of the AEW).

The Naval Ordnance Department was not created until 1891, and not until the early years of this century could the Admiralty have full control over the design and production of its own ordnance. The major gun manufacturers (chiefly Armstrong and Vickers, with Coventry Ordnance Works and later Beardmore's) designed most of the large guns and gun-mountings. The same situation occurred with engines and boilers where the Admiralty was more concerned with improving the power, reliability and economy of existing designs than in creating anything from scratch.

In addition, the Admiralty started the century

with four home Dockyards, each capable of building battleships. The number, capabilities and status of the home Dockyards have fluctuated over the past 80 years. For most of that period they not only built a sizable proportion of the fleet and repaired and refitted most of the rest, they also acted as a check on costs incurred with the shipbuilding industry, as well as acting as a threat of Admiralty self-sufficiency in case industry became too obdurate during negotiations on contracts.

By 1900 almost any British shipyard could build a simple slow freighter, and any engine builder could provide the reciprocating engine and boiler to power it. Warships, however, require more expertise because of their intricate, damage-resistant structure. Small high-speed warships require particular skills, because the balance between light-weight and structural strength is especially difficult to achieve. Except in times of international tension and war, most shipyards specialize in particular types of ship as do engine builders, though most makers of auxiliary machinery and fittings can provide suitable equipment for any need. Yarrow and Thornycroft (now Vosper Thornycroft) shipyards always concentrated on high-speed vessels. Major warships being much heavier for their length than

ABOVE: *An unusual view of the 'island' superstructure of the* Ark Royal *laid down in World War II at Birkenhead but not completed until 1955.*

ABOVE RIGHT: *The launch of the destroyer* Dainty *at the J Samuel White yard in Cowes. These large and sophisticated ships proved to be the last true destroyers.*

RIGHT: HMS Rothesay *photographed by her builders, Yarrow, in 1960.*

LEFT & RIGHT: *Gas turbines being installed in a destroyer at Cammell Laird. The Royal Navy pioneered the use of gas turbines in large ships, using the Rolls-Royce Olympus and Tyne engines.*

BELOW: *Moving a section of a submarine from the welding shop to the building slip.*

BELOW: *Preparing a destroyer for launching, still a job of skill and personal judgement.*

liners or cargo vessels, not all large yards were capable of constructing carriers, cruisers or battleships, because their slipways could not take the heavier loads. Some companies, such as Dennys, only built warships at times of crisis, not because they lacked the capacity but because they could normally obtain a full order book without the help of naval work. Most, however, were very happy to build for the Admiralty at times when other orders were slack, even if they did not do so normally.

The major shipbuilding areas, the Clyde, the north-east coast of England (the Tyne, Tees and Wear), and until about 1910 the Thames, have always had a mixture of firms specializing in different types of ship and equipment. Other areas such as Barrow, Belfast, Birkenhead, and the Solent had only one or two major companies each. There have only ever been two really large British armament firms, Armstrong Whitworth based in Newcastle and Manchester and Vickers based in Sheffield and Barrow. At the time of World War I they were briefly joined by Coventry Ordnance Works (COW) set up by John Brown, Fairfield and Cammell Laird, but this combine ended in 1919.

ABOVE: *The long-awaited 50,000-ton carrier* Ark Royal *was launched at Birkenhead in 1950. She was destined to be the last fleet carrier in the Royal Navy.*

Even Vickers and Armstrong Whitworth finally amalgamated in 1927. These few firms could and did build all the major parts of a battleship. The others bought in armour, guns and often machinery from outside.

Armstrong Whitworth, Vickers and COW (with Beardmore as a never very serious challenger) were the only major gun and mounting manufacturers, and from 1927 Vickers was the only supplier. Armour manufacture was equally restricted, with only the largest steelmakers participating. Specialist marine steam-engine builders for large vessels were almost entirely confined after 1910 to the Tyne, though most large shipyards could build machinery too. Diesels and gas turbines were frequently manufactured outside the traditional shipbuilding industry.

The Admiralty knew which firms were capable of building specific items, and how many items the firm could be expected to build at once, as they maintained detailed lists of suitable manufacturers. Firms asked to be put on the Admiralty List for particular items such as destroyers, lifeboats, or anchor chains. They were then inspected by an officer from the relevant Admiralty department – DNCs for a shipyard, EinCs for machinery and so on. If the quality of the firm's existing work, its plant and workforce were satisfactory, the firm was put on the relevant list. Firms on the Admiralty Lists were reinspected regularly to check that they could still do the work. This system has worked for well over 100 years.

Being on the Admiralty List only meant that the firm was capable of building the equipment. It did not guarantee the firm any orders. The main advantage to industry of being on the list (apart from the possibility of getting work from the Admiralty itself) was the indication of the firm's ability. Most minor navies never had the money or the skilled staff to set their own standards for materials and designs. Instead, they used existing standards set by major navies. Up until the end of World War II, most minor navies automatically used Royal Navy standards, and often turned to British firms on the Admiralty List for building their ships and equipment. Some still do.

The Admiralty never intended to keep companies in business simply because they were on the list. Sometimes orders were placed to keep firms going for political reasons, despite there being no shortage of other firms capable of doing the work. In these cases the Admiralty merely responded to pressure from government. When it was left to the Admiralty, the only reason for giving contracts to keep a firm in business was to preserve special skills or to keep sufficient firms in business to be able to meet future requirements. At times when there have been few orders, the Admiralty has often encouraged firms with special skills to amalgamate to ensure that these skills survive.

The List has always been used by the Admiralty to make sure that firms build equipment to the required standard. The threat of being taken off the List and being deprived of what has often been the firm's major source of business has normally been enough to bring wayward firms back into line. The only major firm to be removed was Cammell Laird. In 1907 Admiralty officials discovered that the firm had been saving money by using inferior materials in place of those specified in their contracts. Cammell Laird was not listed again for more than a year. The Admiralty also insisted that the senior management be completely overhauled. The firm lost a large amount of money and the Admiralty never again had to resort to such extreme measures with a major supplier.

The shipbuilding industry always exercised its own control over the Admiralty in indirect ways. The official mouthpiece of the industry was the Shipbuilders and Repairers National Association, and this took up matters of collective interest with the Admiralty from time to time. However, firms have normally relied on other more potent forms of persuasion. Until recent years the senior managers of the larger firms were often Members of Parliament or even of the House of Lords, and a practice still followed is to invite major public figures in the Commons or the Lords on to the board of directors. This has always ensured that the industry's difficulties will be aired and that pressure can be put on the Admiralty to secure orders for specific firms or regions.

At the beginning of the century most of the chief designers at the major British shipyards came originally from the Admiralty. They had trained at the School of Naval Architects, and many had served for varying periods with the AEW under Froude, father or son. They maintained contact, and there was a constant interchange of information and ideas between the AEW and the shipyards. As private industry built up its own technical base (for example the research unit at Teddington) the Admiralty's lead became less pronounced, but there has always been space in the shipbuilding industry for experienced Royal Naval personnel. They proved invaluable for their contacts and experience of the Admiralty, as much as for their practical and technical expertise. There has also been a reverse flow from private industry to the Admiralty when the Royal Navy has required specific skills or a level of experience not attainable within the Admiralty. This happened much more in the years prior to World War I than since. One small way in which the industry has always been able to help the Admiralty has been to show naval officers who are being sent as naval attachés to embassies abroad what to look for when they go round foreign companies.

By the end of the nineteenth century industry had set up its own technical training, at first in the colleges at Glasgow and Newcastle-upon-Tyne but soon spreading elsewhere. This put personnel in industry on a much more equal footing with those in the Admiralty, and the professional bodies such as the Royal Institution of Naval Architects helped spread knowledge and training. Since 1900 the percentage of design staff in major firms who received their early training from the Royal Navy has steadily decreased. Of course, much of the training for most

staff (at least until the second half of this century) has been conducted within the factories and dock-yards, and has relied heavily on practical experience rather than academic courses.

The year 1900 saw the culmination of 10 years of very large-scale naval building for the Royal Navy. The shipbuilding industry was currently building nearly half of all the world's warships and well over half the merchant ships constructed anywhere in the world. These global figures conceal areas where Britain was facing much stronger competition (for example Germany and France together were well up to the British figures in building destroyers for export), but they did ensure that the Admiralty had few worries – given the money – about coping with any warship-building race.

It was obvious by this time that the scale of out-put from British shipyards was bound to fall. Twenty years earlier British yards had been building over two-thirds of all the world's merchant ships, and rising industrial powers such as Germany had had to build up their own shipbuilding and ship-owning industries in self-defence. As these foreign industries grew in size, and more goods were carried in non-British ships, so the work available to British shipyards diminished. However, the advantages of scale that the British industry had over the rest of the world were considerable. The number of major warships laid down between 1904 and 1914 was less

than in the previous decade, but this was compen-sated for by the increase in tonnage of individual ships.

The Admiralty helped to ensure the contin-uance of a large-scale warship building capability by pursuing a well-thought-out policy of spreading orders around suitable yards. In general, orders were given to firms that had put in low tenders, but they did not go automatically to the lowest bidders. If firms had not had orders for some time, then they were more likely to get orders than ones with a lot of business. Firms often met to discuss these contracts before they were sent in to the Admiralty, and there is some evidence they sometimes raised these tenders in collusion with each other. The method used was to raise the amount of all of the tenders by the same amount, so that the bids remained in the same proportion to each other but the price was higher all round.

Repairs were concentrated in Naval Dockyards (except for two short periods around 1900), and the four home dockyards built enough major warships to keep all of them in business. Even though it has always been notoriously difficult to compare the cost of work in the dockyards and in industry, enough could be learned to enable Admiralty officials to have a good idea of when (and by how much) indus-try was inflating its tenders. Cost-accounting tech-niques at this time were very primitive and even the

ABOVE: *The new Type 22 frigate* Campbeltown *is one of four built to replace Falklands losses.*

ABOVE: *The* Campbeltown *now has her bow section, less than a month later.*

RIGHT: *Preparing the hull of a destroyer for extrusion. This method permits the rapid assembly of prefabricated blocks.*

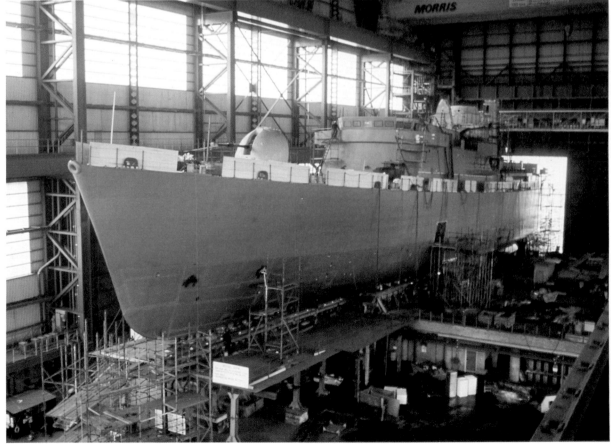

shipyards were not really sure of their true costs – not that this has changed very much in later times! However, it was obvious to the ship-repair industry that warship repair work was not particularly profitable, partly because of the high standards of skill required and partly because the amount of work was not predictable.

This was a time of constant transfer to and from naval and private design departments. The DNC from 1901 to 1912, Sir Phillip Watts, started his career with the Admiralty and served in the AEW. He became the chief designer at Armstrong, and after his spell with the Admiralty as DNC returned to Armstrong as a director. Sir Eustace Tennyson d'Eyncourt, the DNC from 1912 to 1923, had trained at the Admiralty's school of Naval Architecture and served in industry (latterly at Armstrong) before moving to the Admiralty in 1912. Vickers' chief designer was trained by the Admiralty, and when they wanted to reinforce their hold over the design and construction of British submarines Vickers successfully tempted the two leading Admiralty submarine experts away with excellent job offers.

There was very close technical collaboration between the Admiralty and industry. The development of the turbine saw a specialist engine-builder, Parsons, being given the status of main contractor for the first turbine-powered destroyer, HMS *Viper*. Armstrong, the hull-builder, constructed it under a sub-contract. This ensured the best chance of success for the new engine, but was the first time any firm other than a shipbuilder had been the main contractor. Parsons himself was a member of the 1904 Admiralty Committee on Designs that resulted in the *Dreadnought*. In this period, prominent members of the shipbuilding industry sat on a number of such Admiralty committees.

Even before World War I, the Admiralty was prepared to allow a monopoly to grow up if this ensured lower development costs and speedy technological advance. The best example was with submarines, where in the first years of the century Vickers was encouraged to establish a close collaboration with the American firm Holland (later Electric Boat) to develop the submarine as a practical weapon. To make this attractive to Vickers the Admiralty allowed the firm to become the monopoly supplier of submarines to the Royal Navy and it was only a decade later when the technical problems had mainly been solved that the monopoly was broken. This was done by building submarines in the dockyards and by ordering French and Italian designs from other shipyards. It has to be said that Vickers still kept the advantages of their early lead.

As the naval arms race with Germany developed, more and more firms that had never built warships before were brought on to the Admiralty Lists to cope with the ever-increasing demand. They included some of the best known and largest, such as Swan Hunter, which until 1908 had concentrated on large liners and other merchant vessels. This did not mean that all yards, however large, were kept in business. Most Thames-side shipyards, including Thornycroft and Yarrow, either closed down or moved to other parts of the country in the early 1900s because labour and land costs made Thames-side heavy engineering uneconomic. The Admiralty was pressed by Parliament to give orders to Thames Ironworks, the largest yard, and responded with orders for several large warships, culminating in the battleship *Thunderer*. However, when *Thunderer* was complete in 1912 Thames Ironworks closed down.

ABOVE: *The first destroyers were designed and built by industry to meet a broad Admiralty specification. Close collaboration continued until after World War I.*
LEFT: *The 'Tribal' class were a failure, when Fisher pushed the partnership too far, forcing the builders to accept unrealistic specifications.*

There were enough other battleship-building yards and Thames Ironworks was simply too expensive.

Until after 1910, there were relatively few areas of naval design that the Admiralty was concerned about keeping secret. Developments such as quick-firing guns, stronger armour, and new types of engines and boilers were sold to potential enemies without any serious concern, because it knew that with the aid of private industry it was always possible to outbuild any potential foe. This changed abruptly after the start of German naval expansion but the Admiralty still allowed industry to provide consid-

erable technical assistance to Britain's new allies, Japan, France, and Russia. This was mostly in the field of major warships, and another area of assistance was heavy gun mountings. Continued assistance was also provided to Italy (whose major warship yards were controlled by British interests), and from 1912 onwards an entire new dreadnought building yard was built in Spain by Armstrong Whitworth.

For the most part, World War I vindicated the Admiralty's policies towards industry. At the outbreak of war there were four battleships in various

The fleet carrier Ark Royal missed every major operation between 1956 and 1978 but endeared herself to the public and the Navy alike.

stages of completion for foreign navies, and all were taken over. Two, renamed *Agincourt* and *Erin*, were completing for Turkey, but were delayed on Admiralty orders until they could be requisitioned. Two were in a much earlier stage of building for Chile. The most advanced ship was taken over and work restarted almost immediately; she was completed in 1915 as HMS *Canada*. The second was suspended until taken over in 1917; she was completed eventually as the aircraft carrier *Eagle*. Two cruisers for Greece, two coast defence vessels for Norway and a number of smaller warships were also taken over and incorporated into the Royal Navy.

The range of yards with warship-building experience also proved invaluable, particularly in the construction of destroyers and submarines. For the first two years of the war, the dockyards were finishing off existing orders, but from 1916 they concentrated mainly on repairs, leaving new warships mainly to industry, although there was so much repair work that industry did a large amount of this too. After Jutland, for example, most damaged British ships including the *Lion* and the *Warspite*, headed for the Tyne, where they were repaired by commercial shipyards. They had the assistance of a large floating dock that the Admiralty had sent up to the Tyne to bolster its repair and refit capability. The nearest Royal Dockyard, Rosyth, was only partially complete in 1916 and even had it been finished as planned would not have been able to cope with the quantity of work.

To cope with the overload of work at the Admiralty and in industry, considerable changes were made in the way in which ships and equipment were designed. Not only were certain commercial ship designs such as whalers and tugs adopted almost unaltered by the Admiralty, but the DNC's department also handed over a much larger part of ordinary warship design to industry. Large yards were given the basic outline designs for warships and told to produce the drawings for all the yards involved in their construction and they were also made responsible for a much greater proportion of the design of the ship. An example was the *Courageous* class, for which Armstrong Whitworth were the leading yard.

One of the major surprises of the war was the enormous requirement for escort vessels. No more destroyers could be built because most merchant shipbuilders lacked the skills and experience to build turbine machinery and fast highly stressed hulls. The solution was found in a series of slower, simpler, designs, such as the 'Flower' Class and the '24' Class. These could be produced by all but the smallest yards, and their simple reciprocating machinery did not demand scarce, complicated machine tools. Eventually, 167 yards built ships for the Royal Navy in World War I – more than four times as many as had done so at any previous period.

Industry was not only able to take on work for the Admiralty. Prominent members were drafted to assist at a senior level, and the firms also contributed their own ideas. The only purpose-built 'Q-ship'

ABOVE: *Monitors were built hurriedly in 1914-15 to bombard the Belgian coast, using American 14-inch guns and 12-inch guns stripped from old battleships.*

ABOVE: *Large numbers of 'Hunt' class minesweepers were built in 1916-18 and some of these sturdy little ships were still in service in World War II.*

(anti-submarine decoy) was HMS *Hyderabad*, designed and built by Thornycroft partly as a show-case for Thornycroft's own anti-submarine mortars. Armstrong Whitworth had a very close involvement in the development of the early carrier designs including the conversion of the *Furious* and *Eagle*.

There were many difficulties, quite apart from the need for quick results and the drastic shortage of raw materials. There were problems with skilled workers joining the armed forces and many vital workers never returned to the yards. Dilution (making use of unskilled men and women) was imposed on the industry and created problems that management, unaccustomed to these kinds of work-ers, spent much time in trying to solve. The creation of new yards to try to build more ships was not very sensible, too much effort being expended for too little return. The only partial success was on the Tees. Otherwise the time and material employed by the Admiralty would have been better used to improve existing yards. One major difficulty with building large warships had already become apparent before the war. This was that major war-ships had become so large that only certain yards with suitable subsoil, enough room for expansion and sufficient water to launch the ship could build them. Before 1914 both Armstrong Whitworth and Vickers had completely rebuilt their yards to deal with this, but some other traditional battleship builders like Palmers found their yards inadequate. The wartime increase from the 30,000-ton *Queen*

Elizabeth Class and 'R' Class battleships to the 40,000-ton *Hood* was too much for most yards.

Problems were inevitable with the building of merchant ships. Some yards such as Vickers had half-built large liners whose construction had been stopped in 1914, blocking vital slipways throughout the war. Such vessels were not needed for the war, would take too long to dismantle, and were not far enough advanced to launch. One, renamed *Argus*, was finally completed as an aircraft carrier. The sheer numbers of warships being built as well as the shortages of materials meant that cargo ship build-ing was reduced at a time when the submarine cam-paigns were making every cargo vessel vital. There was a constant juggling of new building between merchant and warships to try to deal with this, and there was also a gradual recourse to the USA and Japan to take up some of the lost production.

As the war progressed, the Admiralty's control over the industry became greater. Contracts were simplified to payment of cost plus a standard rate of profit and there was excess profit legislation to mop up the most outragous overcharging. The means for controlling the industry were also considerably increased. A deputy was appointed to the Third Sea Lord to control merchant shipbuilding and the Admiralty began to adopt the first stages of modern cost accounting and organizational method (with a considerable increase in staff) to be able to know what was being done and to take the correct decisions. The development from 1915 of the Min-

ABOVE: *HMS* Manchester *was the first of four 'stretched' Type 42 destroyers, lengthened to improve internal arrangements.*

istry of Munitions temporarily removed day-to-day control from the Admiralty, but in practice its need to obtain suitable ships and equipment in the shortest possible time meant that it still had the major say in what happened in the industry.

At times there were quite severe stoppages due to major strikes, particularly on Clydeside. Some were caused by pre-war problems, others by dilution and wartime shortages. These were very much the province of the Ministry of Munitions and the Admiralty had little say in how they were resolved and how quickly work restarted. It is unlikely that the Admiralty would have had any more success in preventing the strikes or ending them sooner than the Ministry, had it been given the responsibility. For the most part the men and women in the yards worked very long hours to get the ships built or repaired, sometimes even finding themselves in action because they had sailed with a ship to complete vital work.

The period after 1918 was very difficult, both for the Admiralty and for the industry. First, there was a glut of warships from war, many of which had seen hardly any service. Not only did this mean the can-cellation of many wartime orders, but it also meant that there would be less demand for new ships for export until the surplus had been reduced. Financial crises and war-weariness that made the country reluctant to put money into the armed services reduced orders still further.

By the end of 1930 several large firms including Palmers and Beardmores had been closed down. As with a number of other firms Palmers was closed in order to allow stronger firms to survive. Many of the remaining companies – including the two largest, Vickers and Armstrong – amalgamated with the active encouragement of the Admiralty. The need to merge was particularly strong in the more specialized parts of the industry, for example among the armour makers and the manufacturers of optical instruments and periscopes. By a judicious use of orders the Admiralty ensured the survival of all the necessary skills and manufacturing techniques, but at the cost of problems in expanding production when money became available later.

As well as the general lack of orders and the 10-year Rule (the official assumption, annually renewed in the 1920s and 1930s, that there would be

no major war for 10 years), there were additional difficulties created by the various naval limitation treaties. Unlike the last two decades, when individual ship size had increased dramatically (in the case of battleships from 15,000 to 40,000 tons), the effect of the Washington and London Treaties was to decrease ship size. Treaty cruisers at 10,000 tons displaced less than the pre-1905 armoured cruiser let alone later vessels. This further reduced the work available to industry which was still sharing orders with the dockyards. In the interwar years Portsmouth, Devonport and Chatham built no fewer than 19 cruisers and 17 submarines between them.

In these years an irreversible change in the relationship took place. All the firms were so dependent on Admiralty orders that it began to seem that the Royal Navy was not just the senior of two partners. Instead there were signs of a 'master-servant' relationship building up, particularly with the shipyards themselves. This occurred despite the fact that the Admiralty was for the first time beginning to fall behind world leaders in certain areas of applied research. Lack of money meant that promising experiments with light, high-pressure boilers had to be shelved at a time when the United States Navy was perfecting similar systems. The Admiralty avoided the danger, demonstrated by World War II German experience, of opting for new systems without sufficient research, and managed with the reliable (but larger and heavier) existing boilers. At this time industry lacked the resources and the inclination to conduct its own research without Royal Naval backing.

For the firms that survived, the effective ending of the 10-year Rule, late 1933 signified a turning point. Rearmament brought new problems, but no shortage of orders. As a result of the earlier economies, the major difficulty was not so much a shortage of manufacturers as a shortage of plant and skills. A clear example is armour plate. After a

decade when the only armour needed was for thin-skinned cruisers, large quantities were need for the *King George V* Class battleships and *Illustrious* Class aircraft carriers. So great were the difficulties in supplying all that was needed in the short time available that orders had to be given to Czech armour manufacturers to make up the difference.

For most of the Third Sea Lord's department and the shipbuilding industry World War II was in many ways a re-run of the First. The main difference was less friction between the organizations, because many of the same people who knew what had been done in 1918 were still in positions of authority in 1939. Once again the war started with the takeover of warships building for abroad, though this time there was nothing larger than destroyers. Once again any yard that had the skills and equipment built warships.

In this war there was an even greater reliance on the United States to build merchant ships (and landing vessels and escorts), while British yards tried to keep up with the demands for warships for a truly world-wide war. Britain's main contribution on the mercantile side was to provide the designs for most of the mass-produced American vessels (this had also happened in World War I). Once again, civilian designs were adapted for war – the 'Flower' Class corvettes being the most significant of these. Some major warships were built to the lower, civilian, standards of watertight subdivision and structural strength to enable more to be built in a hurry. The outstanding example was the Light Fleet Carriers, some of which remain in service in the late 1980s with India, Brazil and Argentina.

Ships were built to the maximum capacity of the yards. The main problem was not so much lack of resources (though steel shortages did influence production at some points) but lack of skilled men. The yards were unable to build ships in sufficient numbers in early years to keep up with losses, particularly in the case of destroyers. Only when losses

RIGHT: *An aerial view of Yarrow's shipyard at Scotstoun on the Clyde. Warships fitting out include two Type 22 frigates and two Iranian landing ships.*

were reduced, and the Admiralty adopted simplified and standard designs could enough be built. Even if all the yards that had been closed in the 1920s and 1930s had been kept going, there would not have been enough skilled men and manufacturers of all the necessary components to build all that was wanted. The simplified escorts, the 'Loch' and 'Bay' Classes, were exceptionally easy to build in quantity, with angles rather than curves, and hulls that could be made in prefabricated sections. A smaller version, the 'Castle' Class, was built by yards too small for the standard designs. Apart from submarines, the dockyards concentrated mainly on repairs.

In this war, as in the previous one, many workers joined the Armed Forces, but there was a better system for keeping men with vital skills in the firms where they were most needed. Dilution and the use of women workers went more smoothly too (although there were still many difficulties), reflecting the benefits of the experience gained 20 years before. Once again, workers found themselves in action as they completed last-minute jobs, the shipyard workers on the *Prince of Wales* during the Bismarck action being only the best-known example.

The period 1946-87 has seen many changes within the shipbuilding industry, and its relationship with the Ministry of Defence has changed accordingly. Most of the changes have been caused by the constant scaling down of both the industry and the Royal Navy. Immediately after the war there was a short boom in merchant-ship production, and British yards were still producing over 20 per cent of the world's vessels, whereas the figure for the late 1980s is less than five per cent. Warship exports have suffered in the same way. As was the case immediately after World War I, there was a glut of wartime ships available for export. There was also a major shift in the balance of the world's navies. For the first time this century minor navies started to abandon Admiralty standards and began to use those of the United States Navy instead. This means that the previous almost automatic 'buy British' policy no longer operates for many navies or at least not in the same way.

Within the shipbuilding industry hulls have become progressively cheaper and less significant compared with the complications and expense of the armament and electronics. For surface vessels, the hull builders are not totally at the mercy of Admiralty orders, while the partnership with the manufacturers of all the components that go into the hulls has become more equal. Nationalization of the shipyards in the mid-1970s and the denationalization of the warship yards in the mid-1980s had no measurable effect on the partnership between the industry and the Navy. The warship-building industry has been so closely intertwined with the Navy for so long that it would have been foolish to try to change things, and in any case nationalization and the subsequent denationalization have in reality had very little effect.

The main surprise in the past three decades is not the number of yards that have closed but the

number that have remained open. Vickers, the largest, builds large warships and submarines. Swan Hunter builds large and medium-sized surface warships, Yarrow and Vosper Thornycroft build frigates and destroyers, and Cammell Laird builds these and submarines too. American experience using single yards to build large classes has not been entirely happy, but the spread of orders in the British yards has meant that no single one (except Vickers with submarines) has had an adequate production run. This has led to very lengthy building times and high costs. The British have kept so many yards not so much to provide a strategic dispersion (both to provide healthy competition and to avoid the possibility of a catastrophic loss of facilities in wartime) but rather to save jobs in towns that otherwise have very little to offer in the way of employment.

The 1960s saw the final abandonment of new building in the dockyards – the last orders were a series of submarines for Canada at Chatham. Since then Chatham has been closed and Portsmouth vastly reduced in size. The function of Devonport, Rosyth and Portsmouth is now entirely that of refit and repair, and in the late 1980s these are being put out to industry once more. It has always been difficult to work out comparative costs between the dockyards and the shipbuilding industry. The moves to sell the dockyards to private industry in the mid-1980s have failed to provide a conclusive answer, even using the most sophisticated cost-accounting techniques. In the end, the decision to sell or retain them has had to be taken on political rather than economic grounds.

To save expense the Admiralty once again turned to private yards for minor warships of limited combat potential. Hall Russell designs were used as

ABOVE: *HMS/m* Upholder, *first of a new class of diesel-electric submarine, is assembled on the slip of Vickers' Barrow shipyard.*

RIGHT: *Launch of the nuclear attack submarine* Torbay, *fourth of a class of seven.*

the basis for the Royal Naval offshore patrol fleet. A private yard design, the Type 21, also provided the solution to the need for an interim class of frigate while the Admiralty design staff were fully occupied with the more capable Type 22s. Considering the cost and complexity of modern Royal Navy designs, the industry managed to build quite a number of warships for export, but the number of competitors and the long gaps between orders mean that no company has been able to survive on exporting warships alone. Royal Naval orders have been the only way of keeping design teams and construction staff in existence, particularly since there are virtually no merchant ship orders either.

The Falklands campaign in 1982 showed what can still be done when needed by the industry in its partnership with the Ministry of Defence. Ships under construction were rushed to completion – in the case of the aircraft carrier *Ark Royal* a year ahead of schedule. Large numbers of ships were hastily refitted with additional armament and electronics, and battle damage was quickly made good. However, this was all done at considerable expense, and this amount of money is no longer available for the Royal Navy in normal times. Once the campaign was over, the Ministry of Defence returned to its usual policy of doling out just enough orders to keep the shipbuilding industry in existence to be ready for the next emergency, whenever or wherever that might happen to occur.

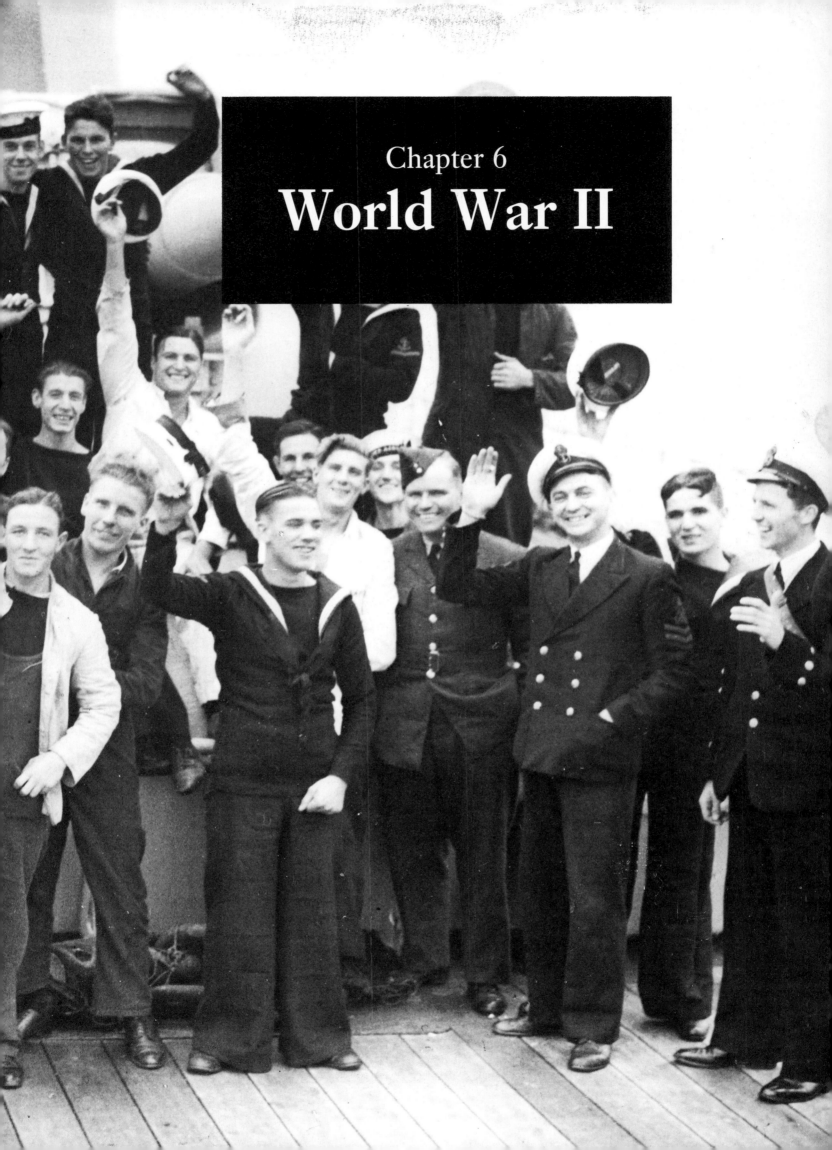

Chapter 6
World War II

In 1939 the Home Fleet returned to the bleak anchorage of Scapa Flow and the minor squadrons moved to their war stations around the British Isles.

To many Royal Navy officers, the war which broke out on 3 September seemed little different from the previous conflict. The overall maritime strategy of the Allies was the same. The Royal Navy's task was to prevent the German Fleet from getting out into the North Atlantic, while the French Navy had the responsibility of containing the Italians. It was a modest, cautious strategy, but given the Allies' weaknesses in other respects it was the one most likely to succeed. In theory a blockade of Germany would weaken her while giving France and Britain a chance to build up their strength.

Some important lessons had been learned since 1918 and this time there was no hesitation over the best method of protecting shipping. Convoying was instituted immediately, although the first of the new corvettes ordered from Canadian and British shipyards would not be ready until 1940. The RAF's Coastal Command immediately began to patrol coastal waters and defensive minefields were laid.

It was the U-boats which drew first blood, sinking the liner *Athenia* within hours of the declaration of war. Two weeks later the new aircraft carrier *Ark Royal* was nearly hit by torpedoes and three days after that the carrier *Courageous* was sunk. It was a salutary warning to the Admiralty not to risk its large carriers on useless anti-submarine patrolling.

On 8 October *U.47* penetrated the defences of Scapa Flow and sank the elderly battleship *Royal Oak* at her moorings. The victim was not a front-line unit, but Scapa Flow's reputation as an impregnable base made the sinking all the more worrying. The most serious consequence was a forced dispersal of the Home Fleet to temporary bases in the west of Scotland, weakening the blockade and exposing the capital ships to further attacks.

The Commander-in-Chief Home Fleet's fears were justified for the battleship *Nelson* was damaged by a magnetic mine in Loch Ewe and the *Barham* was damaged by a torpedo. Had the German Navy been directed more energetically it might have cut the Atlantic supply-line, but the *Kriegsmarine* proved as reluctant to engage British heavy units as its predecessors had in 1914-18. Two armed merchant cruisers, the *Jervis Bay* and *Rawalpindi* were sunk, but on more than one occasion the presence of a single old battleship was sufficient to save a convoy from attack by the modern capital ships *Gneisenau* and *Scharnhorst*.

Although German surface raiders scored isolated successes they were hardly likely to affect the outcome of the war single-handed. But the U-boats were hampered by Hitler's unwillingness to alienate

ABOVE: *The old battleship* Royal Oak *was sunk by* U.47 *in Scapa Flow in October 1939.*

LEFT: *Crew of a twin 4-inch anti-aircraft gun on board the AA cruiser* Cairo *at Narvik, in April 1940.*

RIGHT: *The doomed destroyer* Glowworm *laying smoke across the bows of the heavy cruiser* Admiral Hipper, *8 April 1940.*

PREVIOUS PAGE: *Men of HMS* Ajax *pose for the camera on the ship's triumphant return to Plymouth in April 1940, after the Battle of the River Plate.*

neutral opinion by a wholesale onslaught on merchantmen. The surface campaign suffered a further setback when in December 1939 three cruisers caught the 'pocket battleship' *Admiral Graf Spee* off Montevideo and brought her to battle. The heavy cruiser *Exeter* was badly damaged with all three turrets knocked out, but the 6-inch gunned *Ajax* and *Achilles* fought a brilliant delaying action, using their high speed and the threat of a torpedo attack to force the *Graf Spee* to shift fire repeatedly. As a result the *Exeter* escaped and the *Graf Spee* took refuge in neutral Uruguayan waters.

Intense diplomatic activity and 'disinformation' led the Germans to believe that powerful British forces were close at hand. Hitler lost his nerve and ordered the *Graf Spee's* captain to scuttle his ship, rather than risk capture or sinking in battle. The victory was a small one, but it came at the right time for the Royal Navy which had seemed to the public unable to get to grips with the threat.

Talk of the 'Phoney War' came to an abrupt end in April 1940, when German forces first overran Denmark and then Norway. The First Lord of the Admiralty Winston Churchill had for some time been urging a reluctant government to take action against German iron-ore ships, which avoided the blockade by using Norwegian waters between Narvik and the Kattegat. By coincidence a British minelaying squadron heading for the Inner Leads met German warships escorting invasion troops on their way to Norway.

On 9 April the battlecruiser *Renown* fought a brief and indecisive action with the *Gneisenau* and *Scharnhorst*, and a day later a force of destroyers entered Narvik Fjord to attack enemy destroyers which had captured the iron-ore port. In the resulting First Battle of Narvik two British destroyers were sunk, but two German destroyers were sunk and five damaged. Three days later the Second Battle of Narvik sealed the fate of the survivors when the battleship *Warspite* escorted nine destroyers into the fjord. This time not a single German destroyer escaped and the *Warspite's* floatplane sank a U-boat.

These two stirring actions did not affect the outcome of the Norwegian Campaign, for the ill-equipped French and British troops were soon being withdrawn. With no adequate air cover the ships suffered some losses of which the carrier *Glorious* was the most serious, but in the long term it was the Germans who lost most. The battlecruiser *Gneisenau* was damaged by a submarine torpedo, her sister *Scharnhorst* was similarly damaged by one of the destroyers escorting the *Glorious* and two cruisers and 12 destroyers had been lost.

On 10 May the German Army was unleashed on the Low Countries, smashing through Belgium and Northern France. Outfought and outmanoeuvred, the Belgian, British and French armies collapsed. The remnants headed for the coast, and after only nine days of fighting the Admiralty received an ominous request from the War Office, for 'advice' on the feasibility of evacuating the entire British Expeditionary Force from France. Within 24 hours Flag Officer Dover, Admiral Ramsay had been

INSET: 'Operation Dynamo' included the evacuation of the BEF from all French ports. These weary troops are saying farewell to Le Havre on 13 June 1940.

MAIN PICTURE: The armed merchant cruiser concept was developed into the auxiliary AA ship. The converted merchantman Springbank had the anti-aircraft armament, radar and fire control of a large cruiser, as well as a fighter and catapult.

given instructions to set up 'Operation Dynamo', a massive operation which would eventually stretch from Dunkirk down to Bordeaux.

Although often described as a miracle, 'Dynamo' was a carefully planned operation with capacity, speed and endurance of ships taken into account. By Monday, 27 May over 7000 men had been taken off; two days later the total exceeded 47,000. Although other ports were used until overrun by the Germans the small port of Dunkirk became the main bridgehead, held by a combined Anglo-French rearguard. This force was kept supplied with an average of 2000 tons of ammunition each day by destroyers coming in to pick up troops.

With a fierce land battle raging on the perimeter, and constant bombardment from German artillery as well as air attack, losses were nevertheless remarkably light. Nine British and French destroyers and eight personnel ships were lost, and out of the total of 848 known civilian and minor naval craft, 72 were sunk by enemy action, 163 were lost in collisions and 45 were damaged, but 338,226 men had been rescued.

As Churchill sourly observed during the euphoric reception of the fugitives, 'wars are not won by evacuations', but the Royal Navy and the French Navy had turned a German tactical victory into a strategic defeat. With its entire army captured the British government would have been unable to continue the war, and it is very unlikely that civilian morale could have survived the shock of losing over 300,000 soldiers.

With the British Isles threatened with invasion for the first time in nearly 150 years there was understandable fear that the Germans would cross the Channel within a few weeks. Hitler did, in fact, issue his famous directive on 16 July, instructing the armed forces to prepare for 'Operation Sealion'.

Many reasons have been put forward to explain the fact the 'Sealion' did not happen, most of them unconvincing. The Germans spent a great deal of time and effort to achieve Hitler's aim, but the Luftwaffe's continuing failure to defeat or subdue the RAF made the planners hesitate. Then there was the pessimism of the *Kriegsmarine* which faced an overwhelming preponderance of Royal Navy ships.

Although the British did not realize it, they were reaping the benefit of the losses they had inflicted in Norway. Only two heavy units were available, the heavy cruiser *Prinz Eugen* and the light cruiser *Nürnberg*, backed up by the old training cruiser *Emden*, six destroyers, 19 torpedo boats and 23 motor torpedo boats.

To make matters worse the German Army had no experience of amphibious operations, and could not understand why the Navy voiced so many misgivings. There are those who argue that Hitler 'missed the boat' in the summer of 1940, but in retrospect it is hard to see how 'Sealion' could have worked. The English Channel is a treacherous stretch of water liable to sudden storms. The *Luftwaffe*, despite its bombastic claims, had shown little aptitude for sinking warships at sea, and as long as most of its resources were committed to the air battle with the RAF it could not devote sufficient attention to the destruction of the Royal Navy.

All these factors resulted in the postponement of 'Sealion' on 17 September, followed by deferment on 12 October, but in reality Hitler had abandoned the plan, and his attentions were turning towards Russia.

Italy now showed her hand, declaring war on the Allies on 10 June, but the Admiralty had already sent powerful reinforcements to the Mediterranean. Late in June Force 'H' was formed at Gibraltar under Vice-Admiral Sir James Somerville, with the capital ships *Hood*, *Resolution* and *Valiant* and the carrier *Ark Royal*. Its purpose was to guard the Western Mediterranean and the trade routes from Sierra Leone and Gibraltar.

The French Fleet presented a major problem. Force 'H' was ordered to put 'Operation Catapult' into effect to ensure that the French warships which had retreated to Algeria stayed beyond the reach of the Germans and the Italians. Accordingly Somerville presented four choices to his opposite number Admiral Gensoul: to join the new 'Free French' and continue the fight against Germany, to accept internment in a British port for the duration of the war, to intern themselves in a French port in the West Indies, or to scuttle themselves within six hours. Even though Somerville was prepared to negotiate on one concession, to allow the French ships to 'demilitarize' themselves at Mers-el-Kebir, the conditions were virtually impossible for a proud service to accept, and Gensoul announced that he would not agree to the terms.

Force 'H' carried out its task with efficiency, sinking the battleship *Bretagne* and inflicting severe damage on the *Dunkerque* and *Provence*, but the *Strasbourg* escaped under cover of the pall of smoke over the anchorage. A more diplomatic approach by Admiral Cunningham at Alexandria achieved the surrender of Admiral Godefroy without bloodshed, but Anglo-French relations were badly damaged by the whole tragic episode.

However much bitterness was caused by Mers-el-Kebir and the subsequent abortive Free French attack on Dakar in Senegal, the British Cabinet had achieved its purpose, to demonstrate to neutral

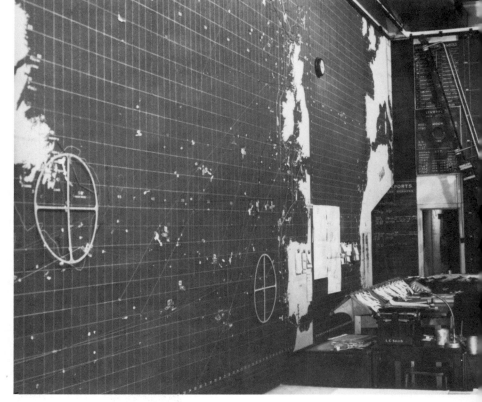

opinion that Great Britain intended to fight on. It was heavy price to pay, but it removed the likelihood of an Axis *coup de main* against the French Fleet.

The North Atlantic supply-line was vital to the British, for it enabled supplies to be imported from the United States and Canada. As in 1914, the first step was to set up a Northern Patrol of armed merchant cruisers (armed ocean liner or AMCs) to prevent neutral ships from carrying war material to Germany and to detect any German warships trying to break out into the Atlantic.

The U-boats were hampered by orders restricting them to the so-called Prize Regulations, which prohibited indiscriminate attacks on merchant ships. By the beginning of 1940 however Hitler's compunction had given way to a virtual sink-at-sight policy. The delay had not been wasted, for the Admiralty had converted a large number of trawlers to anti-submarine vessels, fitting them with guns, depth-charges and Asdic. In April the first of the 'Flower' class corvettes appeared.

The lull ended with the fall of Norway and France. Admiral Dönitz and his U-boat Arm were quick to take advantage, and bases were soon established on the Atlantic coast of France, at Brest, Lorient, La Pallice and elsewhere, while an Italian submarine squadron moved to Bordeaux. From here the U-boats enjoyed shorter routes to the Western Approaches, giving them more time on patrol and avoiding the dangerous waters around the British Isles. It was a totally unexpected reversal of the strategic disadvantages under which the U-boats had laboured in 1914-18.

Although the invasion threat was much less serious than the British believed, their position was alarming. There were far too few vessels to provide the convoys with adequate escorts. Up to the end of

ABOVE: *The Operational Plot of Western Approaches Command, the nerve-centre of the Battle of the Atlantic.*

ABOVE RIGHT: *Admiral of the Fleet Sir Dudley Pound was First Sea Lord until struck down by a brain tumour.*

RIGHT: *The 4-inch gun and crew on the forecastle of a 'Flower' class corvette in the early months of the war.*

May 1940 convoys had been provided with escorts only to a point 200 miles west of Ireland, but between July and October the limit was moved out to 19 degrees West; at that point the escorts moved to a rendezvous with an incoming convoy. The outgoing convoys sailed in formation for another 24 hours before dispersing. Apart from a single armed merchant cruiser, no escorts were available until ships arrived on the other side of the Atlantic.

The new corvettes were beginning to appear in 1940 but in September, a year after the outbreak of war, only 21 new destroyers had replaced the 34 sunk. Battle damage and heavy weather took a heavy toll of escorts and about half the destroyers were out of action for one reason or another. It was to meet this shortage that Winston Churchill asked President Roosevelt to release 50 elderly destroyers to the Royal Navy in return for a 99-year lease on bases in Newfoundland and the West Indies.

Although in poor shape after nearly two decades in reserve the 50 'flush-deckers' (six went to the Canadians immediately) were a valuable addition. Some guns and torpedo tubes were stripped to make way for depth charges, and to commemorate their American origins they were given names of towns common to the Empire and the United States.

The U-boats wasted little time in trying new tactics against the convoys. Night attacks on the surface were almost impossible to defeat without radar, for the conning tower of a U-boat was usually invisible to a ship's lookout. The 'wolf pack' or *rüdeltaktik* called for U-boats to hold off during daylight, but to trail the convoy and wait until nightfall to make a coordinated attack.

Night attacks on the surface posed another problem to the escorts, by nullifying Asdic. As an interim solution ships were fitted with powerful illuminant rockets, but the best solution was a radar set accurate enough to pick up a U-boat. The first such radar set went to sea in a corvette in May 1941 and its production was given top priority. Another important advance was a high-frequency direction-finder sensitive enough to pinpoint a U-boat transmitting back to base.

The U-boats had one chink in their armour. Dönitz had devised a command system which required U-boats to keep his HQ informed of their movements. From Lorient in Brittany he tracked convoys and directed U-boats to the best attacking positions, but these transmissions could be monitored. Direction-finding was a first step towards exploiting this weakness, but since 1940 British cryptographers had been working on methods of deciphering the Enigma coding machines used by the German armed forces. Project 'Ultra' did not yield useful information for the Battle of the Atlantic until mid-1941, but thereafter the stream of intercepts from Bletchley Park became a vital weapon against the U-boats. Sometimes a change in the ciphering arrangements slowed down the flow of tactical information, but Ultra was to remain a key factor until the end of the war.

The surface threat was still serious. The battlecruisers *Gneisenau* and *Scharnhorst* had put into Brest after their last Atlantic foray in 1940. Repeated bombing raids by the RAF failed to put them out of action and the German Navy hoped to push the new battleship *Bismarck* and the cruiser *Prinz Eugen* out through the blockade, disrupt the North Atlantic convoy system and then unite with the two battlecrusiers in Brest. A squadron of three fast capital ships and a heavy cruiser would be powerful enough to require a concentration of the Royal Navy's major units that might be hard to achieve.

ABOVE: *Swordfish on the flight deck of the carrier* Victorious, *being readied for the first strike against the* Bismarck.

ABOVE RIGHT: *HMS Victorious was the second of the armoured carriers to join the Fleet.*

Although the Admiralty was still lacking the help of 'Ultra' intercepts, astute analysis of radio traffic between Bergen and naval HQ in Germany suggested that a breakout was intended in May. Air reconnaissance was intensified, and a cruiser patrol was stationed in the Denmark Strait, the likeliest route for a breakout.

The first radar sighting was made by HMS *Suffolk* on 23 May. Next day the capital ships *Prince of Wales* and *Hood* engaged the German ships, but the flagship *Hood* was destroyed by a magazine explosion; the exact cause remains unknown, and technical historians continue to argue over details. The new battleship *Prince of Wales*, with faults in her main armament being repaired by workmen on board, was in no shape to continue the action and was ordered to disengage. However she had scored two underwater hits in the last hectic minutes and the damage was ultimately to bring about the *Bismarck's* destruction. The German ship was already short of fuel having failed to take on her full capacity at Bergen, and the two shell-hits allowed seawater to contaminate a large amount of her remaining fuel.

The massive sea and air operation which followed is too well-known to be recounted in detail, but it remains a classic of its kind, with capital ships, carriers, cruisers and destroyers performing their roles to maximum effect. The carrier *Victorious* scored a single torpedo hit on 24 May, but failed to slow the *Bismarck*. That night the *Prinz Eugen* broke away and proceeded to Brest without being detected, and next morning the *Suffolk* lost radar contact when the *Bismarck* made an unexpected change of course. Her situation seemed desperate, with the Home Fleet only 100 miles away, but with no idea of where she was. For most of the day the *Bismarck* ploughed through heavy seas, making her way to Brest. Admiral Lütjens had decided that his loss of fuel had made the planned raid into the North Atlantic too dangerous, but his pursuers still believed that he was heading back to Germany.

Then the *Bismarck* made a crucial error, sending a long radio message to Germany. It could not be deciphered, but direction-finding stations in Britain located the source and ships and aircraft were redirected. For some hours the Home Fleet followed the wrong course after the bearings had been wrongly calculated but the error was spotted in time.

To give the Home Fleet time to engage before the major units were forced to return to base to refuel, it was vital that the *Bismarck* should be slowed down. When a Catalina flying boat finally located the *Bismarck* on the morning of 26 May the carrier *Ark Royal* flew off a strike of torpedo bombers. The first attack wave found HMS *Sheffield*, but fortunately no hits were scored. The second wave found their target, and pressed their attack home in appalling weather. Two torpedoes hit, one of which wrecked the *Bismarck's* rudders.

When the Home Fleet flagship *King George V* and the *Rodney* found their quarry next morning she was moving erratically at slow speed. The *Bismarck* fought gamely to the end, but after half an hour lay helpless under a hail of fire. The battleships withdrew, leaving the heavy cruiser *Dorsetshire* to finish her off with torpedoes.

Although the German Fleet was still in being, with the two battlecruisers still safe in Brest and the *Bismarck's* sister *Tirpitz* nearly ready, the *Kriegsmarine's* last hope of using its surface raiders to destroy the North Atlantic convoys was gone. The big ships would remain a nuisance, but the struggle to cut Britain off from the United States must now be left to the U-boats.

An important stage in the Battle of the Atlantic was the passage of the Lend-Lease Bill in March 1941, for it allowed the Admiralty to place large orders for escorts in US shipyards. As President Roosevelt inched his way towards fuller assistance, so the provisions for defending American merchant ships were tightened. This had the dual effect of taking some of the strain off the British and Canadian escorts, but it also increased the likelihood of confrontations between US Navy escorts and the U-boats. At the Atlantic Charter meeting in August 1941 it was agreed that US ships could be escorted by Canadian escorts, and similarly, US warships would escort non-American ships.

The 'Flower' Class corvette programme was now in full swing, and in January 1941 a programme was started to convert some of the older destroyers into 'long-leggers' by replacing one boiler with an 80-ton fuel tank. The corvette was proving too small and slow to cope with U-boats in mid-ocean, so a new type of escort, the 'River' Class frigate, appeared in November 1941. New weapons and new sensors also helped in the fight, but the shipping losses were appalling. By the end of 1939 no less than 755,000 tons of shipping had been sunk; in 1940 nearly 4 million tons (over 1000 ships) were lost; in 1941 1300 merchantmen were lost from all causes, a total of 4,328,000 tons.

Britain's only hope was the United States, but when in December 1941 the Japanese attack on Pearl Harbor brought the United States into the war, the expected miracle did not happen. In spite of all the warnings in 1941 and three attacks on US destroyers off Iceland the US Navy had no workable anti-submarine tactics for the protection of shipping along the East Coast.

The Germans had long since accepted that the United States would sooner or later declare war and had laid their plans accordingly. On 12 December, only five days after Pearl Harbor, Admiral Dönitz unleashed 'Operation Drumroll' by ordering U-boats into the Western Atlantic and Caribbean. With no convoys, all communications 'in clear' and only the occasional high-speed dash by patrolling destroyers, the U-boats were able to inflict heavy losses on a scale resembling 1917.

Not until April 1942 did the US Navy reluctantly admit that the British were right. Convoys were introduced and as an emergency measure 10 corvettes and some trawlers were transferred by the Royal Navy, and orders for a further 15 corvettes and two of the new 'River' Class frigates were placed with Canadian shipyards. Orders for 300 destroyer escorts had already been placed by the Admiralty under Lend-Lease, but these would not be ready until the end of 1943.

By July 1942 the situation in the Atlantic was critical. The losses in American waters were only just beginning to fall, but the Allies now had additional commitments. The enormous losses suffered by Russia led the United States and Britain to offer military aid. This meant more convoys of war material with all the additional hazards of a voyage past the German bases in northern Norway.

Ships heading to and from Murmansk had to run the gauntlet of air raids as well as attacks from U-boats and surface ships. The battleship *Tirpitz* and a number of cruisers lurked in the northern fjords waiting for a good moment to pounce on a thinly defended convoy. Comparatively few of the

convoys were attacked, for the German naval command suffered under strict regulations imposed by Hitler, but on the few occasions when heavy units engaged the results could be disastrous. Convoy PQ-17 suffered the loss of 24 out of 37 ships when the Admiralty mistakenly gave an order to scatter.

What saved the North Russian convoys was the determination of the crews of the merchantmen and the warships. Many of the merchantmen were neutrals, civilians who were untrained for war, but there is no record of any merchant seamen refusing to take a ship to sea.

As the anti-submarine war moved further away from coastal waters one problem became paramount, the need for air cover. Early in 1941 the Admiralty commissioned a number of catapult-armed merchantmen (CAM-ships) to defend the Gibraltar-UK convoys from air attack. Their drawback was that the Hurricane fighter aircraft was invariably 'ditched' after it had shot down the enemy bomber. The idea of a small 'trade carrier' had been around since before the war, but nothing had been done for lack of aircraft.

In June 1941 a captured German banana-boat was commissioned as the escort carrier HMS *Audacity*, with a small wooden flight deck and six Martlet (Wildcat) fighters parked aft. Her career was short but so successful that a request had already gone to the United States for more escort carriers. These ships did not come into service until the following summer, and to supplement them the Royal Navy fitted a number of merchant vessels as MAC-ships or merchant aircraft carriers.

ABOVE: *Under Captain F J Walker RN the sloop* Starling *led her support group in a series of brilliant attacks on the U-Boats.*

ABOVE: *The Hedgehog spigot mortar was the first of a series of new weapons devised for the Battle of the Atlantic. It fired 24 bombs ahead of the ship.*

LEFT: *HMS* Rodney *on patrol in 1943. Deprived of a refit by the* Bismarck's *break-out, she finished the war without a major overhaul.*

As air cover was slowly extended to cover the 'Black Gap' in mid-Atlantic so the task of the hard-pressed escorts was made easier. The best solution proved to be the very long-range Liberator four-engined bomber, which was the first maritime patrol aircraft to have sufficient endurance to 'loiter' over a convoy. The combination of air and sea escort was to account for a growing number of U-boats.

Further progress was made in the autumn of 1942, when the British and Canadians introduced the first support groups. These were groups of escorts not dedicated to any particular convoy, but available to reinforce a hard-pressed convoy. They also contributed by pursuing damaged U-boats to destruction, a task which escorts had previously been forced to ignore on many occasions rather than leave their convoy unguarded.

Unfortunately this steady progress lulled the Allies into false optimism. Against British advice the Americans insisted on a major effort in the Euro-

pean theatre. Rather than be pushed into the 'Second Front' (a major assault in Europe) the British compromised by approving a landing in North Africa. The Allies had sufficient resources to accomplish their objectives on land, but to get the vast convoys of troops and supplies safely across the Atlantic it would be necessary to use escort groups from the Atlantic battle. At a time when they were needed more than ever the new escort carriers, frigates and aircraft would be absent.

As always Admiral Dönitz was quick to take advantage of a mistake, and even the slight slackening of the offensive effort was sufficient to push losses up again. In October 619,000 tons of shipping were sunk, then up to 729,000 tons the following month. Losses fell slightly in December, but that could not compensate for the total losses in 1942: 1664 ships totalling 7,790,000 tons.

To put these figures into perspective, the Allies had only built seven million tons of new shipping.

ABOVE: *Aircraft, when used in conjunction with convoy, were a most potent weapon against U-boats, but it proved necessary to put RAF Coastal Command under the operational control of the Admiralty.*

The deficit of near one million tons was additional to the heavy losses of 1940-1. On the credit side 190 German and Italian U-boats had been sunk, but 1942 was a year in which German shipyards had reached only 85 per cent of the planned output. At the end of 1941 91 U-boats had been operational; by the end of 1942 there were 312 in commission.

In the opening weeks of 1943 it became clear to both sides that the Battle of the Atlantic was reaching its climax. If the shipping losses continued to rise they would outstrip even the resources of the United States. No matter how many victories were won on land, or how many tons of bombs fell on German and Italian cities, if the ships and supplies failed to reach the British Isles the British would be starved into surrender. America would not be defeated but her ability to influence events in Europe would be crippled.

The spring of 1943 was to see a number of fierce convoy battles. In March two convoys were attacked by a wolf-pack of 17 U-boats. In one hectic moment the senior officer of the escort rammed a U-boat, but he and many of his men died when his disabled destroyer was torpedoed by a second U-boat; then within minutes a Free French corvette sank the second U-boat. The two convoys had already lost 17 ships.

Even more serious was an attack by 40 U-boats on two convoys. Even after the two convoys were combined to strengthen their escort, 21 ships were sunk. Shore-based aircraft helped to blunt the attacks, but not until 141,000 tons of shipping had been lost. To the Admiralty it seemed that the convoy system was about to fall apart. Within the first 20 days of March more than 500,000 tons of shipping had been sunk.

Fortunately salvation was at hand and Dönitz was to be proved wrong in his assertion that the U-boat could win the war on its own. The escorts and aircraft released after the 'Torch' landings in

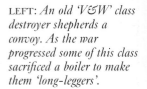

LEFT: *An old 'V&W' class destroyer shepherds a convoy. As the war progressed some of this class sacrificed a boiler to make them 'long-leggers'.*

BELOW: *Loading a Mk VII depth-charge onto a thrower, aboard the corvette* Dianthus.

North Africa were now returning to the Atlantic, and at the same time the U-boats were beginning to slacken their efforts from sheer fatigue. The crypt-analysts had also broken into the latest U-boat cipher just in time, giving vital information to the Admiralty to enable convoys to be rerouted.

The battle between the rival scientists was now as crucial as any made at sea. The German Navy's scientists made a huge blunder in devising countermeasures to the Allies' search radars. First, they missed the significance of high-frequency direction-finding and then they failed to discover that enemy ships and aircraft were now using centimetric wavelengths for their latest radars.

With hindsight we can see that the U-boat offensive failed for much the same reasons which prevailed in 1917. The tonnage figures on which Dönitz based his calculation of the point at which the Allies would crack, were distorted by exaggerated claims. The U-boat ciphers were compromised once again, giving the defenders the inestimable advantage of being able to localize the threat. Added to these factors was the crucial difference in the way in which each side made use of its scientists. The British in particular forged close links between the scientists and the men who had to use their equipment; young officers on leave were sent off to country-house weekends, where they could meet on equal terms with scientists, and this encouraged what is today known as 'feedback'.

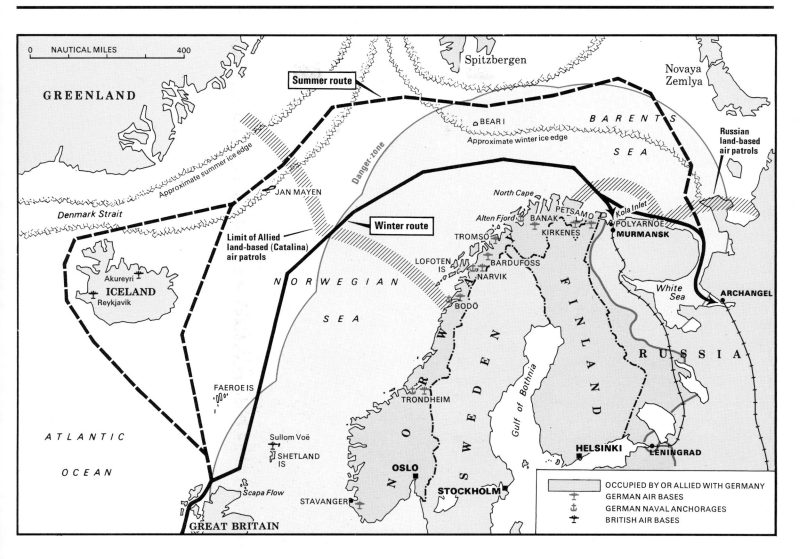

ABOVE: *The entry of Russia into the war imposed a heavy burden on the Royal Navy, which had to convoy supplies to Murmansk.*

RIGHT: *Commander Donald MacIntyre* DSO, *the* CO *of the destroyer* Hesperus, *had the second highest score of U-boats sunk.*

The *Kriegsmarine* had access to the finest brains in Germany, but on a more formal basis. There was also the absurdity of Nazi ideology to complicate matters. To make any important changes it was necessary to dabble in politics, and find a suitable moment to gain the Führer's ear.

The failure of the U-boat offensive was reflected in their losses: 19 in February, 15 in March, 15 in April and 41 in May. On 22 May Dönitz admitted defeat by ordering his U-boats to withdraw for 'retraining', but there was no disguising the scale of the defeat. By the end of the summer Allied shipbuilding finally exceeded the total lost and thoughts turned at last to the counter-offensive.

The U-boats did return to the battle with new weapons as Dönitz had promised. Later in the year they tried to disrupt the North Atlantic convoys using new acoustic homing torpedoes and turning the weight of attack on to the escorts. Fortunately for the Allies the new Type XXI 'electro-submarine' suffered severe delays with the result that only three were at sea by May 1945. Although the morale of the U-boat officers and men never cracked, the losses had diluted the quality of personnel to such an extent that it would never again be possible to attack with the determination shown in the spring of 1943.

The North Russian convoys also benefitted from the easing of pressure in the North Atlantic.

Late in December 1942 a force of eight destroyers fought off an attack by the heavy cruisers *Admiral Hipper* and *Lützow*, giving the British cruisers *Sheffield* and *Jamaica* time to come up in support. Despite the disparity of force (even with the two cruisers the British escort was still heavily outgunned by the German ships) the convoy escaped without loss. Hitler's reaction on hearing of this humiliating fiasco was to order the entire surface fleet to be scrapped, to release its armour for tank-production and its guns for coastal defences.

This extreme reaction forced the resignation of the Grand Admiral Erich Raeder, the only naval leader whose strategic advice Hitler had valued. His post as head of the Navy was immediately given to Dönitz, who found it impossible to make good his own boasts. Instead of scrapping the surface fleet he persuaded Hitler to continue Raeder's strategy of tying down as many Allied forces as possible

Previous surface operations had been ineffective, and the blame could be placed on Hitler's excessively cautious orders but Dönitz was able to get permission for one more operation. The battlecruiser *Scharnhorst* was to be used, and this time Dönitz insisted that he alone should have operational control.

The resulting Battle of North Cape on 26 December 1943 showed that Dönitz and his staff had little more flair than the Führer in running a surface battle. Aerial reconnaissance by the *Luft-waffe* had located the Home Fleet, but the essential phrase 'Including what may be a battleship' was cut out before the message went by teleprinter to the *Kriegsmarine* – only verified facts must be passed to another service. Therefore it came as a shock to Admiral Bey in the *Scharnhorst* when 14-inch salvoes from HMS *Duke of York* started to fall around his ship.

Once again the German force was trying to attack a convoy on its way to North Russia, but this time the scales were weighted in favour of the defenders. Intercepts from Ultra enabled the Commander-in-Chief Home Fleet, Vice-Admiral Sir Bruce Fraser to forecast Admiral Bey's moves. Aware from the signals that Bey's forces had failed to detect another homeward-bound convoy in the vicinity, Fraser was able to weaken its escort to strengthen the target-convoy. He also knew that Bey had lost contact with his destroyers.

The battle was fought in two phases, one in which the close escort of cruisers and destroyers forced the *Scharnhorst* to withdraw, and one in which the Home Fleet flagship *Duke of York* hit the battlecruiser several times and then left her to the destroyers to finish off with torpedoes. Several things distinguished the action; it was the Royal Navy's last big-ship action and the last in the European theatre, it was the first battle fought entirely by radar, and it was fought without the over-rigid centralized command which had marred British tactics

ABOVE: *The battleship* Duke of York *prepares to fire her 14-inch guns as heavy seas break over her forecastle and quarterdeck.*

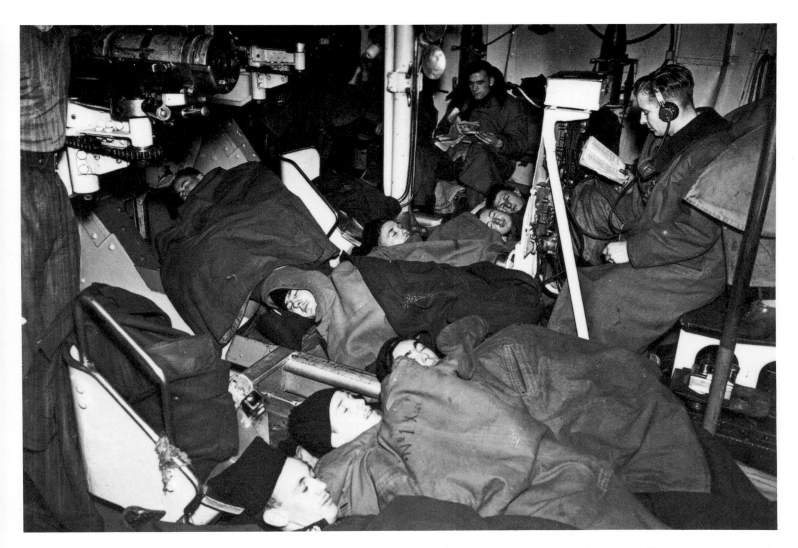

ABOVE: *Royal Marine gun crews snatch some rest in the gun turret of a light cruiser at sea.*

in the past. In fact Fraser had told his commanders that he would fight the battle with open communications, as he preferred the risk of passing information to the Germans to the risk of friendly ships firing on each other in the Arctic night.

Without the *Scharnhorst* there was no longer any serious threat to Allied shipping in Norway. *Tirpitz* had been seriously damaged by midget submarines in September 1943 and although nobody at the Admiralty knew it she would never again go to sea under her own power. In April 1944 an air strike from six carriers, 'Operation Tungsten' scored several hits and caused heavy casualties. Other air attacks were unsuccessful, but when she was moved further south to serve as a floating gun-battery she came within range of bombers based in the United Kingdom. On 12 November 1944 a force of RAF Lancaster bombers hit her with 12,000-lb 'earthquake' bombs and sent her to the bottom. The U-boat Arm remained dangerous to the end, however. A new coastal variety, the small Type XXIII, continued to score successes in British coastal waters until three days before the final collapse.

The Battle of the Atlantic was the hardest ever fought by the Royal Navy in all its long history. Nor can the Merchant Navy's contribution be ignored. Whereas the Royal Navy lost about 9.3 per cent of its total manpower in World War II (as against 9 per cent for the RAF and 6 per cent for the Army), the Merchant Navy suffered 17 per cent casualties.

Although many of the 33,000 seamen were lost in other theatres, it was the Battle of the Atlantic which took the worst toll, not just in numbers but in stamina and morale. Like the Americans, Canadians and other nationalities which made up the world's seamen, they faced death by drowning and burning, starvation in open boats or frostbite. The sea was the constant enemy.

The War in the Mediterranean

The British were on their own after the fall of France and the attacks on the French Fleet, but they were fortunate to have one of their most talented senior officers commanding the Mediterranean Fleet. Like Nelson, Vice-Admiral Andrew Cunningham was to establish his reputation in the Mediterranean in a series of actions in which he led numerically inferior forces to victory by superior tactical skill and leadership.

The Mediterranean was no sideshow for the Royal Navy. Control of the Suez Canal and Egypt denied Germany access to the Middle Eastern oilfields. It was also reasoned that pressure on Hitler's partner Mussolini would strain the Axis partnership and draw off forces from Northern Europe.

The first signs were encouraging. On 9 July 1940 heavy units engaged in the Battle of Calabria, but the Italian Fleet withdrew at top speed. The flagship HMS *Warspite* hit the battleship *Giulio Cesare* at a range of 26,400 yards (15 miles), establishing a record for long-range gunnery which has never been equalled. Although it was not the decisive result which Cunningham wanted, it gave the Royal Navy a moral edge over the Italians.

Then came the news, little more than a week later, that the Australian cruiser HMAS *Sydney* and her destroyers had sunk the light cruiser *Bartolomeo Colleoni* north of Crete, and had driven off her sister *Giovanni delle Bande Nere*.

Despite the threat of invasion in home waters, the Admiralty gave Cunningham the reinforcements he needed for further hammer-blows against the Italians, the new armoured carrier *Illustrious*, the newly modernized battleship *Valiant* and two anti-aircraft cruisers. Cunningham's plan was to strike at the Italians' main fleet base at Taranto, the 'arch' of the Italian 'boot'. Until that fleet was neutralized it would be impossible to send convoys of war material through the Mediterranean, to reinforce the troops fighting the Italians in the North African desert.

The attack on Taranto on the night of 11 November achieved all that and more. Within a space of two hours the battleship *Conte di Cavour* had been sunk and the *Littorio* and *Duilio* had been severely damaged, all for the loss of two Swordfish biplane bombers and two aircrew. It was the world's first carrier strike against a fleet in a defended base, and it showed what could have been achieved if the Fleet Air Arm had been equipped with better aircraft.

Cunningham now had two carriers under his command and soon the Fleet Air Arm was attacking land and sea targets along the North African coast, dive-bombing, mining and torpedoing shipping. One of the lesser advantages of the Taranto raid was the destruction of the seaplane base; without its long-range seaplanes the Italian Navy was robbed of valuable reconnaissance.

In November Force 'H' met the Italian Fleet off Cape Spartivento, while covering the passage of a fast convoy from Gibraltar to Alexandria. Once again the Italian forces used their high speed to avoid action, but they failed to intercept the three fast merchantmen.

The great naval base at Malta had been regarded as indefensible before the war, particularly by the RAF, but it was now obvious that it was vital both as a base to cover ship-movements through the Central Mediterranean and as a platform for offensive operations against the Italian communications with their North African possessions. With these aims in mind the island's long-neglected defences were strengthened as fast as possible and a submarine flotilla was sent out.

The British now became over-confident, and when Italian forces attacked Greece the Cabinet decided to transfer troops from Egypt. The Royal Navy was forced to set up an advanced base at Suda Bay in Crete to cover the shipments of men and munitions. Despite the achievements since June 1940 the British forces were dangerously overstretched and only the feeble performance of the Italian Navy had permitted the Mediterranean Fleet to get away with so much. One example of the weak-

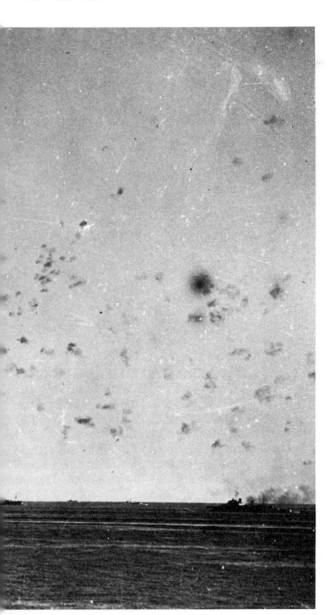

LEFT: *In August 1942 'Pedestal', the last great Malta convoy, battled through to save the beleaguered island.*

BELOW LEFT: *Admiral Sir Bruce Fraser with some of his COs on the quarterdeck of the* Duke of York *after the sinking of the* Scharnhorst.

BELOW: *The 'batsman' watches as a Swordfish comes in to land on a carrier.*

ness of the Royal Navy is the fact that the Italians convoyed over 690,000 tons of shipping to North Africa between July and December, and lost only two per cent to attacks from aircraft and submarines. Nor were Italian countermeasures ineffective – 10 out of 17 British submarines were sunk in the same period.

The Germans were keeping a wary eye on their Italian allies, and now decided to intervene. The specialized anti-shipping air group *Fliegerkorps X* was sent to Sicily in order to sink at least one of the Mediterranean Fleet carriers. On 10 January 1941 they nearly achieved their aim when Ju87 Stuka dive-bombers hit HMS *Illustrious* off Malta. Experts had calculated that two 500-kg bombs on the flight deck would wreck the carrier, but she took three hits and managed to limp into Grand Harbour on fire and heavily damaged. After hurried repairs carried out under intensive bombing she set sail for the United States via the Suez Canal; the damage was so severe that it was another year before she was fit for service.

The British position in the Mediterranean was now so precarious that a new armoured carrier HMS *Formidable* had to be sent out via the Suez Canal – only three months earlier the *Illustrious* had sailed from Gibraltar to Malta safely. But Cunningham showed that he needed only one modern carrier to go back on the offensive, and as soon as he heard that an Italian squadron had been sighted heading for Crete he took his ships to sea from Alexandria.

In the afternoon of 28 March the carrier's aircraft scored a torpedo hit on the battleship *Vittoria Veneto*, and at dusk another attack crippled the heavy cruiser *Pola*. Fifty miles away was the Mediterranean Fleet flagship HMS *Warspite* and two other battleships the *Barham* and *Valiant*. Although some of Cunningham's staff were wary of operating within range of Italian bombers the little admiral decided to continue in pursuit. He knew that the Royal Navy's night-fighting tactics were considerably superior to the Italians', and in addition the *Valiant* and *Warspite* had the latest search radar.

At 10.25 pm lookouts saw three dim shapes less than 4000 yards away. Within seconds the heavy cruisers *Fiume*, *Pola* and *Zara* were shattered by 15-inch salvoes, and were on fire and sinking. Two of the cruisers had been sent back to help their damaged sister *Pola* while the main force made its escape back to Italy.

Here was the decisive battle which Cunningham had sought. Although the battleship had escaped, the loss of three heavy cruisers and two of their escorting destroyers was a severe blow to Italian morale. The Battle of Cape Matapan as it was dubbed was to act as a dampener on Italian plans for many months at a time when the Royal Navy was nearer to defeat than ever before.

Exasperated by the poor performance of their allies in Greece the Germans had attacked with ground and air forces early in April. Suddenly the Mediterranean Fleet was called on to evacuate Greek and British troops to Crete. Then came the

fall of Crete and the Navy's ships were thrown into an attempt to save as many troops as possible.

The task was daunting. With virtually no air cover, the Navy had to prevent a seaborne landing and at the same time rescue large numbers of troops. The first objective was achieved, with heavy losses to a German assault convoy, but in daylight losses to air attack were severe. Two cruisers were sunk, as well as a number of destroyers, and the battleship *Warspite* and the carrier *Formidable* were severely damaged. But in spite of these and other casualties the warships took off more than half the garrison.

Crete has been called the Royal Navy's finest hour. It is said that Cunningham was advised to abandon the troops, rather than lose so many ships, but he replied, 'It takes three years to build a ship, but 300 to build a tradition.' What is undeniable is that the Italian Navy remained totally passive throughout the campaign when even the smallest demonstration might have forced Cunningham to move his ships away from the island. The resolution shown at Matapan had been more than justified.

After the fall of Crete pressure on Malta became severe. Its submarines continued to harass supply-lines between Italy and North Africa but constant air-attacks from Sicily wore down the defending aircraft. In June 1941 three aircraft carriers flew off Hurricane fighters to replace losses and submarines were used to bring in vital spares and ammunition. In July a fast convoy got into Malta, and in September the carriers *Ark Royal* and *Furious* flew in another 49 Hurricanes. The dividend for all this effort was well over 100 German and Italian ships sunk, totalling nearly 300,000 tons.

In another attempt to remedy the situation Admiral Dönitz was ordered to send 10 of his precious U-boats into the Mediterranean between September and November. The intervention was dramatic; on 13 November the carrier *Ark Royal* was

torpedoed and sunk near Gibraltar, and 11 days later the battleship *Barham* was also sunk near Alexandria. Worse was to follow, for in mid-December the light cruiser *Galatea* was torpedoed and the Malta striking force ran into a minefield, losing the flagship HMS *Neptune* and the destroyer *Kandahar*; in addition two more cruisers were damaged. On the night of 19 December an Italian submarine launched two 'human torpedoes' into Alexandria harbour and their two-man crews succeeded in putting limpet mines under the battleships *Queen Elizabeth* and *Valiant*.

With their last capital ships out of action the British now had no major units left but once again their luck held. The two battleships sank upright in shallow water and aerial reconnaissance failed to reveal that they were sunk. The Italians assumed that Cunningham still had two effective capital ships and failed to exploit the chance to destroy British sea power once and for all. However, they did run two convoys to North Africa in time to replenish Field-Marshal Rommel's forces and Malta could do nothing to stop them.

By January 1942 the Eighth Army had recaptured airfields in Cyrenaica, and Cunningham hoped that it might now be possible to run a small, fast convoy through to Malta. In March this was attempted, and this precipitated the Second Battle of Sirte. This time the Italian battle-fleet came out in support, but even without capital ships to back them up Admiral Vian's famous 'Fighting Fifteenth' the 15th Cruiser Squadron, were able to win through. In a rising sea Vian's ships made skilful use of smokescreens to avoid serious damage. By the evening the Italians had given up; the convoy was safe.

The sequel was tragic. Next day repeated air attacks accounted for several ships. The fast transport *Breconshire* was stopped by a bomb, towed into Grand Harbour, but was hit again and sank at her

TOP: *The only known view of HMS/m* Upholder, *the Royal Navy's most successful submarine. She is lying outboard of a later 'U' class boat at Malta.*

ABOVE: *Lieutenant Commander Wanklyn VC, DSO***, CO of the* Upholder, *was the leading British 'ace'.*

RIGHT: *The 'lucky'* Ark Royal *was finally sunk by a single torpedo-hit in November 1941.*

BELOW: *HMS* Indomitable *operating in the Far East in 1944-45, with an Avenger torpedo-bomber overhead.*

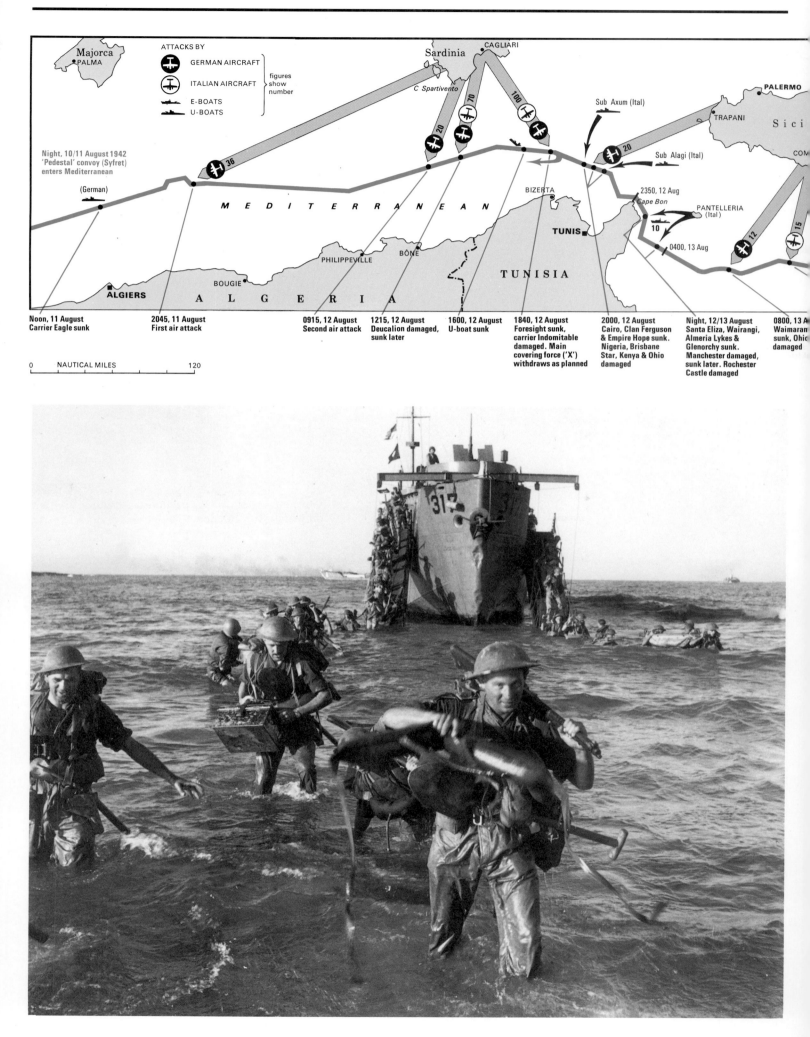

ATTACKS BY

GERMAN AIRCRAFT

ITALIAN AIRCRAFT

figures show number

E-BOATS
U-BOATS

Majorca
PALMA

Sardinia

CAGLIARI

C Spartivento

PALERMO

TRAPANI

Sici

COM

Sub Axum (Ital)

Sub Alagi (Ital)

Night, 10/11 August 1942 'Pedestal' convoy (Syfret) enters Mediterranean

(German)

2350, 12 Aug
Cape Bon

PANTELLERIA (Ital)

M E D I T E R R A N E A N

BIZERTA

TUNIS

PHILIPPEVILLE

BÔNE

BOUGIE

ALGIERS

A L G E R I A

TUNISIA

0400, 13 Aug

0 NAUTICAL MILES 120

Noon, 11 August
Carrier Eagle sunk

2045, 11 August
First air attack

0915, 12 August
Second air attack

1215, 12 August
Deucalion damaged, sunk later

1600, 12 August
U-boat sunk

1840, 12 August
Foresight sunk, carrier Indomitable damaged. Main covering force ('X') withdraws as planned

2000, 12 August
Cairo, Clan Ferguson & Empire Hope sunk. Nigeria, Brisbane Star, Kenya & Ohio damaged

Night, 12/13 August
Santa Eliza, Wairangi, Almeria Lykes & Glenorchy sunk. Manchester damaged, sunk later. Rochester Castle damaged

0800, 13 A
Waimaram
sunk, Ohio
damaged

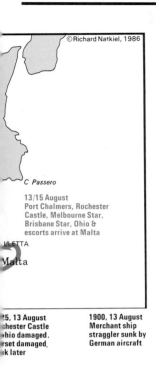

C Passero

13/15 August
Port Chalmers, Rochester
Castle, Melbourne Star,
Brisbane Star, Ohio &
escorts arrive at Malta

VLETTA

Malta

5, 13 August
chester Castle
hio damaged.
rset damaged,
k later

1900, 13 August
Merchant ship
straggler sunk by
German aircraft

moorings. The two survivors got into harbour and started to unload their vital cargoes but were hit and sank at their moorings before they could finish the task. Only 5000 tons out of the 25,900 tons of stores reached the embattled people of Malta.

By August 1942, as plans for the North African landings matured, it was clearly necessary to make a maximum effort to relieve Malta. To get one convoy through it was necessary to provide an escort of two battleships, three fleet carriers, seven cruisers and 20 destroyers, for only 14 fast cargo ships. 'Operation Pedestal' was a four-day battle in which nine merchantmen, a carrier and two cruisers were sunk, and a carrier and two cruisers were damaged.

The high point of the battle was a struggle to get the damaged tanker *Ohio* into harbour. Her cargo of aviation gasoline was essential to keep the defending fighters flying, and she was finally towed to safety with two destroyers lashed alongside to keep her afloat. Despite having caught fire once, her gasoline cargo was intact, and as the other ships brought food and other supplies Malta could fight on.

With the Central Mediterranean secure it was

possible to proceed with 'Operation Torch', intended to catch the Axis forces in North Africa between two fires. The bulk of the troops were provided by the United States but the Royal Navy provided the main naval support. Some losses were incurred but Vichy French resistance was quickly crushed and the troops soon established a bridgehead.

The next step in the counter-offensive was the capture of Sicily, in July 1943. It was a comparatively weakly opposed landing unlike the Salerno landings two months later. British and American warships were subjected for the first time to attack by glider bombs, the first primitive guided missiles.

Italy should by rights have been knocked out of the war. Indeed an armistice was being negotiated on the eve of the Salerno landings, but the Germans moved swiftly to forestall any unilateral negotiations by their allies. This meant that the Royal Navy had to continue to support the Italian campaign for much longer than planned. The ill-fated Anzio landings in January 1944 were meant to shorten the war but merely provided another commitment.

By the end of 1944 the Allies were in control of Italy, but light forces continued the fight against Axis forces in the Adriatic and Aegean almost to the end of the war. What had seemed at times a sideshow had become a four-year war of attrition. Historians continue to debate the value of the Mediterranean campaigns, but there can be no doubt that if the Royal Navy had lost control the Germans would have reached the Middle Eastern oil which they needed.

The Far East

The threat of a simultaneous war in the Far East and in Europe had been dreaded by the Admiralty throughout the 1930s. Although the great fleet base at Singapore had been completed after lengthy bickering, very few reinforcements could be spared for the area.

The battleship *Prince of Wales* and the old battle-cruiser *Repulse* were sent out to Singapore in the forlorn hope that their presence would somehow deter the Japanese. Any hopes that these two ships would affect the outcome were dashed by the news from Pearl Harbor, and it was only a matter of time before they were hunted down. They were caught on 10 December while steaming off the eastern coast of Malaya, and sunk in quick succession by the well-coordinated attack by land-based bombers and torpedo bombers.

The fall of the 'Gibraltar of the Far East' was almost as big a shock, but the sinking of the two capital ships was the inevitable result of a deeply flawed strategy. Much has been made of the 'guns pointing the wrong way', but that can be dismissed as a hasty excuse put up by the Prime Minister to ward off criticism. Inter-service rivalry had prevented the full complement of guns being installed to defend the landward side of the fortress and the heavy batteries were issued only with armour-piercing ammunition. The RAF had successfully opposed any strengthening of the defences with the spurious argument that the money would be better

SIAM

BANGKOK

✠ JAPANESE AIRBASES
0   MILES   200
0   KILOMETERS   300

8 Dec 1941
Jap Fifteenth Army
invades

FRENCH
INDO-CHINA

PRACHUAB

SAIGON

0905 hrs, 7 Dec
Japanese disperse
to landing points

CHUMPHON

Japanese invasion fleet

From Hainan I.

BANDON   *Isthmus*

NAKHON   of

Kra

Intended strike

SINGORA
PATANI

KHOTA BHARU

Japanese submarines
locate Force Z

0200 hrs, 10 Dec

2015 hrs, 9 Dec
Force Z changes
course for
Singapore

3 Japanese
aircraft sighted

1340 hrs, 9 Dec

MALAYA

KUANTAN   10 Dec
Japanese aircraft
sink Repulse - 1233 hrs
& Prince of Wales -
1320 hrs

ANAMBA IS

SINGAPORE

Sumatra   1735 hrs, 8 Dec 1941
Force Z sails

Equator

© Richard Natkiel, 1986

ABOVE LEFT: *'Operation Pedestal' was a desperate effort to shift vital supplies through to Malta before the 'Torch' landings in North Africa.*

LEFT: *Malaya and the 'impregnable' fortress of Singapore fell to a brilliant land, sea and air campaign by the Japanese after the sinking of the* Prince of Wales *and* Repulse.

FAR LEFT: *Men of the 51st Highland Division wade ashore from a Landing Ship Infantry (LSI) during the invasion of Sicily in July 1943.*

spent on aircraft. Ironically the RAF was right; the fate of Malaya and Singapore was decided by the air battle in northern Malaya, but it was the RAF that lost it.

Thereafter the surviving British and Australian units were harried through the East Indies, suffering severe casualties as they tried to hold off superior Japanese sea and air forces. The Battle of the Java Sea on 27 February marked the end of the ABDA (Australian-British-Dutch-American) force. In the space of less than three months the Allies lost two capital ships, five cruisers, a seaplane carrier and 17 destroyers in futile attempts to defend the East Indies. Fortunately the Japanese never achieved their aim of reaching Australia, but until the US Navy stopped them in the Battle of the Coral Sea there was little to prevent it.

The carrier force which had wiped out the US Pacific Fleet had little trouble in destroying British forces in the Indian Ocean. The carrier *Hermes* and the heavy cruisers *Cornwall* and *Dorsetshire* and a number of minor warships were all sunk by air attack. Admiral Somerville's force of old battleships could do little except avoid trouble, making use of its secret anchorage at Addu Atoll in the Maldive Islands.

Individual British and Australian ships operated with American forces in the South Pacific in 1942-3. The carrier *Victorious* was lent to the US Navy for a few months in 1943 to ease the desperate shortage of ships, but a serious British contribution to the Pacific War had to wait until 1944, when efforts were made to rebuild both an Eastern Fleet and a British Pacific Fleet.

The Eastern Fleet was built up early in 1944, mustering the carriers *Illustrious*, *Begum* and *Shah*, and capital ships *Queen Elizabeth*, *Renown* and *Valiant*. On 19 April the British carriers were joined by the USS *Saratoga* in a bold raid on a Japanese base at Sabang in North-West Sumatra. Although the US Navy and the Royal Navy operated well together it came as a shock to the British to realize how much they had to learn from the Americans. The design of the British carriers did not permit the large air groups of the American carriers, but it was also clear that the Americans had a vastly more efficient method of operating aircraft. The US Navy's logistic organization was also considerably better; lacking the chain of bases across the world, the Americans had always paid more attention to a mobile logistic force.

The Fleet Air Arm had long since given up any hope of getting satisfactory aircraft from the overstretched British aircraft industry. Under Lend-Lease a steady flow of rugged and potent aircraft made good the shortage, and the efficiency of the Fleet Air Arm rose noticeably. However, the most useful contribution made by the United States was to take responsibility for training British carrier pilots.

In September 1939 the Royal Navy had only 360 qualified pilots, with another 332 under training. In July 1941 the first trainee pilots went to Pensacola, and by co-opting a number of Canadian and New Zealand trainees surplus to RAF needs it was possible to achieve a total of 1632 naval pilots by mid-1942.

Destroyers of the Eastern Fleet fought the last classic destroyer action of the war. On 9 May submarines reported the Japanese heavy cruiser *Haguro* and an escort of three ships heading northwest through the Malacca Straits. Six days later an aircraft from the escort carrier HMS *Shah* sighted the Japanese force north of Sumatra, following a search initiated by Vice Admiral Walker.

That night the 26th Destroyer Flotilla under Captain Manly Power moved into the attack. At 11 pm HMS *Saumarez* made radar contact at 34 miles and the four destroyers moved into position for a coordinated torpedo attack from all points of the compass. Although the *Haguro* hit the *Saumarez* with gunfire and caused slight damage she could not avoid the torpedoes launched by the destroyers and sank at about 2 am.

The British Pacific Fleet was built up to maximum strength for the final assault on Japan. Four fleet carriers, the *Illustrious*, *Indefatigable*, *Indomitable* and *Victorious* were formed into Task Force 57, and in addition the battleships *King George V*, *Duke of York*, *Anson* and *Howe* were sent out. Although the British effort seemed puny in comparison with the enormous American fleet in the Far East, the British came into their own during the assault on Okinawa.

RIGHT: *HMS Formidable's armoured flight deck being cleared of a kamikaze aircraft. Fire precautions proved as important as armoured decks in limiting damage.*

BELOW: *A motor launch escorting a group of Large Personnel Landing Craft or LCP(L)s.*

The task for the British ships was to stop the Japanese forces in the Ryukyu Islands from attacking the amphibious ships around Okinawa. The British carriers were all hit by *kamikazes*, but their armoured decks and superior fire precautions enabled them to avoid serious damage. The *Illustrious* was replaced by the *Formidable* which was hit twice in two days but remained operational.

Although the British contribution to the downfall of Japan was comparatively small it was none the less significant. The last occasion on which British battleships fired their guns in anger was on 17 July when HMS *King George V* shelled industrial targets round Hitachi 50 miles north of Tokyo.

Home Waters 1944-45

Planning for the liberation of Europe can be said to have started in 1940, immediately after the evacuation from Dunkirk, but serious work started when in May 1943 the codename 'Operation Overlord' was allocated. The Royal Navy would bear the brunt of the naval side, codenamed 'Operation Neptune', for which at least 45,000 extra personnel would be needed. To find the extra numbers it was necessary to lay up four old *Royal Sovereign* Class battleships as

well as five old light cruisers, 40 destroyers and the last of the armed merchant cruisers. Even so manpower was so scarce that Army and Air Force personnel were drafted to make crews for the hundreds of landing craft and other specialized vessels.

A key element of the 'Overlord/Neptune' plan was to seal off both ends of the English Channel, thus preventing the U-boats and remaining light surface forces from interfering with the landing in Normandy. A huge umbrella of air cover would make it virtually impossible for surface units to operate in daylight. So effective was the air cover that during the actual invasion German forces found it impossible to move on moonlit nights.

Then there was the invasion armada of over 4000 landing ships. They ranged from large Landing Ships HQ (LSHs), attack transport and Tank Landing Ships (LSTs), down to fuelling barges and Medium Landing Craft (LCMs). To deal with the new 'oyster' or pressure mine, the Royal Navy built two giant trimarans, named *Cyrus* and *Cybele*, intended for towing across minefields.

An even bigger surprise was the idea to build two artificial harbours. The 1942 Dieppe Raid had shown that it would be impossible to seize and

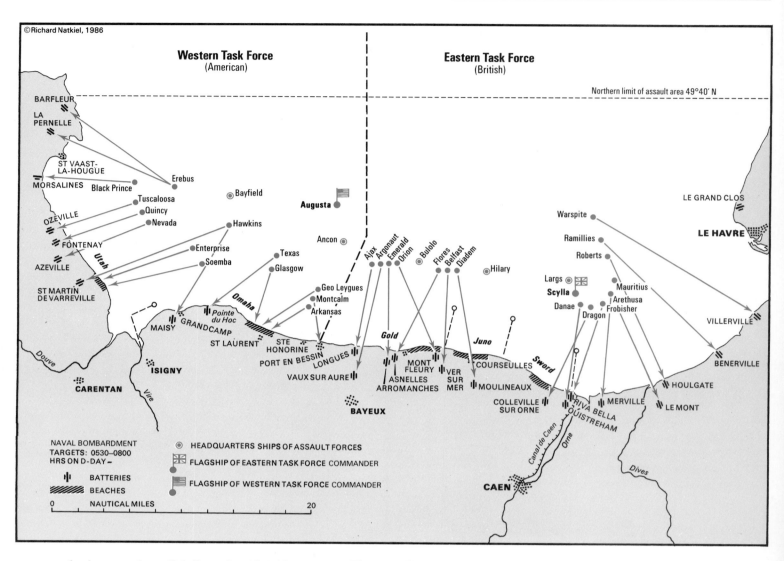

operate a harbour, and two 'Mulberry' artificial harbours were built. They included concrete caissons to act as breakwaters, floating piers and roadways. As things turned out Cherbourg and Le Havre proved to be so severely damaged that they were unable to handle any cargoes for six months.

The assault was timed for the early hours of 6 June 1944. In spite of bad weather the assault convoys arrived on time at the designated beaches 'Juno', 'Gold', 'Sword', 'Utah' and 'Omaha'. A massive aerial bombardment was backed up by an equally massive naval bombardment. Within the first six hours over 130,000 troops were ashore.

Royal Navy warships allocated to 'Operation Neptune':

Battleships 3 (+1 in reserve)
Monitors 2
Cruisers 17
Destroyers 63
Sloops 14
Fleet Minesweepers 89
Small sweepers 133 (+40 in reserve)
Frigates 53
Corvettes 63
A/S trawlers 60
Minelayers 4
MTBs, MGBs etc 360
Seaplane carrier 1
Midget submarines 2

The overall naval plan worked superbly. Despite desperate counterattacks by German naval and air forces the huge mass of shipping lying off the invasion beaches suffered only slight losses. Massive bombing raids wiped out the *schnellboot* base at Le Havre, while the U-boats suffered heavy losses trying to penetrate the 'Cork' barriers at either end of the Channel. On 9 June a force of British, Canadian and Polish destroyers encountered four German destroyers heading for Cherbourg. The Canadian *Haida* and *Huron* chased *T.24* and *Z.24* but failed to prevent their escape, but HMS *Ashanti* and HMS *Tartar* sank *Z.32* and *ZH.1*.

The biggest threat to the Normandy landings was a gale on 19 June. Some 800 landing craft were wrecked, and the American 'Mulberry' at St Laurent was wrecked soon after it had been assembled. The decision was made to salvage what could be saved from the wreckage, and the British 'Mulberry' at Arromanches was expanded.

The Normandy invasion was the biggest amphibious operation of the war and also the biggest land-sea operation ever seen, and its success reflects the quality of planning and execution. Had the air war over northern Europe not suddenly turned against the *Luftwaffe* in the spring of 1944, and had the German High Command not been so divided on how to fight the invasions, losses might have been much heavier.

ABOVE: *The Normandy Invasion in June 1944 was the largest combined operation ever seen. The main bombardment ships and their targets are shown.*

The Royal Navy could look back on six years of war with considerable pride and satisfaction. In spite of pre-war difficulties its administrators had foreseen the threat from submarines. Right to the end, British sonars proved the most effective, and the Navy led the Allies in most aspects of anti-submarine warfare. The Admiralty's pre-war preparations had proved far-sighted, particularly the decision to mass-produce Asdic sets in Canada and the corvette building programme.

The dockyards and commercial shipyards coped well with the demands of the Fleet, in spite of interruptions from bombing, but by 1941 there were signs that capacity was over-stretched. Several major repair jobs notably the carrier *Illustrious* and the battleship *Warspite* had to be given to American yards. Without the help of the American yards there was no way in which the Royal Navy's organization could have coped in 1942-3.

The problems of naval aviation have been dealt with previously. The British armoured carriers were an ingenious solution, but if good aircraft had been available in 1939 there would have been no need for them. The Americans and Japanese were much quicker in grasping the fundamental truth that the carrier's real defence was her air group.

The Fleet Air Arm was saved by American aircraft, but the design of its carriers prevented full use being made of them. Notwithstanding, British naval aviators achieved remarkable victories. Not until 1944 did the US Navy have a night-flying capability, whereas the Fleet Air Arm had developed the technique before the war.

Similarly it was industrial weakness and shortage of money interacting on each other which prevented the development of adequate anti-aircraft guns and fire control. What money there was had been spent on major gun systems and these proved excellent. Undoubtedly the worst weakness showed up in the Pacific where British warships proved no match for American warships in long-distance steaming. British machinery simply burnt more fuel

BELOW: *Assault Landing Craft (LCAs) returning to a Large Infantry Landing Ship or LSI(L) during a pre-invasion exercise.*

per knot than American ships and their machinery was heavier and less economical. The fault lay in the failure to invest in research on high-pressure boilers and lightweight turbines.

In the field of small combatants the Admiralty was subjected to intensive lobbying by the small boatbuilders pre-war. As things turned out, the German *schnellboot* with its reliable diesel engines, long hull and round bilge form proved a far better combatant than the short hulled, petrol-engined, hard chine form favoured by British designers. Against this it must be remembered that Coastal Forces were a luxury for the Royal Navy and could be built rapidly in large numbers when needed.

Strategically, the Navy fought the war as best it could. The Far East commitment led to the debacle which many had predicted, but apart from the possibility that Singapore might have held out longer, what else could have been done? Given the enormous economic assets which Britain still had in India, Malaya and China the Royal Navy was not going to be allowed to withdraw from East of Suez.

If anyone had predicted that France would

ABOVE: *The 15-inch gun monitor* Erebus, *a veteran of World War I, saw action off the Normandy beaches.*

LEFT: *Admiral Sir Bertram Ramsay was the architect of success at Dunkirk and Normandy.*

RIGHT: *Admiral Sir Max Horton KCB, DSO, the C-in-C Western Approaches, examines the surrendered blockade-runner U.532 at Liverpool in 1945.*

capitulate so suddenly in 1940 they would not have been believed. Nor would the Admiralty have been permitted to spend money against the contingency. Therefore the reliance on the French Navy to control the Italians in the Mediterranean was logical. Equally the programme to build coastal escorts as a wartime emergency measure made sense. As we have seen, it was the success of the coastal patrols that forced the U-boats out into the Western Approaches.

The British were not the only people to discover radar, but there is no doubt that they made best use of it, especially in the early years of the war. The pre-war experiments had been correctly understood, and although the equipment produced was crude by later standards it conferred important tactical advantages. In general the Navy was well served by scientists, who continually provided new weaponry in the fight against enemy innovations.

American help was lavish and without it the Navy would not have survived, but one of the hidden benefits of the Great Alliance was the feedback of information to and from the US at all levels. First there was the vital Ultra intelligence, then there was the inestimable value to the US Navy of expertise gained by repairing battle-damage to British warships. In effect most of 1941 was spent in raising the Navy yards in the United States to wartime standards of efficiency. The scientific information was invaluable. The gift of the resonant cavity magnetron enabled American electronics engineers to improve radar design, while British pre-war research in underwater acoustics enabled the first anti-submarine homing torpedo to come into service earlier than it would otherwise have done. But above all a common language and heritage enabled the inevitable rivalry and friction between the navies of the two nations to be overcome.

Losses were very heavy for the Royal Navy and its Dominion partners:
1939 – 1 carrier, 1 battleship, 3 cruisers, 3 destroyers, 1 submarine 1 AMC.
1940 – 1 carrier, 3 cruisers, 37 destroyers, 24 submarines, 3 sloops, 2 corvettes, 4 minesweepers, 9 AMCs.
1941 – 2 carriers, 4 capital ships, 10 cruisers, 1 fast minelayer, 1 monitor, 23 destroyers, 11 submarines, 3 sloops, 8 corvettes, 4 minesweepers, 4 AMCs.
1942 – 3 carriers, 13 cruisers, 49 destroyers, 20 submarines, 6 sloops, 11 corvettes, 9 minesweepers, 1 AMC.
1943 – 1 carrier, 2 cruisers, 2 fast minelayers, 17 destroyers, 14 submarines, 1 sloop, 1 frigate, 5 corvettes, 8 minesweepers.
1944 – 4 cruisers, 18 destroyers, 6 submarines, 2 sloops, 9 frigates, 8 corvettes, 9 minesweepers.
1945 – 2 destroyers, 1 submarine, 1 sloop, 1 frigate, 4 corvettes, 5 minesweepers.

It had been a hard war, and although in August 1945 the Navy was larger than it had ever been its great days were over. Within a year it was to be reduced to a much smaller force. Great Britain's place in the world had changed and its Navy would reflect its diminished status.

Chapter 7
Warship Design

The Edwardian Navy inherited a great tradition of excellence in warship design. Since the late 1880s the Department of Naval Construction (DNC) had been under the guiding hand of Sir William White the Director and had reached a position of pre-eminence which has never been equalled. When White retired in 1901 as a result of ill-health he had been responsible for designing the ships of the Royal Navy for 16 years. He had also shown a rare talent for organization and administration. Yet, only 15 years after his retirement the public and the Navy were echoing Beatty's claim of 'Something wrong with our bloody ships today'.

To understand the apparent paradox it is important to clarify what is meant by 'good' or 'bad' design. All designs must be measured against what is expected of them and what results in practice. Warships are regarded as unsuccessful if they get sunk in battle yet they are all too frequently sunk by more powerful opponents. Warships lose effectiveness rapidly when the pace of technology is fast; as the years pass they are more likely to face threats which did not exist when they were designed.

Warships are all too frequently compared with foreign competitors which are apparently faster, better armed and better protected, all achieved on the same tonnage. Unfavourable comparisons are not helped by the tendency of all navies and shipbuilders in particular to exaggerate the performance of their latest ships. Even when navies and shipbuilders tell the truth, the basis of comparison differs from country to country. Trial speeds may be quoted as the maximum achieved, or as a mean of several runs with and against wind and tide. Tonnage may be quoted as light, standard or full load, with no qualification to warn the critic that the ship is not carrying her full 'payload'.

White himself reacted very strongly to criticism of Admiralty designs, in words which are just as valid today:

'Comparisons . . . have been made from time to time in the press, always to the serious disadvantage of our ships. The inference, of course, is that the designs prepared for the Admiralty are inferior to those prepared by private firms. In other words, that private firms "do more on the dimensions and displacement". No explanation is given of why this should be so, or how the trick is done. It is thought sufficient to tabulate and compare dimensions, displacement, maximum (reputed or estimated) speeds, maximum thickness of . . . armour, numbers and calibres of guns, and bunker capacity (not coal actually carried) at the quoted displacement and speed. Such comparisons are incomplete and most misleading, but they serve their purpose . . .'

Warships tend to last a long time in the days of peace, with the result that they often finish their days performing tasks for which they were not designed. An old constructor's adage has it, 'Never deliberately design a second-class warship, as the passage of time will provide more than enough'. Nor is this phenomenon confined to old ships; in wartime warships frequently perform tasks well outside their original specification.

PREVIOUS PAGE: *The elegant torpedo gunboat* Circe *was one of a number of vessels built in the late 1880s to counter the menace of French torpedo boats.*

The magnificent fleet designed by Sir William White and his department suffered eventually from all these problems. The pace of technical advance, both in what today we call 'platforms' and in weaponry was so fast between 1890 and 1910 that all late Victorian warships and many from the early Edwardian period were out of date by 1914. New machinery, better armour and in particular, vastly more powerful weapons, left White's battleships and big cruisers completely outclassed. To cite only two examples, the diameter of torpedos went up from 14 inches to 21 inches (implying a very large increase in warhead weight) and the battle-range went up from about 4000 yards to 10,000 yards.

A more valid criticism of White's battleship designs was that they were beginning to fall behind their foreign rivals in scale of armament. This was due to the tight financial limits imposed by the Treasury, but White's successor Sir Philip Watts was able to profit by public fear of Germany to get the constraints eased. As size went up so did all-round qualities, as was to be expected.

When Fisher became First Sea Lord in 1904 the DNC's department had already expanded the armament of the standard White battleship by giving it a heavy secondary armament of ten 9.2-inch guns. The next step was to substitute 12-inch guns for 9.2-inch and create HMS *Dreadnought*, an 'all-big gun' battleship armed with 10 12-inch guns. Fisher provided the initiative and political will but Deadman, Attwood and Narbeth translated his enthusiasm into reality. The Engineer-in-Chief, Sir John

ABOVE: *HMS* Aurora, *one of a series of very successful light cruisers ordered in 1912 for service in the North Sea.*

BELOW: *A stark view of the* Dreadnought, *still awaiting turrets and tripod masts.*

ABOVE: *Sopwith 2F.1 Camels parked on the flying-off deck of the* Furious, *probably the seven which raided Tondern in July 1918.*

Durston, supported the adopting of Parsons steam turbines, giving the giant ship three knots more speed than her contemporaries, and Portsmouth Dockyard contributed by getting the ship built in the astonishing time of 14 months.

The *Dreadnought* was a great success, but the attempt to build an armoured cruiser equivalent backfired badly – it was these ships which inspired Beatty's exasperated comment at Jutland in 1916, when three battlecruisers blew up with heavy loss of life. Yet the story of the '*Dreadnought*-type armoured cruisers' (later designated battlecruisers) exemplifies the way in which 'bad' designs come about.

From the designer's point of view the battlecruisers were an undoubted success; the Admiralty (in the person of Admiral Fisher) asked for ships armed with 12-inch guns, capable of 25 knots, and protected to the same scale as existing armoured cruisers (with 6-inch side armour). Despite the formidable technical problems in meeting this specification the three *Invincible* Class cruisers exceeded expectations, being reliable, seaworthy and well armed. The subsequent tactical error in thinking that these huge, overgunned and expensive cruisers could act as fast battleships was by no stretch of the imagination a fault which could be laid at the door of the DNC.

The official naval designer labours under a disadvantage which the private naval architect does not. He has only one 'client', the Navy, and in the long run he can only execute the designs which his naval and political masters approve. In private he and his staff may produce imaginative designs which are more cost-effective, more powerful, or much faster than the 'official' designs, but cannot force the Navy to accept them. A commercial naval architect, in contrast, often has a portfolio of designs which are on offer to prospective customers, and these are modified to suit specific enquiries.

Although the *Dreadnought* and the *Invincible* were both brilliant conceptions, the pressure of the Anglo-German arms race prevented any rational assessment of their qualites. To sustain the building programmes a further six near-copies of the *Dreadnought* were built. They were followed by three more ships which showed scarcely any improvement and had several disadvantages including a very awkward arrangement of guns and thinner armour. The design of the *Invincible* was similarly repeated in the *Indefatigable*, with the added length to improve arcs of fire for the midships guns.

The *Dreadnought* was completed in December 1906 and the first *Invincible* in June 1908, yet the first of the follow-on battleships was started as early as December 1906 and the *Indefatigable* in February 1909. It was not conducive to good design to build naval ships at such a pace and little or no attention was paid to foreign competition. Not until the 1909

ABOVE: *Loading 15-inch shells aboard HMS* Queen Elizabeth. *Poor AP shells robbed the Grand Fleet of a decisive victory in 1916.*

Programme was it possible to make any radical improvement in the fighting qualities of British battleships. The four *Orions* re-introduced the 13.5-inch gun, giving them much greater range and hitting-power. Unlike the *Dreadnought* and her successors, all five twin turrets were on the centreline and armour protection was improved. The major weaknesses were an awkward layout of the tripod mast, subjecting the fire control platform to excessive smoke interference, and a restriction on beam which made the ships vulnerable to underwater damage.

The battlecruiser equivalents of the *Orions*, the *Lion* class were in contrast a poor design. The layout of guns and tripod mast was bad, with the midships turret masked by superstructure and funnels. To make matters worse, the 700-foot hull was thinly armoured against shellfire. At Fisher's instigation the press was given inflated figures for speed and protection thereby camouflaging their weaknesses, but war service was to expose their shortcomings all too soon.

With small improvements the design of the *Orion* was repeated for the next two classes of battleship but for the 1912 Programme another change was approved. The *Queen Elizabeth* Class ships were given 15-inch guns to ensure superiority over foreign ships for some years to come, and in response to recommendations from the Naval War

College speed was increased to 25 knots. In effect the battlecruiser had given way to the fast battleship, a more battleworthy type of warship. Despite the haste of the programme the new 15-inch gun was a great success, even more accurate than the 13.5-inch, with longer range. The ships again suffered from restricted beam, giving them less resistance to underwater damage than the German contemporaries and battle experience was to show that their magazine-protection was also inferior. On the other hand, the substitution of oil fuel for coal began a revolution which was copied by all navies. The fact that five saw front-line service in World War II is sufficient proof of their value to the Royal Navy.

During the same period cruiser design was in a state of flux. The small scouts built as contemporaries of the *Dreadnought* proved too small and too light for ocean work, but served well in the North Sea as leaders for destroyers. Fisher disliked cruisers, so no ocean-going types were started until 1909, but the ships which resulted were sound. On an initial displacement of 5000 tons it proved possible to mount 6-inch guns and achieve a speed of 25 knots. The 'Town' series of 19 ships (including four built for Australia) saw a steady progression of fighting power, as the mixed armament of 6-inch and 4-inch guns gave way to a uniform armament of eight or nine 6-inch guns. In battle British light cruisers proved far better than their German equivalents, and the 'Towns' gave good service for many years.

Destroyers had been a British invention, and after an initial period of panic-building, a more robust design had emerged, the 'River' Class. Further development was hindered rather than helped by Admiral Fisher's enthusiasm for destroyers. He insisted that the next class must steam at 33 knots (as against 25 knots in the 'Rivers') and must use oil fuel. Despite such an enormous jump in speed the builders were allowed only 11 days to submit tenders, and as a result costs rose sharply. The trials were not successful suggesting that design had been forced ahead too rapidly. Several of the new destroyers, the original 'Tribals', had difficulty in reaching their contract speeds and all were very uneconomical.

Fisher's other incursions into the field were even worse. A new class of torpedo boat or light 'coastal' destroyer proved too flimsy to work with the fleet. A project for a very large, fast destroyer produced the 2390-ton *Swift* which repeatedly failed to make her contract speed. Despite Fisher's belief

that she would replace the cruiser as a fleet scout she was too lightly built to serve with the fleet and very expensive.

The lessons were learned however and succeeding classes reverted to the qualities of the 'River' design: a robust hull and a realistic sea speed. By 1914 British destroyers were as successful as any in the world, rugged and well armed for their size. Although the Admiralty pursued a policy of standardizing basic features, and built over 100 largely similar destroyers between 1908 and 1914, there was a lot of encouragement to builders to make innovations. In each class 'specials' tried out such ideas as gearing (for economy), longitudinal framing (to improve hull strength) and even the first high-speed diesel (not a success).

Although the 'Town' Class cruisers were well thought of, the steadily rising speed of destroyers dictated a need to replace the scouts with ships capable of leading flotillas. There was also a shortage of cruisers capable of scouting for the fleet, and the DNC was asked to produce a 'North Sea' type, capable of 30 knots.

RIGHT: *HMS* Acheron, *an 'I' class destroyer at sea in 1917, a good example of the pre-1914 destroyer.*

BELOW: *HMAS* Sydney *and the rest of the 'Town' class were probably the most successful cruisers of their day.*

This was a stiff specification, almost impossible to match with the technology of the day, but the *Arethusa* design for a 'light armoured cruiser' was an outstanding technical achievement. Although cramped and overweight as a result of wartime additions it won a formidable reputation and started a new line of development.

The Admiralty's policy on submarines was shrewd and well judged. After keeping a wary eye on foreign developments, particularly in France, negotiations were started in November 1900 to build Holland-type boats. Private industry, in the form of Vickers Sons & Maxim, was given a free hand and by 1909 a total of 60 boats had been laid down. Unfortunately Fisher saw their main role as harbour and coast defence, so all the early boats were too small for 'overseas' patrolling. Not until the 'D' Class was much attention paid to the problems of endurance and habitability but thereafter progress was rapid. The 'D' Class introduced the diesel engine, and a hull of nearly double the displacement allowed much greater endurance. The next class, the 'E's rectified any teething troubles in the 'D's and bore the brunt of wartime operations in the North Sea, the Baltic and Mediterranean. Over 50 were built.

Dissatisfaction with the Vickers monopoly led the Royal Navy in 1911 to buy two foreign designs, one French and the other Italian. This bold experiment was unfortunately ended by the outbreak of war; the boats were not thoroughly evaluated and were transferred to Italy in 1915-16.

When war broke out in August 1914 it was assumed that hostilities would be over by Christmas. The Cabinet immediately stopped work on battleships but gave approval for greatly expanded construction of the light cruisers, destroyers and submarines. Fisher, who was brought back from retirement as First Sea Lord then persuaded the Cabinet to allow the construction of two more battlecruisers, claiming that their value had been enhanced by the Battle of the Falklands. Spare 15-inch gun mountings for the suspended battleships were to be installed in two new ships to be called *Renown* and *Repulse*.

The result was a repetition of the original mistakes made with the *Invincible* Class, and showed how little Fisher understood the latest technology. He tried to emulate the *Dreadnought* by demanding that these novel and complex ships should be built in a year and insisted on a scale of armour equal to the *Invincible*.

The ships took over 18 months to build, but when we recall the wartime conditions under which they were built and the novelty of the design, they were a remarkable achievement. Like the original battlecruisers they achieved what their designers had been asked to do, but when they joined the fleet after the Battle of Jutland there were no illusions about their fighting value.

Without second thought Fisher placed orders in 1915 for three more battlecruisers, but to avoid the Cabinet ruling against capital ships he called them 'large light cruisers'. This time he saddled the fleet with ships of obviously dubious value. On a displacement of about 22,000 tons the *Courageous* and *Glorious* carried four 15-inch guns, while the *Furious* was to have only two 18-inch guns. HMS *Furious* lost one 18-inch gun before she went to sea to allow her to serve as an aircraft carrier, but she was not a success and went back into dockyard hands in 1918 for further conversion.

The *Arethusa* design was already under development and for the rest of the war a series of progressive improvements were made. The mixed armament was replaced by uniform 6-inch guns, rising from two in the early classes to six in the final 'stretched' design. Similarly torpedo armament increased from four to a dozen 21-inch tubes to meet wartime needs.

This policy of standardization worked so well that only two new designs were approved during the war. Five *Cavendish* Class were built for commerce-protection on a greatly expanded 'Town' design, and in response to false intelligence reports three very fast ships, the 'E' Class, were ordered.

A similar policy was followed in destroyer-construction. The latest pre-war design, the 'M' Class, was put into quantity production with only minor changes. In 1915 a change was made to geared turbines to improve economy, but little change was made to the basic design, apart from improvements dictated by war experience. To free light cruisers for other work, a new type of slightly enlarged 'flotilla leader' had been ordered in 1914, and this innovation proved successful.

Another erroneous intelligence report in 1916 led to the building of much more powerful destroyers. To save time a new flotilla leader design was repeated, and out of this programme emerged the 'V&W' Classes totalling over 50 ships. They and the contemporaty flotilla leaders of the *Scott* and *Shakespeare* Classes enjoyed such a high reputation in other navies, that in the post-war years the design was to be copied around the world.

The 'E' Class submarine design was similarly put into quantity production, and served with distinction. However, a number of other designs were built with varying degrees of success. In response to urgent requests from the Grand Fleet attempts were made to produce 'fleet' submarines capable of operating with the battlefleet. These efforts culminated

in the ill-fated 'K' Class, whose record of catastrophic accidents should not conceal the remarkable technical achievement which they represented. They were much larger than anything built previously and made nearly 24 knots on the surface. They also carried the heaviest armament yet seen in a submarine.

Even more bizarre were the 12-inch gunned 'M' Class, but when in 1916 a new standard submarine was designed, the 'E' type was used as the basis for expansion. The freaks were remarkable, but the keynote of British submarine design in 1914-18 was reliability and cost-effectiveness.

Space does not allow a detailed discussion of all the auxiliary warships produced during the Great War, but every conceivable type was built, from 18-inch gunned monitors down to landing craft. Most of the specialized designs were prepared with the help of industry but one Admiralty design is worthy of mention. To meet the need for a general-purpose escort, minesweeper and fleet tender, the DNC produced the 'Flower' Class sloop. Built on mercantile lines they proved rugged and versatile foreshadowing the corvettes of 1939-45 in their role as utility convoy escorts.

Post-war there was great interest in putting right what were seen to be the faults of capital ship design. The *Hood*, the only capital ship laid down and launched during the war, was rightly seen to be pre-Jutland in her standard of protection, and the DNC was anxious to build a new generation of ships incorporating the lessons of war.

ABOVE: *The ill-starred 'K' class were an outstanding technical achievement, but the tactical concept was badly flawed.*

ABOVE RIGHT: *Initially the 16-inch turrets of the* Nelson *and* Rodney *were made so safe that they could not function properly until modified.*

BELOW: *The 'County' class cruisers proved well able to absorb wartime additions. HMS* Norfolk, *for example, has numerous additional AA guns and radars.*

The country's parlous finances could not support such a programme and in 1922 the Washington Treaty came into effect limiting both battleships and cruisers in displacement and gun-calibre. However unpopular the treaty might be to navalists it had the benefit of concentrating designers' minds on weight-saving. A huge and novel design for a fast battleship known merely as the *G.3* was successfully remodelled to conform to the 35,000-ton limit imposed by the treaty. HMS *Nelson* and HMS *Rodney* sacrificed speed to achieve an impressive scale of protection for the first time in many years. Although considered outlandish by many they were in fact the most powerful battleships of the inter-war years and technically ahead of foreign contemporaries.

To meet the treaty conditions a new type of 10,000-ton cruiser armed with 8-inch guns came into vogue. The British version, the 'County' Class, attracted severe criticism because of its apparent weakness, but from today's standpoint it was a fair compromise between speed, endurance and gun-power. None of its contemporaries achieved any better balance on the legal tonnage; some were faster, some had more guns, and some displaced considerably more than 10,000 tons. As with the battleships, weight-saving became a prime objective of the designers, with beneficial results for later ships.

The policy on destroyers was to achieve numbers and reliability, rather than individually powerful but expensive units. As a result British destroyers showed little improvement over the best ships built in the final months of the war. A reluctance to invest in high-performance steam machinery was to prove short-sighted as was the later failure to invest in the development of diesels, but British destroyer and submarine machinery was reliable and rugged.

Despite the shortage of money several interesting developments were achieved. The cruiser-minelayer *Adventure* had the first diesel-electric propulsion system and also adopted the transom stern which had been recommended by the Admiralty Experiment Works at Haslar. The transom was not a success in HMS *Adventure* as it produced eddies which sucked each freshly laid mine under the stern, but it did become a highly successful feature of later cruisers and destroyers. The critics of the 'County' Class heavy cruisers failed to note that they were given an unusually heavy anti-aircraft armament in addition to having a dual-purpose main armament.

An attempt to produce a monster cruiser submarine failed, largely due to her unreliable (German) diesels and thereafter design reverted to medium size. The early 'O' Class suffered from leaky external fuel tanks but when riveting was replaced by welding the problem disappeared. The two surviving 'M' Class ships were converted, one to operate a small seaplane and the other to lay mines. Both proved successful although *M.2* was lost tragically in 1932.

Design of all major warship types continued to be hamstrung, not only by successive disarmament treaties but by financial constraints. The Treasury's

notorious Ten-Year Rule effectively curtailed development of capital ships and aircraft carriers at a time when the Royal Navy should have been demanding up-to-date designs.

The post-war DNC's department had to grapple with new problems created by aircraft carriers. The world's first carrier designed from the keel up, HMS *Hermes*, was completed in leisurely fashion in 1924, a year after the conversion of the ex-Chilean battleship HMS *Eagle*. Experience with these two ships helped in the conversion of the light battlecruisers *Courageous* and *Glorious*, which joined their half-sister *Furious* to make up a trio of fast and comparatively capacious carriers.

As the war clouds gathered over Europe the long-delayed rearmament programme began, but the DNC and his staff were hampered by the decay of Britain's naval armaments industry. The new battleships of the 1936 Programme were given 14-inch guns because it was too dangerous to risk delay by changing to 16-inch, given the weakness of the armaments industry. To compensate for the lighter gun a very complex quadruple mounting was designed, introducing fresh problems.

The same difficulties beset the new carrier *Ark Royal*, which had been laid down in 1935. To keep the tonnage down the designers resorted to a number of devices, but for all her technical ingenuity her operational efficiency was hampered by lack of good aircraft. The armoured carriers which followed her were even more ingenious and carried very heavy batteries of medium and close-range guns, but they also sacrificed aircraft capacity for protection, and suffered from lack of suitable aircraft.

In 1934-5 the first of a new series of 10,000-ton light (6-inch gunned) cruisers was laid down. The new 'Town' Class was a reply to the Japanese *Mogami* and American *Brooklyn* Classes and marked the abandonment of medium-sized (7000-ton) cruisers. Their successors, the handsome 'Colony' Class, were cleverly designed to accommodate the same armament of 12 6-inch guns on only 8000 tons, sacrificing only half a knot in the process.

The aircraft threat was fully recognized. During the Abyssinian Crisis two of the old 'C' Class light cruisers were rearmed with 4-inch guns and multiple pom-poms, but clearly a modern hull with modern weapons would answer the fleet's needs better. In 1937-9 11 *Dido* Class were laid down, elegant ships which displaced 5600 tons and carried five of the new twin 5.25-inch dual-purpose gun mountings. They suffered in two ways: the gun mounting and its fire control were not a great success, and the hull was too small to permit any great degree of resistance to battle damage. As with so many designs of this period, the twin villains were the long 'holiday' in procuring new ships and equipment, and the need to keep tonnage down to comply with limitations imposed by international treaties.

The popularity of 'super-destroyers' abroad finally persuaded the Admiralty to move away from the standard 'A' to 'I' design, which had been built since the mid-1920s. The 16 'Tribal' Class laid down in 1936-7 doubled the previous armament by the simple process of adopting twin 4.7-inch guns in place of singles, but torpedo armament was halved to four 21-inch tubes. The theory was that the 'Tribals' would bring more gunpower to fleet

ABOVE: *The 'J' class destroyers reintroduced longitudinal framing (first tried in 1913) and achieved a good balance of speed, gunpower and torpedo armament.*

RIGHT: *The new 'Town' class cruisers were built to match the Japanese* Mogami *class, but never met them in battle.*

defence, but as usual it was considerations of cost which drove the Admiralty to limit displacement to 1850 tons. On such modest displacement it was impossible to mount a balanced armament, and industry could not supply a dual-purpose high-angle/low-angle mounting, so the new twin 4.7-inch guns were limited to 40-degree elevation.

Although handsome and well-liked, the 'Tribals' were hardly in the forefront of technology. In the next class the DNC persuaded the builders to change to longitudinal framing as had been tried in HMS *Ardent* in 1913. This method, well known in large ships, gave much greater strength to the hull. A new pattern of Admiralty three-drum boiler permitted the number to be reduced from three to two, and by placing these back-to-back the designers reduced funnels to a single uptake. This limited the silhouette and gained valuable deck-space for more armament. The 'J' or *Javelin* design was a better one than the 'Tribal', carrying a balanced armament of three twin 4.7-inch gun mountings and 10 torpedo-tubes, all on 160 tons less. A total of 24 were built to this design, but in the 'L' and 'M' Classes an attempt was made to provide a dual-purpose armament. However the twin 4.7-inch Mk XI was over-complex, and the mounting only permitted 55 degrees of elevation, still insufficient for air defence.

To meet the desperate shortage of destroyers it was decided in 1938 to build a new class of small escort destroyers quicker to build and using less steel. The 'Hunt' Class were virtually a scaled-down 'J' hull armed with twin 4-inch anti-aircraft guns and (it was hoped) three torpedo-tubes and a multiple pom-pom. For once the Constructors over-reached themselves; in the haste of the rearmament programme suddenly gathering momentum a major error in the calculations was made. Only when the prototype HMS *Atherstone* was nearing completion did it become obvious that the ship was seriously overloaded. One twin 4-inch mounting and the tubes were removed and after re-ballasting the fault was rectified, but the next batch had their hulls 'kippered' while on the stocks, with two feet more beam.

As with the larger warships, numbers were made up by pressing some of the older ships into service, and 20 'V&W' hulls were modernized to a similar standard, with 4-inch AA guns and modern fire control.

The steady development of submarines had paid dividends and by 1939 three good designs were in service, tailored to meet all future requirements. The 842-ton 'S' Class was suited to the North Sea, while the 1300-ton 'T' Class was intended for overseas patrolling. Both types were distinguished by fast diving times, and the 'T' had an unusually heavy bow salvo of ten 21-inch torpedoes. To supplement them it had been planned to build unarmed 'U' Class training boats, but at the last minute it was decided to arm them as prototypes for a new class of coastal submarines.

Although escort development had proceeded slowly, producing a series of improvements, the sloops were considered too complex for wartime mass-production. Accordingly the Admiralty col-

ABOVE: *Many amphibious warfare designs were created in Britain, but construction was largely undertaken in the USA.*

BELOW: *The Type 12 frigate of the 1950s (here HMS* Lowestoft*) was the outcome of studies initiated in 1944, to establish a first-rate anti-submarine escort.*

FAR RIGHT: *HMS* Pollington. *The 'Ton' class wooden-hulled coastal minesweeper, designed to meet post-Korean War needs, has served for over 30 years in a variety of roles.*

laborated with Smith's Dock to adapt a whale-catcher design for use as a coastal escort. The 'Flower' Class which resulted were dubbed corvettes but because of Treasury restrictions orders could not be placed until the outbreak of war.

Once war broke out there was little scope for innovation, all proven pre-war designs were put into mass-production. The task of DNC's personnel became more one of interpreting battle damage and adding new equipment than the introduction of new designs, for obvious reasons, but it was none the less vital. Alarming losses such as the *Hood*, the *Prince of Wales* and the *Ark Royal* had to be correctly analysed partly to maintain morale in the fleet but particularly to prevent repetition.

Another important task for the Constructors was to supervise the enormous number of conversions, from anti-submarine trawlers up to large armed merchant cruisers. In each case the weight of additions had to be correctly calculated. According to the official history of the Royal Corps of Naval Constructors (RCNC), some 1700 small ships were taken in hand, in addition to 51 ocean liners and large numbers of merchant ships converted to auxiliaries of all sorts.

The need to build up Coastal Forces rapidly was met by a judicious partnership between the DNC and small private boatyards. As in so many other areas design was hampered by the weakness of British industry; engines were imported from Italy until 1940 and then American Hall-Scott and Packard engines had to make good the shortfall. British designs were generally inferior to the German craft, but the short, hard chine hull suited the British yards and a longer round-bilge hull did not appear until late in the war.

Of far greater significance to the war effort was the enormous fleet of amphibious craft created. The talented constructor Rowland Baker produced the outline Tank Landing Ship (LST) design and the Dock Landing Ship (LSD), which were built in the USA, while literally scores of specialized minor landing craft types were designed and built in the United Kingdom.

The post-war years saw a steady contraction of the Royal Navy, but paradoxically the burden on the designer has become much greater. While budgets shrink the cost of equipment is rising steeply. Each new design comes under intense bureaucratic scrutiny with the result that the design phase becomes very protracted and expensive. Yet with so much money involved a rushed decision can prove very expensive – even a badly designed ship will be in service for a quarter of a century.

The old pre-war enemies of good design, cost and tonnage-limits are still there and it is surely no coincidence that the 'unsuccessful' designs are those which have suffered most from these constraints: the carrier *CVA.01*, the Type 42 air defence destroyer, the Type 21 frigate and the 'Bird' Class small patrol vessels. All four suffered from a greater or lesser degree of political influence or arbitrary size limits; the carrier grew hopelessly complex and expensive, while the Type 42 and Type 21 failed the strictest test of all, battle.

In stark contrast the mainstream of frigate-design has been a great success. As early as 1944 the Naval Staff asked the DNC to look ahead and draw

up designs to meet post-war threats. Out of these studies emerged the Type 12, a truly magnificent hull form designed to avoid panting and slamming, and at the same time large enough to accommodate a powerful anti-submarine and defensive armament. One proof of good design is versatility; the Type 12 *Whitby* was developed into the *Rothesay*, and then after considerable reworking, into the *Leander* Class general-purpose frigate. Critics of current Ministry of Defence designs are apt to talk of a Golden Age when British frigates were widely exported but in practice most of these export successes turn out to be Type 12 and *Leander* orders.

The Royal Navy is often accused of reluctance to embrace new technology but it has pioneered several developments. Early post-war experiments with gas turbines led to the world's first large warship driven by gas turbines in 1968. The need for non-magnetic hulls led to the introduction of glass-reinforced plastic (GRP) in the 1970s. Long before that the contribution to aircraft carrier design of the steam catapult, the angled deck and mirror landing sight were widely acknowledged. It is not so well known that the Royal Navy was the first customer for the French Exocet anti-ship missile.

The decision to build nuclear submarines involved a huge investment and progress was speeded up by the purchase of an American reactor for the first boat, appropriately named *Dreadnought*. Since then the highly specialized skills have been developed, with a new generation of pressurized-water reactor, the PWR2, about to come into service. The Trident missile submarines although armed with an American weapon represent in every other respect the most advanced features afloat.

In recent years the RCNC and the Director-General, Ships (the successor to the old DNC) have been subjected to a surprising amount of ill-informed public criticism. As the record shows, British warships have not been badly designed in the past, and there is little evidence to suggest any sudden reversal of performance. The Royal Navy gets the warships it asks for, and if it transpires that the Staff Requirement has been incorrectly drawn up, or was based on incorrect intelligence, that can hardly be blamed on the Constructors.

One of the fallacies of the critics' arguments is that hull-forms are the key to cheapness – the argument runs that a minor change in length/beam ratio will cut frigate costs by as much as 50 per cent. This is not true. The hull nowadays costs about 10 per cent, as against machinery, weapons and equipment which cost 90 per cent. To quote a distinguished former member of the Naval Staff, 'If you want a Navy which can fight a Third World country, we could do it for about £100 million a year, but you [the politicians] tell us that we are facing the Russians, and that sort of Navy costs more'.

LEFT: *HMS* Dreadnought *ushered in the nuclear age for the RN, and has been as revolutionary as her predecessor in 1906.*

Chapter 8
The Navy Post-1945

Post-war adjustments

Since 1945 British seapower in all its aspects – naval forces, merchant shipping and shipbuilding – has declined to an extent unparalleled in the nation's history of the past 300 years. Dissolution of the Empire, economic factors and above all the development of strategic nuclear weapons all contributed to this retrenchment.

The Royal Navy had retained its pre-war organization virtually unchanged until 1957 and the aftermath of the Suez Crisis, when Defence Secretary Duncan Sandys' Defence Estimates commented that 'the role of naval forces is somewhat uncertain' in total war. There were the Home, Mediterranean and Far East Fleets and independent squadrons under their own flag officers in the East Indies, South Atlantic, West Indies and South America, while the Persian Gulf had a frigate squadron under a Commodore. To support this almost world-wide naval presence there were the dockyards at Portsmouth, Devonport, Chatham, Rosyth, Portland and Sheerness and others overseas at Malta, Gibraltar, Trincomalee, Singapore, Hong Kong, Simonstown (South Africa) and Bermuda.

During the war years recruiting of career sailors had been halted and the 'Hostilities Only' ratings were being steadily released, so that the total of 790,000 officers and men in the Service on VJ-Day had dwindled to 492,000 by April 1946. Ships on Foreign Service Commissions normally spent at least two and a half years overseas so that when commissioning it was essential to ensure as far as possible that all the ship's company had at least this amount of time left to serve. Forty years ago there could be no question of putting a man whose service was expired onto the next flight home – getting him home and arranging for his relief to join could take many weeks. It all depended on sailing dates of the troopships which shuttled servicemen and women, and Army and RAF (but usually not naval) families between home and overseas.

Finding sufficient sailors for ships overseas made reductions in the complements of those in home waters inevitable and by early 1948 the Navy League was pointing out that only 66 of the 120 battleships, carriers, cruisers, destroyers, submarines and minesweepers the Navy Estimates for that year claimed as 'operational' could really be so described. The League noted that the Home Fleet had been reduced to a single cruiser and four destroyers.

At the time of Japan's surrender the Navy had had some 9000 ships in commission but by late 1946 about 840 warships had been deleted from the Navy List and 5700 returned to their commercial owners. In addition, 727 warships in various stages of construction had been cancelled. Among them were three 50,000-ton carriers the *Malta*, *Gibraltar* and *New Zealand*. The size of these ships, comparable to contemporary US carriers still in service more than 40 years later, could have enabled the Navy to retain the ability to operate fixed-wing aircraft into the twenty-first century.

But even after such massive reductions the 1948-9 Navy Estimates showed that the fleet still had five battleships, 13 carriers of various types, 31 cruisers, 117 destroyers, 180 frigates, 65 submarines, two monitors, three fast minelayers and 65 minesweepers. Many of these ships were, of course, in reserve.

In 1945-6 the Mediterranean was the main area of tension. The civil war in Greece had only just ended but Yugoslavia was still in dispute with Italy over the status of Trieste. In Palestine the increasing flow of Jewish illegal immigrants posed a considerable problem for the Navy whose task it was to see that the influx of refugees from former occupied Europe did not swamp the indigenous Arab population and exacerbate an already tense situation.

But it was in international waters off newly Communist Albania that an incident occurred that was a pointer to the deteriorating relations between the free world and the Communist states. British warships had previously been shelled by Albanian shore batteries but in October 1946 the destroyers *Saumarez* and *Volage* ran into a minefield in the Corfu Channel. Forty-four sailors in the two ships died and it was later established that the mines were of German make but had been very recently laid. The International Court at The Hague later ruled that Albania was culpable although Yugoslavia had actually laid the mines. Some £5 million in Albanian gold in London was seized by the British government against payment of the £800,000 compensation awarded by the International Court but not a penny has ever been paid either to the dependents of those killed or to the permanently maimed.

The American Bikini Atoll atomic bomb test in the Pacific had shown that warships, even when of obsolete design and with no crews on board to take action to counter damage, could still withstand a nuclear air burst very much better than had been supposed. A subsequent underwater detonation proved more lethal, with the enormous tidal wave it generated, and the resulting deluging of the target ships with highly radioactive water particles. In Britain the 12-year-old cruiser *Arethusa*, with no crew on board, was bombarded with gamma radiation from a barge alongside at Spithead in an attempt to see how future ship designs might be modified to afford crews greater protection against radiation. Much thought was given to provision of air-conditioned citadels in future ships in which crews could live and fight when their ships were in areas of radioactive fall-out or where there was a risk of chemical or biological weapon attacks. A five-year series of trials with biological germ warfare weapons began in 1949, many of them in the Bahamas on board the tank landing ship *Ben Lomond* which had been converted into a mobile laboratory.

Although the potential threat was clearly that from the Russian Navy, it was to be the Russians' huge ally Communist China which was the first to begin overt hostilities when the frigate *Amethyst* was severely damaged by field guns some 140 miles up the Yangtse river. The ship was on her way to Nanking some 60 miles further upstream to relieve the

PREVIOUS PAGE: *HMS* Cavalier *was preserved in 1972 as the last classic destroyer in the Royal Navy. Despite modifications she still resembles the original 'J' class of 1937.*

ABOVE: *The carrier* Ark Royal *and her task group operating with Brazilian warships during a 1975 goodwill visit to Latin America.*

RIGHT: *The passing of the old order;* HMS *Duke of York arrives at the breaker's yard in 1957.*

destroyer *Consort* as guardship for the British embassy. The Nationalist government was waging a bitter and unsuccessful war against Mao's forces who claimed the frigate was carrying Nationalist troops.

Nineteen of the frigate's crew were killed including the captain, Lieutenant-Commander Skinner. The *Consort*, assisted by the cruiser *London* and the frigate *Black Swan*, tried to rescue the *Amethyst* and tow her off the mudbank on which she had run aground, but had to give up after suffering damage and a further 25 killed. The frigate remained trapped from mid-April 1949 until the end of July when, under the command of Lieutenant-Commander J S Kerans, she slipped down the river at night, sinking a Communist gunboat and ramming a boom across the river on the way. British reaction to the incident was swift and as a first step it was decided to restore the Far East Squadron's organic air power, which had been withdrawn in 1947. The light fleet carrier *Triumph* was despatched from the Mediterranean to Hong Kong and other ships soon followed.

In January 1949 an agreement was signed between Britain, Argentina and Chile not to send warships below 60 degrees South into Antarctic waters in the summer season.

It was hoped that this would reduce minor territorial disputes; for example, the previous year, an Argentine officer had tried to deliver a note of protest to the cruiser *Nigeria* for her intrusion into 'Argentine waters'. The cruiser responded by delivering a reciprocal protest note to two Argentine naval tugs. There were to be several more incidents of this type up to 1982.

The demise of the battleship as the capital ship was underlined with the announcement in 1949 that the fleet carrier *Implacable* would replace the battleship *Duke of York* as flagship of the Home Fleet. Another break with tradition was the disappearance of warrant officers who would in future be commissioned and would mess with other officers in the wardroom. It took 20 years before this step towards greater 'social equality', which few had wanted, was reversed. Curiously, the reason given was the same on each occasion: to encourage more senior men to stay in the Service. One further sign of changing times was the comment in that year's Navy Estimates debate in the House of Commons that 300 refrigerators were to be installed in operational ships.

An even more significant portent for the future in 1949 had been the first major Western European Union exercise at sea involving ships and aircraft from Britain, France, the Netherlands and Norway. The agreement establishing the North Atlantic Treaty Organisation had been signed in April 1949 and moves to give the Treaty real military backing were gaining impetus. One important reason was the deteriorating situation in the Far East, where in the summer of 1950 the North Koreans launched a massive attack on the South and rapidly overran most of the country Britain was quick to follow the US lead in providing help to South Korea.

RIGHT: *A Sea Fury is catapulted from the deck of HMS* Glory *in Korean waters.*

BELOW: *Light fleet carriers bore the brunt of the British and Commonwealth naval contribution to the Korean War.*

The Korean War

By July 1950 a combined British-US naval task force had been set up and the cruiser *Jamaica* soon distinguished herself by sinking five out of six North Korean motor torpedo boats attempting to attack her. Once again events emphasized the importance of seaborne air power. The Allied carriers were able to take the war to the enemy by attacking the lengthy lines of communication in the north. The Royal Navy's light fleet carriers *Triumph*, *Ocean*, *Theseus*,

and *Glory* as well as their Australian sister ship *Sydney* had all been involved for varying periods by the time the North Koreans agreed to an armistice in 1953. Relying entirely on piston-engined Sea Furies and Fireflies, the Navy was not to get its first operational jet fighters at sea until the carriers' air groups appeared to be totally outclassed by the Communists' jets. But despite being some 200 knots slower, a Sea Fury flown by Lieutenant Peter Carmichael from HMS *Ocean* shot down a MiG-15 in an engagement in which two more were damaged without any loss among the British aircraft.

At home Parliament was told that the first two new-design frigates would be laid down in 1950 as would 41 new wooden minesweepers. Work was also to start on the first 3200 naval married quarters and pay and pensions were to be improved. To help offset the increased expenditure, these measures would require a number of shore establishments to be closed as well as the Bermuda dockyard. The recall of reservists and particularly the retention and sometimes overseas drafting of men due for release, caused a growing tide of discontent that was evident in cases of malicious damage in 12 ships including four submarines. Such incidents were to continue sporadically into the 1960s.

In January 1950 there was a disastrous accident when the submarine *Truculent* was sunk in a collision in the Medway with the loss of 64 sailors and Chatham dockyard workers on board. It was found afterwards that the number of sets of Davis escape apparatus on board was far fewer than the number of men embarked.

By early 1951 the gravity of the international situation was reflected in British defence spending. The Navy Estimates were increased by 40 percent to cover, among other things, a future construction programme of 300 ships with particular emphasis being put on coastal and inshore minesweepers. They were to have a designed life of 15 years – but some will still be in commission in 1990. Some 60 ships were brought forward from the Reserve Fleet for operational service and more ships in reserve were to be refitted and put in a state preservation.

But this massive rearmament programme overlooked the fact that British industry was unable to carry it out now that the economy was no longer geared to war. Finding spare shipbuilding capacity, especially for steel ships, in an industry whose order books were already full with mercantile work was not easy and delays were inevitable in the laying down of some ships. There were delays too in steam turbine manufacture, and diesel engines in some new minesweepers caused problems. The last of the 24 new frigates, the construction of which was approved under the 1951 Programme, was not completed until 1960.

In terms of equipment, work on developing gas turbines was progressing in a number of craft and in the early 1950s two gas turbines were sold to the US Navy for trials in a 1700-ton destroyer escort. Development of new aircraft was continuing apace but the lack of a British equivalent to the US Navy's airborne early warning (AEW) aircraft was recognized with the purchase of 45 American Skyraiders for this specialised task (and yet some 30 years later

the conversion of nine elderly Sea King helicopters for AEW was considered adequate to meet the Navy's needs).

The Americans' predominance at sea was accepted by Mr James Callaghan, the Financial Secretary to the Admiralty who told Parliament, 'The balance of seapower has tilted away from us very dramatically in the last 10 years. For the first time in many hundreds of years our Fleet has been outdistanced and outpaced by the Fleet of a friendly ally. At the same time there has been a profound change in the strategy of the defence of these islands. We are now to a large extent part of the Continent'. He continued, 'We must remember all the time that our own large Merchant Navy is working throughout the whole of the seas of the world. It is our job, therefore, to preserve a balanced fleet of ships of all types quite distinct from the forces that must be put into our North Atlantic Treaty contribution. This is what the Government proposes to preserve.'

Mr Callaghan's belated recognition that the Royal Navy was now clearly the 'junior partner' to the US Navy did not prevent a political row of some magnitude over the appointment of an American admiral as the first Supreme Allied Commander Atlantic with Mr Winston Churchill in Parliament leading the opposition to the appointment.

In Malaya, Third Commando Brigade Royal Marines was among the security forces fighting the Communist guerillas. The Navy was also active with ocean minesweepers patrolling the coasts to prevent arms being smuggled in by sea from mainland China.

ABOVE LEFT: *Arming a Seahawk for an attack on Egyptian positions, during the Suez operations of 1956.*

ABOVE RIGHT: *A Seahawk returns safely to HMS* Albion *with a damaged fuel tank.*

RIGHT: *New fast patrol boats were built in the early 1950s but development was cut short when Coastal Forces disbanded in 1957.*

In the Gulf, Persian Premier Mossadeq's demand for the nationalization of the Anglo-Iranian Oil Company's huge Abadan refinery caused the cruiser *Mauritius* to be sent to lie off the port to protect British lives and interests. She and other warships were to remain there for many weeks – which was no picnic since few ships at this time had air-conditioning and the number of refrigerators on board was scarcely adequate. *Mauritius* was eventually ordered to evacuate the remaining British subjects from Abadan.

During 1951 the first of the new carriers, the *Eagle*, was commissioned as was the *Daring*, the lead ship in the last class of conventional destroyers built for the Navy. In the Home Fleet the battleship *Vanguard* was to be relegated to a training role and the four remaining *King George V* Class battleships were to be mothballed. A new Royal Yacht, to be named *Britannia*, was ordered to replace the 52-year old *Victoria and Albert* but as she would not be completed until 1954 the liner *Gothic* was fitted out for the planned 1952 Royal Tour.

The year was marked by another major tragedy when the submarine *Affray* was lost in the Channel with 75 men on board including a number of Royal Marine Commandos. As the boat's last position was not known the search for her involving 40 ships was a protracted one. The wreck was found by sonar and positively identified by an underwater TV camera from the deep diving ship *Reclaim* long after any

hope for those on board still being alive had been abandoned. This was the first time TV had been used in this way. The submarine had been flooded because the 'Snort' underwater breathing mast had snapped off (this mast had allowed the diesel engines to be used when the boat was submerged at periscope depth). The steel tube used for the mast was of a specification which the manufacturers had warned the Admiralty was quite unsuited for the kind of stresses it might encounter.

Egyptian demands in late 1951 for the total withdrawal of British forces from the Suez Canal Zone were backed up by strikes of Canal workers and threats of sabotage against ships in transit. The Navy moved in promptly and by the end of 1951 had passed 2600 merchant ships of 16 million tons through the Canal as well as providing security for installations and ships in transit.

In 1952, off Australia's Montebello Islands, the first UK atom bomb was detonated inside the frigate *Plym*, reducing her to a few fragments.

For the Fleet Air Arm 1952 saw the culmination of steam catapult trials on board the maintenance carrier *Perseus*; experiments had begun in 1949 in considerable secrecy. New and heavier aircraft could now be launched with almost nil wind over the flight deck, as some launchings by the ship while at anchor off Rosyth proved. Another British invention, the angled deck, whereby an aircraft missing the arrestor wires could fly off again over the carrier's port side without ploughing into the parked aircraft at the forward end of the flight deck, was tried out for the first time later in the year. This trial was held on board the American carrier *Antietam* and HMS *Warrior*, the first British carrier to use it, was not ready until the following year.

Development of naval helicopters was proceeding apace and following the installation of a landing platform for a Dragonfly on the stern of Royal Fleet Auxiliary (RFA) *Fort Duquesne* the previous year, the first naval Whirlwind squadron, 848, was formed in late 1952 for service with the ground forces in Malaya.

However, there was evidence of trouble to come with the naval equipment programme in other areas. Official utterances made much of how modern technology was allowing cost reductions in new construction by reducing margins of hull plating thickness and the use of lighter materials. Yet within five years 12 of the new frigates were to require hull strengthening and another six had to have their hull plating replaced. Lack of research in metallurgy was also to lead to severe problems with the nuclear submarine programme. Construction costs were rising, and in 1952 a destroyer was costing £700 a ton compared with £150 a ton in 1914. The First Lord, Mr Thomas, admitted that the naval rearmament programme was slowing down due to production difficulties and the worsening balance of payments – so much so that at the end of the year Prime Minister Winston Churchill announced that defence production costs were to be pegged at £600 million a year. This was £150 million below the previous government's planned figure and £250 million

below their estimated figure for 1953-4. The national economic problem was thus making its first real impact on the Navy's rearmament programme – something that was to continue without let-up for a further 30 years until momentarily relaxed during the Falklands Campaign.

Traditional, albeit infrequent, tasks continued and while on her way home after seven years in the Far East the frigate *Alacrity* was called upon to put a 24-man armed boarding party aboard the British tanker *Athelduke* after her captain had called for the Navy to put down a mutiny on board. In 1952, 12 of the crew of 18 in the minesweeping motor launch *P.2582* died when a Dutch jet fighter crashed on board during an exercise off Den Helder. The following year there were 32 casualties on board the cruiser *Swiftsure* when she was rammed by the new destroyer *Diamond* off Iceland in a NATO exercise. It was this occasion which give rase to an immortal exchange of signals in which the *Swiftsure*'s captain in response to his signal 'What do you intend to do now?' received the reply: 'Buy a farm!'

In Korea, where in mid-1953 the Communists had agreed to an armistice, the British and Australian carriers had flown 25,000 sorties with the loss of 21 aircrew killed in action and 14 in accidents out of 480 who had taken part. Apart from some Sunderland flying boats there had been no RAF participation in the conflict.

But all this did not inhibit Lord Trenchard, the 'Father of the Royal Air Force', from claiming in a House of Lords debate that '£100 million a year' could be saved by scrapping the carriers and over-

ABOVE: *The Type 14 frigate HMS* Dundas *in 1977. The Type 14 was a utility version of the Type 12, armed with the same ASW weaponry but possessing only half its power.*

seas bases and relying instead on long-range aircraft. In a subsequent debate the same year he went further and said that 'if aircraft carriers go to sea they are going to sea to be sunk'. The land-based bomber would always get through – why the carrier-based one could not he did not explain. Nor did he say how short-range land-based fighters would protect ships at sea from air attack. Not only are his views, with some updating to take into account new weapons, still those publicly voiced by some senior serving RAF officers but they were also at the nub of government defence policy in the late 1960s.

Replying in a letter in *The Daily Telegraph* Admiral of the Fleet Lord Cunningham of Hynd-hope wrote that the belief that airpower alone could achieve victory was based on two fallacies. These were that a British government would agree to using nuclear weapons at the outset of a war, while against an enemy with well-defended and widely dispersed resources 'the decisive and immediate success so confidently promised from atomic bombing may well prove illusory.' He went on: 'no one who has twice come through the ordeal of seeing Britain's sea communications very nearly severed and the country brought to the verge of defeat can ever forget the simple, but easily forgotten, saying that: if we lose at sea we lose the war.'

In 1953 the Queen held her first Fleet Review to mark her Coronation. In all, 197 Royal Navy ships participated – over 40 more than had been assembled for her father's Coronation Review in 1937 but almost twice the number in the Silver Jubilee Review 24 years later.

Despite evidence world-wide of Communist-inspired military activity it was still something of a bombshell for the British public to learn from Mr Thomas, the First Lord, in the 1953 Navy Estimates debate that the Royal Navy had now slid to third place in the world league, as the Soviet Navy with 20 cruisers, over 100 destroyers and 350 submarines was now second in size only to the US Navy, and continued to expand over the next two decades.

Of more immediate concern to potential future naval officers was the decision to scrap the 16-year-old entry to Dartmouth introduced by Labour in 1948. Instead a committee had recommended a return to the earlier traditional 13-year-old entry but the government eventually ruled that the entry age be raised to 18.

Technical developments in the mid-1950s included the introduction of the mirror deck-landing aid in the carrier *Illustrious* and subsequently in operational carriers, the construction of the first post-war class of four midget submarines and trials with High Test Peroxide fuel for torpedoes. The last was to prove disastrous – a torpedo blew up in the submarine *Sidon* alongside the depot ship *Maidstone* at Portland, causing 13 deaths.

The same year Admiral Earl Mountbatten arrived at the Admiralty as First Sea Lord and not long after the post of Chairman of the Chiefs of Staff Committee was created with Marshal of the RAF Sir William Dickson as the first incumbent. This was to be the prelude to the creation of a combined Defence Ministry in 1964 in which the three service Ministries were merged.

By 1956 a number of major changes in the Navy's organization were in train. From 1957 officers in the various specialized branches were to be merged into a single list thus abolishing the separate career structures for Engineering, Electrical and Supply and Secretariat as well as Seaman specialists. For ratings the port divisions of Portsmouth, Plymouth, Chatham and Fleet Air Arm were to go. This meant that promotion opportunities were improved as a man no longer had to wait until there was an opening in the next higher rate within his port division.

In the 1956 Navy Estimates debate mention was made of the start of work on a marine nuclear power plant at Harwell. Britain was a latecomer to nuclear propulsion having concentrated on development HTP for submarines following on German wartime research.

In April 1956 there was considerable government embarrassment when retired diver Commander Lionel ('Buster') Crabb, who had led the search for the missing submarine *Affray* five years before, went missing after diving in Portsmouth harbour. Crabb, whose dive was not authorized by senior intelligence officials, was trying to discover whether the Russian cruiser *Ordzhonikidze*, then in the port having brought the Russian leaders Khruschev and Bulganin for an official visit to Britain, had controllable pitch propellers and other unusual features below the waterline. However, this turned out to be a minor irritation for the government in relation to subsequent events.

The Navy's next major challenge arose in July that year when Egypt seized the Suez Canal. The Admiralty responded immediately by stationing Mediterranean Fleet ships off Cyprus. One former Royal Navy destroyer, bought by Egypt was prevented from sailing from Portsmouth, although her sister ship was allowed to depart – without any ammunition. Troop reinforcements were moved by warship from Britain to Cyprus but despite the urgency of the situation the build-up of forces was leisurely. It was not until late August that it was announced that men due to leave the service were to be retained, and another two months elapsed before a joint Anglo-French task force was reported to be at sea. The British ships were spearheaded by the carriers *Eagle* and *Bulwark* operating Sea Hawk and Sea Venom fighters and Wyvern strike aircraft; these had to provide all the fighter cover as Cyprus was too far away for RAF fighters. On board the training carriers *Ocean* and *Theseus* were the men of 45 Commando Royal Marines and they were to be put ashore by Fleet Air Arm Whirlwind helicopters in the first 'vertical assault' to be staged at sea.

Once the troops were established ashore the minesweepers led the way for other ships to enter Port Said. French and British cruisers and destroyers had earlier provided gunfire support but the Egyptian response was minimal.

In the Red Sea the cruiser *Newfoundland* was hit twice at night after challenging a ship which failed to reply. She then returned the fire and sank what turned out to be the Egyptian frigate *Domiat* which was probably about to lay mines. Sixty-nine survivors were rescued. Shortly after this the frigate *Crane* was attacked by four Israeli jet fighters in the Gulf of Suez and succeeded in shooting one down. She was most likely mistaken by the Israelis for a similar ship serving in the Egyptian Navy,

Significantly, in the early stages of the crisis a number of ships in reserve were prepared for operational service. The Admiralty was clearly thinking in terms of a protracted campaign. Naval salvage ships with crews in civilian dress and under United Nations control were to stay in the Canal until early the following year, removing ships that the Egyptians had scuttled to block the waterway.

Concerned by inadequacies shown up at Suez and the need to cut costs, in 1957 the government and the Defence Minister Duncan Sandys published a sweeping Defence Review. Measures included winding up the Royal Naval Volunteer Reserve Air Squadrons, followed by merging the RNVR with the RNR. The Review's primary object, although it was never spelt out, was to save money by increasingly relying on nuclear weapons. Conventional forces could be drastically cut as they would have little part to play in a nuclear exchange. This applied particularly to the Navy and over a five-year period its manpower was to be reduced from 128,000 to 75,000. The Reserve Fleet of some 550 ships was to be scrapped or sold.

Overseas, Trincomalee dockyard was to close when the East Indies and Far East stations were merged, while the post of CinC America and West Indies was to be abolished; Hong Kong dockyard was to be closed and Simonstown handed over to the South African Navy. Several naval air stations at home were to close and were followed in 1958 by the closure of dockyards at Portland and Sheerness.

By the end of 1957 the government began to appreciate that its cuts had been too drastic and the First Lord said that the Service would now have 100,000 men and women by 1962. It was also announced that, in the light of the success of the *Ocean* and *Theseus* at Suez, the carrier *Bulwark* was to be converted into a commando carrier, later followed by her sister ship *Albion*. Trials of the first naval anti-aircraft missile, Seaslug, had begun the previous year in the converted maintenance ship *Girdle Ness* but, offsetting these developments, a new naval helicopter and the naval SR.177 rocket assisted fighter were cancelled.

This massive British maritime retrenchment triggered an immediate response by Moscow. In 1957 the Soviet Navy greatly expanded its deployments in places as far apart as the American Atlantic coast and southern Africa.

By 1958 it was being officially recognized that the extremely adverse response to the Sandys White Paper in NATO required some placatory remarks. That year's Navy Estimates stated that 'The oceans cover over 70 percent of the world's surface. Taking first the interests of these islands and of the Commonwealth, nothing is more important than that merchant shipping should be able to pass freely and safely across them. Our very existence in peace and

The cruisers Blake *(seen in 1979) and* Tiger *were rebuilt between 1965-72 as helicopter-cruisers, with a huge hangar aft to accommodate four Sea Kings.*

war depends upon this freedom. The same freedom means no less to the alliances which are helping to knit the free world together. Between the countries of these alliance is the sea. It can unite them if the countries of the free world maintain mastery of it; but the alliances will be divided and will fall apart if that mastery is lost. It is the business of the Navy, as it always has been, to help retain it.' In direct rebuttal of Sandys' paper the previous year, the statement added: 'uncertainty about the course and direction of global war, which applies to all the fighting services, does not therefore restrict the role, the shape, or the size of the future Navy.'

But despite such stirring restatements of the Navy's role, the 820 ships in the fleet in 1957 had dropped to 228 a year later, the same number that had been lost to enemy action at the height of the

war in 1942. Other cuts were to include paying off the Navy's Rhine and Elbe squadrons.

Overseas the Navy's many tasks continued, ranging from aid for the Sultan of Oman, anti-piracy and slave-trading patrols in the Persian Gulf, to support for the hydrogen bomb tests at Christmas Island and reinforcement of the Belize garrison and the forces in Libya. More troops were moved to Cyprus because of the continued unrest on the island and civilians evacuated from the Lebanon, while the overthrow of the monarchy in Iraq resulted in some 500 sorties being flown by aircraft from the *Eagle*. She covered the movement of British troops to Amman at the request of the Jordanian government. The autumn of 1958 saw a rise in tension off the Icelandic fishing grounds where a 12-mile territorial limit had been declared and was being ignored by British trawlers. Royal Navy ships were called in after an Icelandic Coastguard cutter had fired blank rounds to scare a British trawler and the 'Cod War' was to continue intermittently until 1960. There were to be other, increasingly bitter 'Cod Wars' with Iceland in 1973 and 1976.

In 1959 the first sections of the first British nuclear submarine *Dreadnought*, were laid down on the slipway at Vickers' Barrow shipyard. Her reactor was bought from America in order to speed her entry into service. It also enabled a rapid build-up of knowledge and experience among officers and ratings. There were changes of equal significance affecting the Navy's sailors – some 25 per cent of all officers were now being promoted from the lower deck compared with only some 18 per cent 10 years earlier. This proportion was to continue to rise so that by the 1980s it was 33 percent.

By the end of the 1950s the Far East was an increasingly important part of Britain's foreign policy and was finally to eclipse the Mediterranean. Late in 1959 a squadron of minesweepers left Malta for Singapore where they were to conduct patrol duties in the East Indies and it was also announced that for the first time since 1947 the Far East Fleet was to have a submarine squadron.

At the beginning of 1960 the newly converted commando ship *Bulwark* sailed for the Far East where she was to be joined by increasing numbers of ships over the next few months. It was also announced that two new amphibious ships *Fearless* and *Intrepid* were to be built. The *Dreadnought* was launched and the *Vanguard*, last of the Navy's battleships, was sent to the shipbreakers.

The Portland spy case in early 1961 involved the theft of highly classified documents from the Underwater Weapons Establishment and Moscow gained information on both British anti-submarine weapons and submarine design.

Although the effects of the Sandys Axe continued to be felt with the closure of the Nore Command in 1961, a classic example of the Navy's role in foreign policy was provided in the Gulf. Fearing she might be invaded by Iraq, Kuwait appealed for British assistance and within 24 hours 750 men of 42 Commando Royal Marines had gone ashore from the *Bulwark*. Within a very short time air support was being provided by fighters from the *Victorious* which also controlled RAF fighters ashore. Nine days after Kuwait's request 5700 British troops were ashore. No Iraqi attack took place and the deployment ended successfully in October 1961.

BELOW: *The 26 Leander class general-purpose frigates were developed from the Whitby and Rothesay Type 12s. HMS* Jupiter *in 1978.*

INSET: *HMS* Salisbury *was one of four aircraft-direction frigates built in the 1950s.*

LEFT: *The Type 21 frigate* Antelope *and the missile destroyer* Devonshire *exercising in close company, seen from HMS* Ark Royal *in 1978.*

BELOW LEFT: *The design of the 'County' class destroyers was successful but the bulk and the handling problems of the Seaslug missile imposed severe penalties.*

BELOW RIGHT: *The long-awaited second-generation air defence missile Sea Dart underwent exhaustive trials in HMS* Bristol *in the 1970s.*

At the beginning of 1962 the first all-British nuclear submarine, *Valiant*, was begun at Barrow. A few months earlier *Ashanti*, the first frigate designed to operate a helicopter, had been inspected by MPs on the Thames. The fact that the helicopter was too big for her hangar was demurely concealed.

Defence policy for the next five years was spelt out in a White Paper which called for commonality of aircraft between the Navy and the RAF. Prospects for progress on these lines appeared good, with both Services showing interest in the supersonic Vertical/Take-off and Landing (V/TOL) aircraft the P.1154; but despite this identity of interest nothing happened, and within four years the Navy had ordered the conventional American Phantom fighter.

A new problem was the confrontation with Indonesia whose government was increasingly opposed to the newly established Malaysian Federation. This was made clear first in Brunei where a force of Indonesian guerrillas, described by the British as 'Communists' had clashed with police and had to be overcome by Commandos put ashore by Far East Fleet ships.

There was also indirect help for the Americans in Vietnam from the Royal Navy with the chartering of two ex-German heavy lifting craft to assist in clearing wrecks in the various ports. Under the Wilson government this assistance was to be extended further to include the refuelling by RFA tankers of American warships in the Indian Ocean on their way to Vietnam. In late 1962 Harold Macmillan and President Kennedy signed the Nassau Agreement under which Britain was to get the American 2500-mile range A3 Polaris submarine-launched strategic nuclear missile following the Americans' cancellation of the air-launched Skybolt missile. Before the year was out the Admiralty had laid down a five-year target date for completion of

the first of four submarines, armed with 16 missiles, which was to cost £70 million. The first, *Resolution*, began sea trials in 1967 'on time and to cost'. The total programme was to cost some £300 million of which three-quarters would be spent in Britain on the missile warheads, the submarines and their reactors, leaving manufacture of the missile bodies and the submarines' inertial navigation systems to the Americans. Later it became clear that the Americans' share of the work was nearly a third of the programme.

In early 1963 the first deck landings took place at sea on board the *Ark Royal* of the P.1127 V/TOL aircraft, the forerunner of the Sea Harrier.

The Navy's conventional submarines were continuing their experiments in navigating under the Arctic icecap begun by the *Finwhale* in 1961. Divers from the deep-diving ship *Reclaim* were now working regularly at depths as great as 450 feet. Trials went well using free-ascents rather than breathing apparatus for escapes from 200 feet by survivors from sunken submarines. The ultimate aim was to increase the escape depth from submarines to 500 feet or more. Mine-hunting sonar was to show its worth in the sweeping of the southern North Sea for live wartime mines. The first ship so fitted, HMS *Shoulton*, was able to detect an object the diameter of a paint pot on the seabed.

The war with Indonesia intensified in 1963. Two Fleet Air Arm helicopter squadrons were active in both Sabah and Sarawak in North Borneo and flew 3500 operational sorties in the first six months of the year while coastal minesweepers maintained patrols around the coasts. On her way to reinforce the Far East Fleet in early 1964 the carrier *Centaur* was diverted to East Africa where the Royal Marine Commando, supported by her aircraft and the guns of the destroyer *Cambrian*, were instrumental in putting down mutinies in Africa.

LEFT: *The commando carrier* Bulwark *at anchor off Tromsö after landing 42 Royal Marine Commando in a NATO exercise.*

RIGHT: *HMS* Ark Royal *in Grand Harbour, Malta in 1970.*

The British government, facing a general election, was not prepared to apply any real pressure that might end the conflict with Indonesia. In September the carrier *Victorious* was on her way from Western Australia to Singapore and a direct course would have taken her through the Sunda Strait, well within range to attack the Indonesian capital Djarkarta. As she neared Indonesian waters there was panic in the city and senior officials began fleeing in large numbers. Had the carrier's aircraft been flown over the city as a display of strength the regime would have quite probably collapsed, but instead the ship was diverted some 700 miles to the east and the confrontation avoided.

In 1963 President Kennedy proposed that all the NATO powers share in a mixed-manned force of ships equipped with surface-launched Polaris missiles. In an unsuccessful trial the US destroyer *Claude V. Ricketts* was manned by contingents from the British, Netherlands, West German, Italian, Greek, Turkish and US navies for 18 months. Despite this unpromising experiment, the NATO navies were later to form a conventionally equipped multi-national squadron of frigates, and also a squadron of mine countermeasures vessels.

Late in 1964 there were reports that the Americans had offered four *Essex* Class carriers as a cheaper alternative to the building of new carriers in Britain. The American price for a single carrier with 70 aircraft was £5 million. (A comparable offer of two carriers was made by President Reagan to Mrs Thatcher in 1981.) But in Britain the government had already embarked on economies, with the cancellation of plans to build a fifth Polaris missile submarine and the Royal Navy's first icebreaker to have been named *Terra Nova*. Instead a Danish cargo ship was converted for Antarctic patrols and renamed *Endurance*. More significantly, it became

known that the government was leasing the Indian Ocean island of Diego Garcia to the Americans. According to US Navy sources, this was to be part of a chain of island bases to be established by the two nations.

Rhodesia's Unilateral Declaration of Independence was to be a major commitment for the Navy, but a frustrating one. The Navy provided air cover over neighbouring Zambia by patrols from its aircraft carriers. AEW Gannets assisted frigates on the lookout for ships attempting to break the blockade and run prohibited cargoes for Rhodesia into the Portuguese East African port of Beira. The purpose of the patrol was undermined when a tanker captain who refused to stop was, on advice from London, allowed to proceed. None-the-less, the patrol was to continue for a further nine years.

The most important event of 1964 was the decision in the government's Defence Review to abandon plans for a new generation of carriers of which the first, *CVA-01*, had already been approved by the previous government. This decision had a profound long-term effect both on the Navy and on national defence strategy.

The argument was that defence spending had to be reduced from seven to six percent of the Gross National Product. While British forces were to retain commitments outside NATO where their presence 'by itself is a deterrent to local conflict' they would not in future 'take part in major operations of war outside Europe except with the co-operation of allies'. This last point was something of a concession to the Navy Minister, Christopher Mayhew, who had resigned before the Review's publication on the grounds that pegging defence spending at £2000 million was an arbitrary figure which took no account of increasing commitments. He and the First Sea Lord, Admiral Sir David

RIGHT: *The last Gannet Airborne Early Warning Flight, aboard* Ark Royal *in 1978.*

FAR RIGHT: *One of* Ark Royal's *Phantoms takes the wire in the Mediterranean, on the last leg of the last commission.*

Luce, who also resigned, both felt that the RAF could not provide adequate defence for both the fleet and merchant shipping. The entire Admiralty Board had, with only one exception, also wanted to resign but Luce had persuaded them to stay, to maintain continuity in the command of the Navy.

At a press conference Mr Healey, the Defence Secretary, said that conversion of the three *Tiger* Class cruisers to carry a small number of helicopters was to go ahead (eventually only two were converted) and planning their successors was underway. These were to emerge in 1972 as the *Invincible* Class 'through-deck cruisers' (the word carrier was by then politically too emotive) but in fact they were small carriers.

The existing carriers would remain in service into the 1970s. The argument against a new generation of carriers was precisely that which the Air Staff in the Defence Ministry had submitted to Mr Healey the previous autumn – that carriers were of value only for supporting amphibious operations against a sophisticated enemy and outside the range of supporting shore-based aircraft. Even with one new carrier and the existing *Ark Royal* and *Eagle* the cost of the three would be £1400 million over a 10-year period. A month later Mr Wilson, the Prime Minister, was to give the same figure for the cost of three

new carriers. For 25 years the entire fleet had been designed and built around the carrier and now it was to go with nothing to take its place. Rather surprisingly the Defence Estimates flatly contradicted the Review, stating that the carrier was the most important unit in the fleet.

Following the Review the Admiralty Board set up the Future Fleet Working Party whose reports said that nuclear weapons now made the escalation of limited wars by the Super Powers 'unlikely'. But in five years, without either a reduction in commitments or any increase in warship construction, the fleet would be unable to safeguard Britain's overseas interests and her shipping. It also considered that organic air support would continue to be vital at sea. This last point was rejected by the Admiralty Board.

Metal fatigue problems were now manifesting themselves in some nuclear submarines and high-tensile steel was bought from America as British industry could not produce it. To save costs of future warships there was much talk in the Defence Ministry of a standard NATO frigate design during 1966. Conversion was to start during the year in replacing the steam turbine in the frigate *Exmouth* with an Olympus gas turbine to test it at sea.

The first military space satellite communications terminal opened at Christchurch, Hampshire, in June 1966 and the initial trials of the Ships' Satellite Communications Terminal (SCOT) began on board the frigate *Wakeful*.

By 1967 the reduction in the Navy's forces overseas and at home made it logical to have only two fleets. The Far East Fleet would cover an area east-

BELOW: *Although nominally a sister of HMS* Eagle, *the 'Ark' differed in many details.*

ABOVE: *One of* Ark Royal's *Buccaneer bombers landing. Both Phantoms and Buccaneers were handed over to the RAF after the ship paid off.*

wards from the Red Sea, with its headquarters at Singapore, while the Western Fleet covered the Atlantic and Mediterranean from the old Home Fleet headquarters at Northwood, Middlesex. The flag of the CinC Mediterranean was hauled down for the last time on 5 June 1967, something that the Dutch, French, Spaniards, Austrians, Germans and Italians had failed to do in a long history of conflict dating back over 300 years.

The Navy's commitments remained considerable with rising tensions in the Middle East as Russian arms flooded into Egypt. This required the retention of the carrier *Victorious* in the Mediterranean while in Hong Kong the *Bulwark* put her commandos ashore to deter unrest which arose as the Cultural Revolution on the mainland got underway. Some of the helicopter crews were surprised to observe on landing the Red Stars on some soldiers' caps – fortunately the Peking government did not choose to make political capital out of the Royal Navy's accidental 'invasion' of their territory and Whitehall kept the incident firmly under wraps. The *Bulwark*'s sister ship *Albion* sailed ostensibly for the

ABOVE: *The Fleet Air Arm uses the two-seater Hunter (foreground), a two-seater Sea Harrier and the standard Sea Harrier for training.*

LEFT: *HMS* Broadsword *was the first of the powerful Type 22 frigates, intended to replace the* Leander *as the standard ASW ship.*

RIGHT: *The elegant Type 21 frigates replaced the Navy's diesel-engined frigates in the 1970s.*

Far East in May 1967 and her return only six weeks later attracted no press comment. During this time the ship had been standing by off Nigeria to land 41 Commando Royal Marines to rescue British subjects caught up in the Biafran civil war – 20 years later there is still no official acknowledgement of this event either.

The Fleet Air Arm, both fixed-wing aircraft and helicopters, had been operating in the Aden Protectorate since the early 1960s mostly against both Moscow- and Cairo-backed rebels in the Radfan. But by 1966 it was clear that Britain would quit and late the following year a task force that included three carriers and all four amphibious ships was assembled off the colony to cover the final withdrawal of British forces.

Other cuts at this time included the premature scrapping of the carrier *Victorious* after a fire on board and the abandonment of plans to buy American F-111 aircraft, which were to replace the carriers and their aircraft, and US Indian Ocean bases.

One problem was to find a new role for the amphibious forces. *Bulwark* was sent to Norway to land Commandos in a NATO role to support the Northern Flank. Unfortunately there had been no time to adapt her helicopters for Arctic conditions and an unexpected June blizzard kept them firmly on deck while the Marines laboriously made their way ashore in the ship's four small landing craft. But the exercise did show that helicopters armed with anti-tank missiles were potent weapons against missile-armed fast attack craft. The sinking of the Israeli destroyer *Eilat* the previous year by such craft of the Egyptian Navy had created a measure of sensitivity to the anti-ship missile threat.

During another NATO exercise in the far north later in the year it was disclosed that senior American naval officers had put forward a proposal that the Alliance should take over the British carriers *Ark Royal* and *Eagle* in order to ensure they were not lost to the West. The idea, though still-born, showed how concerned were Britain's allies by the government's policy.

When questioned about fears that the Russians might try to fill the gap to be left by Britain's East of Suez withdrawal, Mr Healey said he did not think so at least until the Suez Canal, closed during the 1967 Arab-Israeli war, was reopened. In March 1968, less than two months after his remarks, the first Russian squadron arrived to visit Indian ports and in 1969 they established a permanent naval presence – though the Canal was not reopened until 1975.

The Russians were starting to flex their muscles at sea. One of their submarines intruding in the clearly defined naval exercise area off Londonderry was forced by Royal Navy frigates to surface after a prolonged hunt. During the same period, a poaching Russian trawler was arrested off Shetland by a Fishery Protection Squadron minesweeper and escorted into Lerwick but the case failed in court for lack of evidence.

Many of the effects of the government's policy only came to light gradually, although the transfer of

Singapore dockyard to the island's government in December 1968 was well publicized. In September 1968 it became known that in 1966 plans for a replacement for the Navy's AEW Gannet aircraft had been cancelled, a decision which the former Director of Naval Air Warfare in the Defence Ministry described as being 'something that may one day be recognized as a greater national loss than either the TSR2 or the F-111'. The decision was to contribute to the deaths of many servicemen in the Falklands 14 years later.

On 1 July 1969 the Navy formally assumed responsibility from the RAF for maintaining the British nuclear deterrent; the first of the Polaris submarines *Resolution* having begun her initial operational patrol a year earlier.

ABOVE: *The only reminder of Coastal Forces was a trio of fast target craft, including* HMS Cutlass.

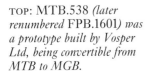

TOP: MTB.538 *(later renumbered* FPB.1601*) was a prototype built by Vosper Ltd, being convertible from MTB to MGB.*

At home the deteriorating situation in Northern Ireland called for obsolete depot ships being used as temporary jails and barracks. Around the coast the minesweeper *Wotton* began anti-gun running patrols and this and other security tasks by the Navy were to continue without respite in the waters around the Province into the 1980s.

Two links with the past were severed in 1969. The posts of CinC Portsmouth and Plymouth were abolished and replaced by that of the CinC Naval Home Command at Portsmouth responsible for all naval shore training establishments, the Reserves and other personnel matters. In Scotland the Navy's last two coal-burners, the boom defence vessels *Barrage* and *Barnard*, paid off at the end of the year.

Other traditional activities continued. At the Royal Naval Detention Quarters at Portsmouth men could now talk together at meal times but they had still to pick oakum.

By 1970 the recruiting position was improving a little but Mr Healey was still trying to justify his carrier policy by claiming that keeping one carrier in the Far East was costing £170 million a year. Even his supporters in the media had to accept that such a figure was a 'fudge' and included the cost of a naval aircraft repair yard and Singapore dockyard.

To prove that it still believed in maintaining a world-wide capability to aid allies the government staged a large-scale air reinforcement exercise in 1970 in the Far East. Royal Marines would take part operating from *Bulwark* but there would be no British carrier. However, there was the small Australian carrier *Melbourne* and it was her few fighters which alone provided air support for the initial amphibious assault when the RAF's Phantoms failed to put in an appearance. That a carrier should be required under the exercise plan was a curious admission.

The British election campaign aroused enormous interest at the Singapore base since the Conservative leader Mr Heath had promised to retain a residual British military presence in the Far East. As each Conservative victory at the hustings was chalked up in the Naval Headquarters it was cheered by watching Malay, Chinese and Indian clerks, sweepers, drivers and others. In the event, the Heath government kept a frigate at Singapore as the British naval element in the combined Commonwealth ANZUK forces.

The entire Singapore base was in fact handed over to the island republic's government in 1971 and the offer by Mauritius of an alternative site for a base was rejected. Some time previously the idea of joint development of a base in Western Australia with the RAN first proposed by Admiral Jellicoe as far back as 1921, had also been rejected.

During the election campaign the government announced massive spending plans at both Devonport and Portsmouth dockyards where a number of drydocks would be covered over to give all-weather working on warship refits – in the event only the Devonport scheme came to fruition. There was some embarrassment for the government in the opening stages of the campaign when the Pentagon disclosed that in 1967 there had been a joint plan for the two nations' carriers to form a task group to contest the Egyptians' closure of the Canal and the Gulf of Aqaba. Downing Street's response was to claim that at no time had Britain contemplated *unilateral* action in the 1967 war.

Before the end of the year the new Heath government decided to retain the carrier *Ark Royal*, which had just completed a £30 million refit. Exocet anti-ship missiles were also to be bought from France to give the Fleet some of the offensive capability that it was losing with the reduction in carrier aircraft.

In June the 47,000 ton RFA tanker *Ennerdale* struck a reef off the Seychelles and sank, fortunately without loss of life. She was the biggest naval-owned ship to be lost in peace or war.

The last rum issue was made to the Navy's sailors on 31 July 1970. The tot, an eighth of a pint of 98 per cent proof spirit, was available free daily for all ratings aged over 20 and was served neat to Petty Officers (commissioned officers did not receive it except when 'Splice the Mainbrace' was ordered, usually by the Sovereign) or with added water for junior ratings. In compensation the 'Sailors' Fund', usually known as the 'tot fund' was set up with money it was calculated the Treasury would save. This is used to buy equipment and amenities to improve the sailor's life, particularly ashore. A new scheme was also introduced that would even out the time a sailor spent at sea and served ashore, where he could live or be near his family. By this time the maximum length of separation a man could expect from his family was limited to nine months under the 'harmony' rules.

The following year the first of the new *Invincible* Class carriers, designed to operate Sea Harrier fighters and helicopters, was ordered; she was launched by Queen Elizabeth at Barrow four years later. But the order for the first batch of Sea Harriers was not placed until 1975 because of economic problems facing both Conservative and Labour governments. In 1973 the world's largest glass-reinforced plastic ship, the mine-hunter *Wilton*, was completed but was not followed by the first of the larger GRP built 'Hunt' Class until 1979. *Wilton* and two older MCM vessels were involved in 1974 in the arduous and protracted task of clearing the Suez Canal of mines. Although not one mine was found, large quantities of other explosive ordnance were recovered or destroyed by the ships' divers.

By this time the growing offshore North Sea energy industry was a cause for concern over its security, and after initial conversion of a patrol vessel nine ships were eventually built for this task and fishery protection duties.

The new Labour government undertook a new Defence Review in 1975. This called for cancellation of any long-term plans for replacement of the Navy's amphibious ships, a measure not rescinded until December 1986. Other measures were to include cutting one-seventh of the Navy's destroyers, frigates and MCM vessels and of one-quarter of its conventional submarines; the number of minesweepers for RNR training went down from 11 to six. Plans were abandoned for nine destroyers and frigates, several MCM vessels, a fleet maintenance ship and four other support vessels. Residual naval forces were also to be withdrawn from the Mediterranean and the Caribbean. The remaining British naval staff were withdrawn from South Africa thus severing the last defence links with that country. In the Far East the frigate *Lowestoft*, guardship with the ANZUK force, was ordered home as she was in the midst of rescuing refugees from Vietnam.

What was extremely disturbing at this time was the post-election disclosure that, while Ministers were absent at the hustings, Defence Ministry and Foreign Office civil servants had been preparing to 'rubber stamp' a Soviet request to establish 'support facilities' for their weather ships at Greenock, overlooking the British Polaris base at Faslane and the US Navy's similar establishment at Holy Loch. Facilities were also requested at Gibraltar and both would have been approved had a routine report not been carefully read by a member of the Naval Staff in the Defence Ministry who drew it to Ministers' attention.

The Turkish invasion of Cyprus in 1975 involved the *Hermes* and other ships evacuating large numbers of refugees including a Soviet ballet troupe who gave an impromptu performance on an RFA's flight deck.

By 1976 the Fleet was smaller than at any time for 80 years and contraction continued with the frigate guardship at Hong Kong being withdrawn. There was tragedy, too, when the RNR-manned coastal minesweeper *Fittleton* was lost with 12 of her crew in a collision with the frigate *Mermaid* in the North Sea.

In 1977 Ministers, on the advice of Treasury civil servants, tried to renege on a commitment to pay Supplementary List (Short Service) naval pilots and observers £5000 gratuities after 12 years' service. Instead, they would receive most of the money in the form of a pension at the age of 60, so saving the Treasury a tidy sum. Rear Admiral John Roberts, the Flag Officer Naval Air Command, made the plan public knowledge forcing the government to drop it. But this climb-down did not prevent something similar being tried again when naval pilots, hurriedly brought home from foreign postings during the Falklands conflict, were refused financial help to defray the cost of bringing their wives home, even though they had no idea how long they might have had to leave them on their own overseas.

Towards the end of the 1977 training started for the Services' most unusual post-war task: replacing

LEFT: *HMS* Hermione *entering Portsmouth. The* Leander *design was widely regarded as the best escort produced by any navy since World War II.*

ABOVE: *HMS* Ark Royal *became widely known as a result of the TV series 'Sailor'.*

RIGHT: *One of the successful* Leander-Class *escorts, HMS* Ariadne *comes into harbour.*

striking firemen up and down the country. At Poole, for example, the naval firemen were soon achieving a faster response time than the normal civilian crews. The eventual settlement of the dispute served to underline the appallingly low level to which the Services' pay had dropped with some sailors' families on such low rates that they qualified for rent relief.

Besides pay the Navy was being starved of money for spares, including such things as sonobuoys used for routine but essential peacetime tracking of Russian submarines and sonar equipment in frigates. Such was the inflexibility of the Treasury rules that money underspent in one area of the defence budget could not be switched to another nor could it be held over until the next financial year. Unspent funds went back to the Treasury which then cut the next year's budget.

At the end of 1978 *Ark Royal*, the last of the Navy's conventional carriers, was paid off for scrap and it was announced the name would be revived for the third of the *Invincible* Class carriers.

The Conservative government elected in 1979 immediately paid off a number of ships in order to relieve the now acute manpower shortage – arising mainly from poor pay. The following year the government decided to adopt the American Trident ballistic missile as the eventual replacement for Polaris. Initially the 4000-mile range C4 version was chosen, but in 1982 it was decided to adopt the 6000-mile range D5.

Following the outbreak of the Iran-Iraqi War in 1980 and Russia's invasion of Afghanistan a Royal Navy force of four destroyers or frigates with two supporting RFAs was established in the Arabian Sea. By 1986 this force was also playing a traditional role patrolling inside the Gulf to deter attacks on British-owned merchant ships.

ABOVE: *In 1967 the abandoned chemical carrier* SS Essberger Chemist *was sent to the bottom by torpedoes from the nuclear submarine* Dreadnought.

LEFT: *A Sea King helicopter drops a Mk 46 anti-submarine torpedo.*

June 1979 saw the delivery of the Fleet Air Arm's first operational Sea Harrier. The 'ski jump' ramp fitted in the three *Invincible* Class ships and the *Hermes*, at a trifling cost, greatly increased the Sea Harrier's launching velocity, thereby improving range and payload.

In 1980 the latest in a long line of official reports on how the Royal Dockyards' management might be improved and costs reduced was produced by Mr Keith Speed, the Navy Minister, and recommended retention of the three dockyards at Portsmouth, Devonport and Chatham as well as Gibraltar.

In April 1981 reports began circulating that the number of destroyers and frigates was to be cut from 59 to 32, the two remaining amphibious assault ships *Fearless* and *Intrepid* were to be scrapped and only two carriers would be retained with the sale of *Hermes* to India and of *Invincible* to Austrailia. The Royal Marines would be disbanded and the Navy's manpower cut from 66,400 to 47,000. At the end of April when giving evidence to the Parliamentary Defence Committee, the Defence Secretary Mr John Nott was asked: 'Have you discussed with SACLANT (the Supreme Allied Commander Atlantic) the effect of reducing the number of anti-submarine warfare vessels in EASTLANT (the NATO Eastern Atlantic area) in view of the fact that he has said there are far too few and the lessons of the last two wars illustrated the danger, and if you have had such discussions what have been the results?' To this Nott replied: 'We have not had any discussions with SACLANT because we do not have any proposal to do any such thing'.

Exactly eight weeks later he told Parliament in a defence White Paper that the number of operational destroyers and frigates would be cut to 42; the carrier *Invincible* was being offered for sale to Australia; Chatham dockyard would be closed; Portsmouth much reduced and Gibraltar handed over to commercial contractors; naval manpower would be cut by 10,000 by 1984 and probably by further 8-10,000 by 1991. This second batch of cuts, together with that of a further 10 frigates by the end of the decade, was not made public at this time nor was the cancellation of plans for construction of a new class of missile destroyer the Type 44. Only the amphibious ships and the Royal Marines were reprieved thanks to a prudent invitation to Nott some weeks later to witness an amphibious exercise. It had already been announced that the Navy's Antarctic ice patrol ship *Endurance* would be withdrawn without replacement at the end of the 1982 season.

Before the publication of the White Paper, Mr Speed, in a speech to his constituents, said that for about 23 percent of the defence budget the Navy and RAF maritime air supplied 70 percent of the NATO forces in the Eastern Atlantic, whereas for 40 percent of the budget British ground and air forces provided 10 percent of Allied forces in central Europe.

BELOW: *HMS/m* Dreadnought *leaves the scene of the sinking of the* Essberger Chemist.

LEFT: *HMS* Beaver,
second of six 'stretched' Type
22 frigates ordered since
1979

ABOVE: *HMS* Finwhale
was one of eight Porpoise
Class diesel-electric
submarines ordered in the
early 1950s.

Speed was immediately sacked for 'disloyalty' to the government and for failing to have his speech approved beforehand by Nott. Thus for the first time in its history the Navy was left with no political representation, something that the Prime Minister soon found so convenient that she made it a permanent arrangement for all three Services. In March 1982 Speed, with the author, then Naval Correspondent of *The Daily Telegraph*, formed the British Maritime League, the aims of which were to keep the decline in every aspect of Britain's maritime resources in the public eye and to put forward possible solutions.

Admiral Sir Henry Leach, the First Sea Lord, suggested that the £800 million then being spent on 25,000 civil servants and in the support of 79,000 families of British servicemen in Germany each year might be a better area in which to consider spending cuts, rather than the Navy's front-line forces; but his arguments were to no avail.

Some three months after the publication of his White Paper Nott said in an interview in the *International Defence Review* that the most senior Admiral in NATO ('he's not British' and was presumably American Admiral Harry Train, the Supreme Allied Commander Atlantic) had told him that the Royal Navy's dockyard resources were 'excessive', 'I would rather have a hundred escorts – frigates and destroyers – than fifty'. Nott said, 'Of course I'd rather have a hundred. I'd rather have five hundred. But the only way in which we could have kept the frigate and destroyer numbers up would have been by sustaining four dockyards'. Clearly it was money not national security, that was of any importance.

As the 1981 Review progressed Admiral Leach wrote to Mrs Thatcher: 'To cut the Navy in haste before a proper, objective assessment has been made both at national and NATO levels, would be to leap into the dark and would involve taking a grave risk with the security of the nation on an arbitrary basis which has not been fully substantiated. It will markedly reduce our flexibility for meeting the unforeseen and thus reduce the options for future governments. In my view it would be neither wise nor responsible to proceed in this way.'

It was indeed fortunate for Mrs Thatcher and her government that, by April 1982, too short a time had elapsed since the start of the Review for a serious reduction to have taken place in the ability of the Navy to meet the unforeseen.

By the mid-1980s the number of UK-registered merchant ships had reached a point where it was clear to all except the government ministers concerned that in a future crisis there would not be enough ships to sustain the nation's economy and to meet NATO commitments such as helping lift American reinforcements to Europe and providing naval auxiliaries. In the words of Sir Frederic Bolton, President of the British Maritime League, the government clearly believed a future war would be so short that the nation could rely on its strategic stockpiles of food, fuel and raw materials without recourse to seaborne imports. This would be a virtual invitation to an aggressor to ensure a protracted conflict knowing that after about three weeks British leaders would face the choice of national starvation and surrender – or national suicide by the initial use of nuclear weapons.

Chapter 9
The Falklands War

LEFT: *HMS* Brilliant, *which fired the first Sea Wolf in anger in May 1982. The missile-launcher is in front of the wheelhouse, with the Exocet anti-ship missiles on the forecastle.*

PREVIOUS PAGE: *HMS* Hermes *returns from the Falklands, rusty after hard steaming as the Task Force flagship.*

BELOW: *The nuclear submarine* Conqueror *sank the* General Belgrano, *hitting her with Mk 8 torpedoes.*

For the Royal Navy the year 1982 was probably one of the most momentous since World War II. In that year it was called upon to undertake operations the like of which had not been seen since 1945, exceeding even its involvement in the Korean War in the early 1950s and the Suez Crisis of 1956.

In an eagerness to cut defence commitments overseas some members of the government and the Secretary of State for Defence, John Nott, were advocating major reductions in the strength of the Navy. These proposed reductions would have made it virtually impossible for the Navy to carry out its allotted tasks. The withdrawal of HMS *Endurance* from Antarctica can also be said to have led to the Argentine decision to invade the Falklands. Not since 1944 had the Navy been tasked with carrying out operations so far from a secure base against a fully alert enemy.

The South Atlantic War of 1982 can be divided into four phases:
(1) The despatch of the Task Force south to recapture South Georgia and protect the sea lines of communication.
(2) Gaining control of sea and air space around the Islands.
(3) An amphibious assault.
(4) Support of the Army ashore and maintaining total control of the sea to prevent the Argentines from resupplying their troops still in the islands.

Within hours of Argentina invading the Falkland Islands on the night of 1 April, the logistic ship *Sir Geraint* had sailed from Plymouth for the South Atlantic, loaded with war stores. At the time of the invasion the carriers *Hermes* and *Invincible* and the assault ship *Fearless* were in Portsmouth. Within the three days the ships were made ready for sea by dockyard personnel working round the clock, and the two carriers sailed on 5 April. They were to play a major role in forthcoming events proving yet again that in a conflict at sea out of range of shore-based support, it is imperative that the fleets have at their disposal an integrated and reliable air capability. The old carrier *Hermes* was nominated as the flagship of the Task Force flying the flag of Rear Admiral 'Sandy' Woodward, a submariner who was then Flag Officer, First Flotilla.

Aboard the two carriers were three squadrons of Sea Harrier fighter aircraft – 800 Squadron *Hermes* (12 aircraft), 801 Squadron *Invincible* (8 aircraft), 899 Squadron (*Hermes/Invincible*). These were supplemented on 18 May by 809 Squadron, which allocated four aircraft each to 800 and 801 Squadrons, and three squadrons of Sea King helicopters. These included 820 Squadron (*Invincible*) with nine Mk 5 ASW aircraft, 826 Squadron (*Hermes*) with nine Mk 5 ASW aircraft, 846 Squadron (*Hermes*) with Mk 4 transport, some of which were based on the assault ship HMS *Fearless*.

The Task Force sails –
South Georgia recaptured

Once the decision to recapture the Falklands had been taken there was an explosion of activity throughout the whole of Britain. There have been many who criticized both the Government and the services for not having been prepared for such an eventuality. Such criticism was unjust, for within an incredibly short space of time a major Task Force was assembled and sailed 8000 miles into enemy-controlled waters without any nearby friendly base to fall back on in the event of failure.

As the Task Force sailed a major effort was undertaken to requisition merchant shipping suitable for use as troop and equipment transport and to carry the vast amount of supplies to the South Atlantic that would be required to keep the Fleet operational and continuously at sea over 4000 miles from the nearest base.

The prodigious feat of requisitioning or chartering and converting a large number of merchant ships was successfully undertaken at very short notice, without undue disruption of the economy.

There was great need for these merchant ships, the Fleet Train being too small to maintain such an enormous Task Force for an indefinite time. Naval overseers, draughtsmen, engineers, shipyard and dockyard workers, not to mention numerous companies large and small up and down the country worked round the clock. It was necessary to inspect, survey, measure, prepare drawings, manufacture items large and small, cut, prepare and weld all manner of fixtures ranging form large helicopter landing pads to small rigid mountings for machine guns, bunks, shelving for stores and repainting the ships for the task ahead.

Among the first of the merchant ships to be requisitioned was the P & O luxury liner SS *Canberra*, taken over while cruising in the Mediterranean. As she sailed north, her cruise cancelled, an army of workers assembled and built two helicopter landing platforms to be installed over what had been a luxury swimming pool and other recreational areas. As they carried out their task men of 40 and 42 Commando Royal Marines and the 3rd Parachute Battalion, boarded the liner and she sailed just two days later on 9 April.

On 12 April the British Maritime Total Exclusion Zone, in effect a war zone although not announced as such, for there was no formal declaration of war, came into effect. Two days previously units of the Task Force had reached Ascension Island. Although a British possession, the tiny island had long ago been leased to the US. President Reagan granted the UK permission to use the base as a staging post for warships and transports going south and for the RAF to use Wideawake airfield for long-range strikes and supply flights. This facility proved invaluable especially for the Task Force and the Transports. So hurriedly had the forces sailed that in many of the merchant ships stores had been loaded with little attention to unloading priorities. Many items had to be reallocated to other ships. The Task Force resumed its voyage on 16 April.

RIGHT: *Sending the Task Force to the Falklands was a major logistical problem, as this map illustrates.*

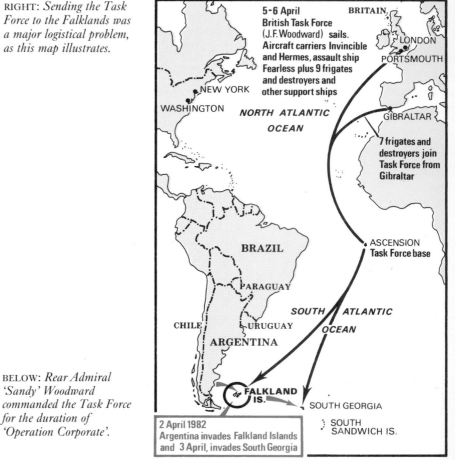

5-6 April British Task Force (J.F. Woodward) sails. Aircraft carriers Invincible and Hermes, assault ship Fearless plus 9 frigates and destroyers and other support ships

7 frigates and destroyers join Task Force from Gibraltar

ASCENSION Task Force base

2 April 1982 Argentina invades Falkland Islands and 3 April, invades South Georgia

BELOW: *Rear Admiral 'Sandy' Woodward commanded the Task Force for the duration of 'Operation Corporate'.*

On 12 April, the destroyer *Antrim*, frigate *Plymouth* and RFA *Tidespring* with units of 42 Commando Royal Marines and detachments of the Special Boat Service (SBS) and Special Air Service (SAS) aboard, had sailed south to carry out Operation Paraquat – the recapture of South Georgia. They were soon joined by RFA *Fort Austin* which had sailed direct from Gibraltar after participating in exercise Spring Train. On 14 April they joined up with the ice patrol ship *Endurance* which had been monitoring events in the South Atlantic while eluding Argentine forces.

The small group, known as Task Group 317.9, was ordered to land on South Georgia on 21 April. To cover the landing force and prevent interference by Argentine units the nuclear submarine *Conqueror*, with SBS troops aboard, had been ordered to patrol off South Georgia. Another small spearhead group led by HMS *Brilliant*, and comprising *Coventry*, *Glasgow*, *Sheffield*, *Arrow* and RFA *Appleleaf* was ordered to carry out patrols three days' sailing time north of the Falklands in an effort to draw Argentine naval and air units into action and destroy them before the main landings on the Falklands took place. It was a plan of classic simplicity – to mop up enemy outposts first and achieve sea and air control around the main objective before the main amphibious assault.

On the morning of 21 April three Wessexes from *Antrim* and *Tidespring* lifted off to initiate the Operation Paraquat landings. The weather soon degenerated into atrocious conditions which led to the loss of two of the Wessexes. In fact the threat of storm damage not only to aircraft, but also to units of the Task Force was most serious, with the nearest repair facilities 4000 miles away at Gibraltar. Eventually the SAS troops landed from the *Tidespring* and *Antrim* had to be evacuated. At another

ABOVE: *A Navy Sea King lifts a load of stores from the runway at Wideawake airfield at Ascension.*

RIGHT: *The ro-ro ferry* Norland *leaves Portsmouth for the South Atlantic on 26 April 1982.*

point 10 miles southeast of Grytiviken two squads of SBS landed from the *Endurance*. They fared little better and were also evacuated on 23 April after their craft were damaged. In the afternoon of the 23rd the *Endurance* picked up coded transmissions indicating the presence of an Argentine submarine within 100 miles, believed to the *Santa Fé*. By this time some of the SBS had established themselves ashore while on 24 April another effort was made to put the SAS ashore, this time successfully.

Meanwhile the ASW frigate *Brilliant* had been ordered to leave her spearhead group and go to the support of the South Georgia force; anti-submarine cover was urgently needed. The *Conqueror*, which had been ordered to leave the South Georgia area on 22nd to screen the spearhead group was ordered to reverse track and return to South Georgia, arriving in the area on the same day as HMS *Brilliant*.

At 0730 on 25 April the frigate *Plymouth* intercepted a radio transmission that gave a clear indication that the Santa Fé was leaving South Georgia. She had arrived at South Georgia and disembarked

stores and a few troop reinforcements. Helicopters were launched soon after and the Wessex 5 from HMS *Antrim* sighted the submarine and attacked with depth charges. The submarine suffered serious damage, which prevented her from diving. The next to attack was a Lynx from HMS *Brilliant*, followed by the Wasp from the *Endurance* armed with AS12 missiles. One of the missiles struck the submarine's fin but because of its light GRP construction, failed to actuate the fuse mechanism. The submarine, now damaged and with a terrified crew on board, continuously harried by the helicopters keeping up a hail of light machine-gun fire, and firing more AS12s, headed back for Cumberland East Bay on South Georgia. Having ascertained that the *Santa Fé*, now alongside a jetty at King Edward Point, was probably no longer seaworthy the intended landings began. Helicopters ferried the troops ashore, and the *Antrim* and *Plymouth* provided support with the 4.5-inch guns, more for effect than with any intention of destroying Argentine troop concentrations. By 1730 on 25 April it was

ABOVE: *A Sea Harrier hovering above the SS* Atlantic Conveyor. *Containers were used to provide a 'windbreak' for the helicopters.*

all over, and the Union Flag once more flew proudly over Grytviken. The capture of South Georgia was an important first step in the operation, as it was to be an important staging post and supply centre for the troopships and RFAs of the Task Force.

Gaining air and sea control

With South Georgia secured *Brilliant* and *Plymouth* were free to rejoin the spearhead Task Group 317.8 tasked with regaining sea and air superiority inside the Total Exclusion Zone (TEZ).

Following a raid on Port Stanley airfield by the RAF, Royal Navy Sea Harriers launched more sustained strikes against the Argentines who were by now fully aware that they could expect further attacks and had their defences ready. Two strikes were launched from the *Hermes*, nine Sea Harriers of 800 Squadron against the airfield at Port Stanley and three against the grass airstrip at Goose Green. While the Sea Harriers from *Hermes* carried out the bombing strikes six other Sea Harriers of 801 Squadron from *Invincible* armed with Sidewinder missiles maintained a combat air patrol (CAP) ready to intercept any Argentine aircraft which might attempt to attack the Harriers. All the aircraft faced heavy anti-aircraft fire but returned safely from the raid, one suffering only slight damage from a 20-mm shell which passed through the fin.

The Argentines launched a number of raids by Daggers against the Task Force, all of which failed to penetrate the CAP. While this intense aerial activity was taking place Sea King ASW helicopters maintained a continuous anti-submarine defensive screen some dozen miles ahead of the Task Force. Three other Sea Kings flew off north of the Falklands and joined the frigates *Brilliant* and *Yarmouth* in hunting for an Argentine submarine operating in the area, thought to be the Type 209 *San Luis*.

Later that afternoon the Argentine Air Force mounted another intense raid this time using the Canberra bombers and Skyhawks as well as Dag-

ABOVE: *A Mirage flies low over a logistic ship offloading in San Carlos Water.*

RIGHT: *Bombs fall among transports and amphibious ships. Fortunately most failed to detonate.*

gers. One of the Daggers was shot down by a heat-seeking Sidewinder missile and the other severely damaged, being eventually shot down by its own forces as it attempted an emergency landing on Port Stanley airfield. Another group of three Dagger aircraft peeled off to attack the *Glamorgan*, *Arrow* and *Alacrity* returning from a bombardment of the airfield. Flying very fast and low the aircraft penetrated the radar screen undetected and attacked the ships before they could react. Fortunately the ships received only very slight splinter damage from cannon fire, the *Arrow* being worst hit and *Alacrity* shaken by a near miss from a bomb. Following this a modern Type 22 frigate armed with Sea Wolf SAMs was detailed off to escort units carrying out bombardment missions.

Further raids against the Task Force led to another Dagger being downed by a Sidewinder while at dusk six Canberras roared in at low altitude on a bombing run. Before they could execute their raid they were bounced by the CAP and one of the Canberras was shot down by a Sidewinder.

And so the first day's full-scale fighting ended, the first round obviously having gone to the British Task Force, which had also inserted SAS and SBS patrols into the two main islands of the Falklands from the submarine *Onyx*. One thing it had proved was that the British pilots were much better at air-to-air combat than their Argentine counterparts. In skilled hands the AIM-9L Sidewinder was a deadly weapon and the Sea Harrier proved more than a match for the Dagger at medium altitude.

The following day, 2 May, was an unmitigated disaster for the Argentine Navy. It suffered a major loss which was to paralyse all further thought of major action by their navy. It left the British firmly in command of the sea, but still having to fight doggedly against unfavourable odds to ensure command in the air.

Throughout 1 May the Argentine cruiser *General Belgrano*, escorted by the two Exocet-armed destroyers *Hipolito Bouchard* and *Piedrabuena*, had patrolled an area southwest of the Falklands, between Isla de los Estados and Burdwood Bank. To the northwest, in the area near to the base at Comodoro Rivadavia, the carrier *Veinticinco de Mayo* with a sizable surface escort was preparing to carry out a major airstrike against the British Task Force scheduled for 2 May.

The Argentine naval forces were well placed to catch the Task Force in a gigantic pincer movement pivoted about the Falkland Islands with the *General Belgrano* ideally positioned to prevent any reinforcements or possible amphibious assault forces attempting to invade the Islands from South Georgia. She was also well placed to destroy any damaged units from the Task Force which might attempt to reach the haven of South Georgia.

By dawn on 2 May the Argentine carrier was in position to launch her air group against the British Task Force some 200 miles to the southeast. Wind conditions were not favourable for a catapult launch, however, and the proposed aerial attack had to be abandoned.

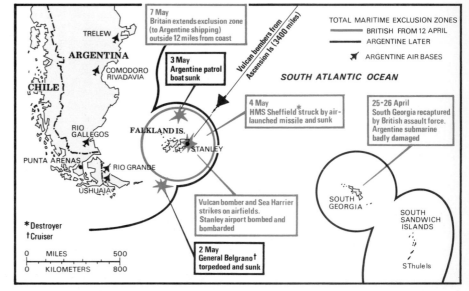

Meanwhile, unbeknown to the *Belgrano*, the submarine *Conqueror* (which had already disembarked its SBS troops) had detected the cruiser and been shadowing her at long range for at least two days. Following an exchange of signals with London the threat was deemed to be such that although the cruiser was some 36 miles outside the TEZ the *Conqueror* was ordered to sink her. Three unguided Mk 8 torpedoes were fired at the cruiser, one of which blew a great hole in her bows, another hitting her in the engine room. She began to settle by the stern and sank two hours later, with the eventual loss of 360-70 of her crew of 1042 in worsening weather conditions. The older Mk 8 torpedoes were used in preference to the modern Tigerfish Mk 24 torpedoes carried by *Conqueror*, as the latter would be needed for any subsequent action against submarines. The *Conqueror* was hounded for some two hours after the attack by the two escorting destroyers. Late in the evening of 2 May a Sea King Helicopter sighted the two armed tugs *Alferez Sobral* and *Comodoro Somellera* engaged in searching for survivors. The tugs fired on the helicopter which called up the Task Force for assistance. Two Lynx, armed with Sea Skua anti-ship missiles, were despatched. The Lynx from *Coventry* claimed to have sunk the *Somellera* with a Sea Skua while the *Glasgow*'s Lynx severely damaged the other tug.

The day of 4 May 1982 is one that will always be remembered by the Royal Navy. For it was then that Argentine Super Etendards, each armed with an Exocet anti-ship missile, carried out a text-book attack. Their target was the Type 42 destroyer *Sheffield*.

Coming in low, the aircraft each launched a missile. At the time the *Sheffield* was only in second-degree readiness rather than at full-action stations, in order to give the crew a short respite. The UAA-1 passive detection gear had been temporarily switched off to enable the ship's SCOT satellite communications system to be used; electro-magnetic interference from SCOT blanketed the UAA-1. *Sheffield* was not completely blind however for she still received radar data from the *Hermes*. For

ABOVE: *The theatre of operations stretched from the coast of Argentina down to South Thule in Antarctica.*

ABOVE RIGHT: *4 May 1982, the frigate* Arrow *plays hoses on the burning destroyer* Sheffield, *while a Sea King brings in spare firefighting gear.*

RIGHT: *A tranquil moment in San Carlos Water. A Sea Harrier is temporarily parked on the flight deck of an LPD, and the ammunition ship* Elk *and an LSL are in the background.*

a brief moment a radar contact was observed but
disappeared before identification could be definitely
established. Shortly after the UAA-1 picked up a
radar contact, but for various reasons, although it
indicated that an airborne radar had locked on to
Sheffield, this was not identified as a hostile threat.
The first indication that the ship was the subject of a
missile attack was when two officers on the bridge
spotted the flame and trail of smoke of the missile.
They only had time to shout a warning before the
missile struck the destroyer amidships four seconds
later. Penetrating the starboard side the missile
passed between the operations room and forward
machinery room. Although the warhead failed to
detonate the impact and friction as it passed through
the side plating set fire to a fuel tank. Serious fires
broke out, and the intense heat set the PVC cabling
on fire with catastrophic effects. Also set on fire
were many other plastic-based materials and almost
immediately thick black clouds of highly toxic fumes
including deadly phosgene and chlorine were released. It was these deadly fumes that were responsible for many of the fatalities, including all those in
the machinery control room, the damage control
centre and the galley, all of whom were asphyxiated.

The fires quickly gained a hold which damage-
control parties were almost powerless to counter, as
all power had been lost. Without power the ven-
tilation system ceased to operate and the fumes
quickly seeped throughout the whole ship, and left
the fire fighting parties unable to use the fire pumps.
To help fight the fires the frigate *Arrow* came alongside and passed hoses over while helicopters
winched down portable generators. Smoke
impeded all fire fighting attempts and it was decided
to abandon ship and take off the remaining survivors.
The gutted hulk finally foundered on 10 May.

With the sinking of the *Belgrano* and the loss of
the *Sheffield* there was no doubt that this was now
full-scale war which would be fought between the
air and sea forces operating around the Falklands.

The next few days were relatively quiet for the
Task Force and no major action took place,
although there were minor skirmishes in which further Argentine small craft were destroyed and bombardments continued. On 12 May the Argentine Air
Force returned to the fray. A raid by eight Skyhawks
was mounted against British warships bombarding
Port Stanley airfield. Both sides gained considerable experience from this raid. Fortunately for the
British, the Argentines failed to appreciate the
major reason for this determined raid not achieving
results. It was an old-fashioned bombing raid, for
which, after the loss of the *Sheffield* the British were
prepared. The low-level attack was directed against
the *Brilliant*. The *Brilliant* engaged the attackers
with Sea Wolf missiles; two of the attackers were
downed and a third crashed into the sea while trying
to avoid missiles. As the fourth Skyhawk pulled
clear the second flight of four ran in, three of them
concentrating on HMS *Glasgow* and one going for
HMS *Brilliant*. At this inopportune moment *Brilliant*'s Sea Wolf system malfunctioned, but the
bombs missed and struck the water.

One of the other Skyhawks scored a direct hit on
Glasgow. A 1000-lb bomb struck the destroyer amidships and passed clean through her hull to explode
in the sea clear of the ship. Fortunately *Glasgow* only
suffered superficial damage, and damage-control
parties soon made temporary repairs before the ship
withdrew to South Georgia to carry out more extensive repairs.

This action was interesting from two points of
view. First, it showed that while the Sea Dart system
was effective against aircraft at higher altitudes it
was not as effective as had been hoped against low-
flying targets. Obviously the Argentine pilots had
accurately assessed the weaknesses of the Type 42
as the Argentine Navy possessed two identical sister
ships. Further it was found that when engaging low-
altitude targets the gun control radar was severely
inhibited by surface clutter which adversely affected
the accuracy of the 4.5-inch gun in an anti-aircraft
role.

The Argentines failed to appreciate that
although determined low-level attacks were able to
penetrate the British defences, the bombs were released at an altitude too low to enable the fuzes to
arm themselves before they struck their target.

On the night of 14 May some 45 men of the SAS
and a small naval gunfire and communications party
from HMS *Hermes* were landed from three Sea
King HC4 helicopters on Pebble Island near to the
entrance to Falkland Sound. Supported by gunfire
from HMS *Glamorgan* they carried out a daring raid
on the air strip at Pebble Island destroying 11 aircraft
and a vital radar installation which could have given
the Argentines warning of forthcoming landings at
San Carlos.

LEFT: *One of* Fearless's *LCMs returning from the Falklands, loaded with Scimitar and Scorpion light armoured vehicles.*

BELOW LEFT: *HMS* Intrepid *looks spic and span after the Falklands, but only three months earlier she was stripped and rusty, ready for sale to Argentina.*

The decision of where to carry out the amphibious assault to retake the Falklands was made on board HMS *Fearless* on 10 May, the place chosen being Port San Carlos. Fortunately, the Argentines had selected other places as more likely landing sites for the assault they knew was bound to come.

The assault force began to gather on 18 May. Harrier reinforcements brought south aboard the converted air transport *Atlantic Conveyor* were transferred to the two carriers. Seven ships were detached from the Task Force to join the assault force to provide air defence and gunfire support for the troops going ashore. Late on the evening of 20 May the assault force began its final run into San Carlos Water prior to the landing on 21 May.

The assault force comprised the assault ships *Fearless* and *Intrepid*, the logistics ships *Sir Galahad*, *Sir Geraint*, *Sir Lancelot*, and *Sir Percivale*. The ferries *Europic Ferry* and *Norland*, and the *Canberra* carried the bulk of the troops for the main assault. The replenishment and stores vessels *Fort Austin* and *Stromness* made up the rest of the assault force. As escort the destroyer *Antrim* and frigates *Ardent*, *Argonaut*, *Brilliant*, *Broadsword*, *Yarmouth* and *Plymouth* were detached from the Task Force.

The first ship to enter San Carlos Water was the frigate *Plymouth*, designated to provide gunfire support for the troops as they went in. In the event this was not required for the assault met minimal resistance and by mid-morning the troops were well established ashore.

Apart from the *Plymouth*, which remained in San Carlos Water with the amphibious force, all the other escorts were disposed to block off the northern and southern entrances to the landings from

Argentine attack. To the north in Falkland Sound the *Broadsword* and *Argonaut* were on ASW patrol, to the south were *Yarmouth*, *Brilliant* and *Ardent*. The DLG *Antrim* patrolled the entrance to the Water ready to provide further gunfire support if required and deal with any aircraft which might break through and try to attack the landing ships.

The first Argentine reaction to the landings came from locally based Pucáras ground attack aircraft and Macchi 339s carrying out reconnaissance. In mid-morning a powerful raid was mounted by 16 Skyhawks escorted by Dagger fighters which attacked the landing forces in waves of four. The force was provided with CAP for air defence from the main Task Force.

As the first wave went in the ships in the Sound loosed off everything in their armoury at the attackers, the *Antrim* even firing an obsolete Seaslug missile as a deterrent. In this first attack the *Antrim* was struck aft by a 1000-lb bomb which failed to explode. The frigates *Broadsword* and *Argonaut* suffered slight damage from cannon fire.

The air attacks continued throughout the daylight hours. The *Argonaut* was attacked by six aircraft and struck by two 1000-lb bombs. Fortunately both failed to explode, but they caused heavy damage.

Immediately after this attack *Ardent*, in the most exposed position, was attacked. Further attacks on the frigate sealed her fate. Having been struck by

ABOVE: *A bomb falls near the RFA* Stromness *in 'Bomb Alley'.*

ABOVE LEFT: *LCM(9)s from HMS* Fearless *head for the beach at San Carlos.*

LEFT: *The burnt-out wreck of the LSL* Sir Galahad *was torpedoed by the* Conqueror *after hostilities were over.*

seven 1000-lb and five 500-lb bombs which exploded and two others which failed to detonate, *Ardent* was little more than a floating hulk and the crew abandoned ship to be rescued by HMS *Yarmouth* which came alongside. *Ardent* finally sank some six hours later.

But the Argentine pilots had not had everything all their own way. During the day losses sustained included five Skyhawks (four by Sea Harrier CAP), five Daggers (four by Sea Harrier CAP, one by Seacat missile), two Pucára (one by Sea Harrier CAP, one by Stinger portable missile), two Pumas and one Chinook (destroyed by an RAF Harrier).

Fighting during this first day proved beyond all doubt that no naval force could operate anywhere with any degree of security unless provided with adequate air cover, which the Royal Navy was hard put to provide.

As for the assault, this had succeeded beyond all expectations for two reasons: it faced virtually no resistance from Argentine land forces and the Argentine Air Force had been forced to devote all its efforts to dealing with the British escorts, which suffered heavily as a result. Had they concentrated on the vulnerable amphibious force the planned assault might have turned into a disaster.

Having spent the next day regrouping and assessing their successes and failures, the Argentine Air Force returned to the attack on 23 May. This time they varied their methods of attack and successive pairs of Daggers and Skyhawks attacked the ships and the troops ashore. HMS *Antelope*, which had joined the force in San Carlos to make up for losses, was singled out for attention and struck by two 500-lb bombs. They failed to denote, and a fire which started was brought under control. Later, one of the bombs detonated as a bomb-disposal expert tried to render it safe. An uncontrollable fire spread rapidly and the explosion of the *Antelope* against the night sky provided the world with a sobering and unforgettable news picture. *Antelope* was abandoned and sank next day.

Six Argentine aircraft were also destroyed the same day, five of them by Sea Harriers of the CAP.

On 25 May, Argentine Independence Day, the air attacks reached their peak, with an almost kami-kaze-style ferocity. The destroyer *Coventry* was attacked twice, to the north of Falkland Sound; three bombs from the second attack penetrated deep into the hull before exploding. The *Coventry* began to list heavily and the crew abandoned ship before she rolled over and sank.

Later in the day it was the turn of the Task Force operating northwest of the Falklands to come under attack. The attack was carried out by two Argentine Navy Super Etendards armed with Exocet missiles. Flying in low the aircraft launched two missiles at the carriers. Chaff decoys were launched and one Exocet was decoyed away but it locked on to the air transport ship *Atlantic Conveyor* and exploded below decks starting an intense fire which spread rapidly. The ship had to be abandoned and foundered on 30

BELOW: *The wrecked and burning hulk of the* Atlantic Conveyor *was left to drift after she had been abandoned. On 31 May Argentine Navy Super Etendards wasted their last Exocet on her.*

ABOVE: *HMS* Invincible *surrounded by small boats on her return in August 1982. Despite Argentine claims she showed no sign of damage from missile hits.*

May. This was a terrible blow, for although the Sea Harriers she had brought south had all been transferred to the carriers, the *Atlantic Conveyor* still carried on board three large Chinook heavy lift helicopters, six Wessexes and a Lynx as well as vast quantities of stores essential for the planned advance across the Falklands.

Supporting the Land Campaign

On 28 May the main focus of operations switched to the land as the troops moved out of the beachhead in two directions, but the Navy's task was not over. A daring leap-frogging move to land troops at Bluff Cove on the southeast of the island turned to disaster on 8 June. During the previous night the LSL *Sir Tristram* had landed Rapier missile batteries and a large quantity of ammunition. For various reasons the second LSL, *Sir Galahad*, had not disembarked her Welsh Guard by daylight. Before the troops began disembarking the Argentines mounted an air raid with five Daggers and five Skyhawks. On the way in to the attack from different directions the Daggers passed over Falkland Sound where any possibility of surprise was lost as HMS *Plymouth*

spotted them. The Argentine aircraft attacked *Plymouth* instead hitting her with four bombs, none of which exploded. The remaining five Skyhawks carried on to attack the two LSLs – three selecting *Sir Galahad* and two *Sir Tristram*. *Sir Galahad* was struck by two bombs which exploded, setting fire to the ship and turning her into a wreck. *Sir Tristram* was also set on fire and severely damaged, but was subsequently salvaged and repaired. A total of 57 troops and crewmen were killed and 46 injured.

A little way up the coast HMS *Fearless* was also attacked and one of her landing craft was sunk. After this there were no further attacks against the Task Force. But the Navy had still to suffer casualties.

On the night of 11-12 June HMS *Glamorgan*, while carrying out a night bombardment of Argentine positions near Port Stanley was struck by an Exocet missile fired from a land-based launcher at a range of some 18 miles. Again the missile failed to explode, but the destroyer was badly damaged and 13 of her crew killed.

Three days later it was all over, and General Menendez surrendered his Argentine troops on the Falklands.

Chapter 10
The Future

Those who regard history as an endlessly repetitive cycle would find much to confirm that theory in the public reaction to the events of 1982. The initial anger at the invasion gave way quickly to an absurd outbreak of jingoistic fervour. Then came the shock of reality when the shooting war had started.

There was understandable dismay at the apparent ease with which the Argentine Air Force and Navy aircraft penetrated the Task Force's defences. What was less easy to justify was the rush to blame the Navy's designers for these faults. The press latched on to the use of aluminium alloy for superstructures, and publicized alleged stability problems caused by the adoption of gas turbines in place of steam power. Fierce denunciation of the French as 'merchants of death' ignored the fact that the Royal Navy had been the first purchaser of the Exocet anti-ship missile, and had sent several Exocet-armed ships to the Falklands.

Warship design is poorly understood, even by naval officers, and in the hands of laymen its principles are very soon distorted. Amid demands to take ship design out of the hands of the Royal Corps of Naval Constructors and give it to private designers, nobody remembered that the use of aluminium in British warships had only been permitted in one class – privately designed in the 1960s. Nor, as a Parliamentary enquiry discovered, did the loss of two of that class, the *Antelope* and *Ardent*, result from the use of aluminium. Similarly, closer investigation revealed that the rumour about stability was related, not to gas turbines, but to a problem with marine growths in oil fuel. Older frigates designed to float oil fuel on seawater ballast were forbidden to use water ballast in peacetime. Naturally this restriction did not apply in wartime or in an emergency.

PREVIOUS PAGE: *The nuclear-powered submarine is the most formidable fighting vessel that the Royal Navy possesses. Here a* Dreadnought-*Class boat puts out to sea.*

LEFT: *The destroyer* Manchester *'takes it green' during the Far East leg of the 'Global 86' round-the world deployment.*

RIGHT: *HMS* Hermes *in 1983, during her last commission. In 1986 she was sold to India and became INS* Virat.

ABOVE: Battleaxe *coming alongside* Invincible *during exercises in the spring of 1985.*

LEFT: *HMS* Boxer *was the first of the 'stretched' Type 22 frigates, enlarged to provide more processing capacity for data from new sonars.*

The design of a new frigate, designated Type 23, was well advanced in 1982 and the opportunity was taken to incorporate many Falkland Islands lessons. The hull was divided into five smoke zones rather than three, and the Sea Wolf missile system was given a second tracker to enhance its air defence capability.

The Sea Wolf missile had been designed to cope with anti-ship missiles, but in the light of Falklands experience it was decided to provide ships with an additional 'layer' of air defence in the form of a close-range gun system. The American Navy's 20-mm Phalanx 'Gatling' gun system had been rushed into service in June 1982, but after prolonged evaluation the heavier Dutch Goalkeeper system was bought. Like the Phalanx it uses a rotary gun to direct a steam of solid projectiles in the path of an incoming missile. The first Goalkeeper was delivered at the end of 1986.

In 1981 it had been decreed that the Navy's ships would no longer get 'mid-life' refits, but this ill-judged economy was soon overturned. The welcome news was announced that the weaknesses of the Type 42 destroyers would be remedied. They would receive the new air defence radar designed for the Type 23s and would also be rearmed with Phalanx 'Gatlings' and possible Sea Wolf missiles. In January 1987 Type 42s received two Phalanx guns each.

Although the subject of electronic warfare (EW) remains highly secret, the failure of HMS *Sheffield's* passive defences brought the EW specialist 'out of the closet' to some extent. Commercial equipment was bought as a stopgap in 1982, but work on a new system was accelerated for the Type 23 and other ships. More important, EW training was given a higher priority.

The Fleet Air Arm's long fight for survival had been amply vindicated by the air battle over the Falklands. In addition to replacements for the losses of aircraft and helicopters, sufficient new Sea Harriers were ordered to provide two squadrons of eight aircraft each by 1988. At the same time the existing aircraft were to be modernized, with an improved radar and new air-to-air missiles.

Although the sale of HMS *Invincible* was rescinded the decision to run only two carriers air groups remained in force. In theory as each carrier goes into refit her air group transfers to the new carrier coming forward to replace her in the Fleet, but in practice it results in great strain on the aircrews and maintainers. The Fleet Air Arm tried this idea in the 1960s, and the result was a steady flow of highly specialized ratings and officers leaving the service for good.

The long-term damage done is not confined to the strain on men and aircraft. Aircrew need time to rest and practise new tactics, a task which is best done after a period at sea followed by leave. A rapid turn-around may look efficient on paper but it tends to be counter-productive.

Keeping HMS *Invincible* prevented the nightmare of trying to run a Fleet Air Arm with only two ships. The third of the class, *Ark Royal*, was cannibalized to get HMS *Illustrious* to sea at the end of Operation Corporate, but the delay in completion did enable a number of improvements to be made. Her ski-jump was extended, the number of close-in weapons was increased to three (two in her sisters) and the stowage of torpedoes and sonobuoys was increased by 50 percent. HMS *Invincible* went into Plymouth Naval Base in 1986 for a two-year refit to bring her up to the same standard.

Although the four ships lost in action in 1982 were Type 21 frigates (*Antelope* and *Ardent*) and Type 42 destroyers (*Coventry* and *Sheffield*) the Navy Board asked for four more Type 22 anti-submarine frigates. They were, however, to be redesigned with a more flexible weapon-fit to enable them to undertake general-purpose duties. In practice this resulted in the provision of a 4.5-inch gun forwards, eight Harpoon anti-ship missiles in place of four Exocets, provision for the new large EH101 helicopter, and the first Goalkeeper close-in weapon system. The first of class, the *Cornwall*, received her Goalkeeper in February 1987. To commemorate the Falklands losses two of the previous *Boxer* group were given the names *Coventry* and *Sheffield* instead of 'B' names.

Pre-1982 these big frigates had been heavily criticized but in battle their combination of size and excellent anti-submarine capability proved most useful. They had the seaworthiness to cope with the worst weather, an air defence system which proved deadly and an excellent passive long-range sonar. Only two, *Broadsword* and *Brilliant*, went to the South Atlantic in 1982 but both acquitted themselves well.

The *Cornwall*, *Cumberland*, *Campbeltown* and *Chatham* will bring the total of new frigates to 14, in three batches. The next design is the Type 23

PREVIOUS PAGE: *HMS* Invincible *firing a Sea Dart missile. At the after end of the flight deck, and alongside the missile launcher are Phalanx 'Gatling' guns for short-range defence against missiles.*

RIGHT: *The Westland AEW Sea King helicopter provides naval forces with long-range airborne early warning of threats from low-flying aircraft and surface vessels.*

LEFT: *The old destroyer* Devonshire *goes down after being hit by a Tigerfish torpedo during 1985 trials.*

PREVIOUS PAGE: *The Type 42 destroyer HMS* Sheffield, *a victim of the Falklands conflict. Past-Falklands, the Type 42s received a new air defence radar and improved Close In Weapon System (CIWS) defences.*

ABOVE: *HMS* Trafalgar *leaving Barrow on trials. She and her sisters are the latest SSNs in service, and will be followed by the SSN-20 design in the 1990s.*

RIGHT: *The RN puts its faith in simulation to provide cost-effective training. The 'Tactician' submarine command trainer has been installed recently at HMS* Neptune, *the submarine base at Faslane.*

'Duke' Class, slightly smaller but intended to provide even better anti-submarine qualities. The lead-ship is HMS *Norfolk*, and orders have been placed for *Argyll*, *Salisbury* and *Lancaster*.

The Type 23 is claimed to be the most advanced ship of its type in the world. Its superstructure is designed for minimum radar-reflection, and its machinery is designed to reduce noise to the lowest possible level, to gain maximum effect out of the towed sonar array. In addition the ships will be the first armed with the vertically launched version of the Sea Wolf.

By 1987 the older surface warships had nearly all gone to the scrapheap or had been sold to overseas navies. The last of the 'County' Class destroyers HMS *Fife* was partially disarmed for training duties, the last of the early Type 12 frigates had nearly all gone, and the first of the *Leander* Class had been put on the Disposal List.

After many years of neglect the mine warfare forces are being replaced and upgraded. As for the frigates, the big but very capable 'Hunt' Class mine countermeasures vessels (MCMVs) had been widely criticized when they first appeared, but the ability of two of them to steam 8000 miles to Port Stanley showed the soundness of the design. These 725-ton ships are still the largest glass-reinforced plastic ships in the world, and are regarded as the most sophisticated minehunters in the world. Inevitably they are very expensive and two new classes were ordered, to undertake simpler tasks at a reasonable cost. A dozen steel-hulled Fleet Mine-sweepers (MSFs) had been built to sweep deep-laid mines and a new class of GRP single-role mine-

hunters has been ordered.

The story of the Royal Navy's Submarine Service follows much the same pattern as the surface fleet but with one important difference. The nuclear attack-submarine (SSN) and the nuclear ballistic missile submarine (SSBN) are the capital ships of today's Royal Navy. The prototype HMS *Dreadnought* was taken out of service some years ago. But the five *Valiant* and *Churchill* Classes will continue in service for some time. The six *Swiftsures* have been followed by the *Trafalgar* Class since 1983. When the seventh boat, *Triumph*, joins the Fleet in 1990, the next class designated *SSN-20* will be under construction.

Despite bitter opposition from the anti-nuclear lobby the British Government pressed ahead with its plans to replace the Polaris missile system as the nuclear deterrent, and the first of four *Vanguard* Class SSBNs was ordered to 1986. They are designed to operate the same Trident D5 6000-mile range missiles as the US Navy. As each *Vanguard* Class becomes fully operational from 1991 onwards one of the *Resolution* Class Polaris boats will be withdrawn. A greater degree of reliability will, it is hoped, reduce the burden of maintaining one SSBN on patrol at all times.

Since 1981 all British SSNs have been rearmed with the American Sub-Harpoon missile in addition to torpedoes, giving them much greater punch against surface targets. In 1986 after many years of teething troubles, Flag Officer Submarines announced that the Tigerfish Mod 2 torpedo had passed all tests with flying colours, removing doubts about his submarines' weaponry. The next generation, the Spearfish, promises to be a more lethal weapon against the latest Soviet submarines, with a speed of 55 knots down to a depth of 3000 feet.

The Trident SSBNs and the new *SSN-20* design will have a new British-designed pressurized-water nuclear reactor, the PWR2. With 20 years of experience behind it, the new reactor and steam plant will be more powerful, quieter and have a longer core-life.

For many years the Royal Navy's submariners talked of an all-nuclear force but in the 1970s it became apparent that the tempo of training could not be maintained unless replacements for the diesel-electric *Oberon* and *Porpoise* Classes were ordered. There was another equally important reason for building a new class of diesel-electric hunter-killer boats (SSKs). Only SSKs can operate in shallow waters and for reconnaissance missions in hostile water their exceptional quietness is unmatched by an SSN.

The first of a new class of SSK, the *Upholder* was ordered in November 1983 and she was launched just over three years later. Three more, the *Unseen*, *Ursula* and *Unicorn* were ordered in 1986 and an eventual total of 10 boats is planned. One unusual feature of these boats is the use for the first time of a French sonar showing an admirable degree of European collaboration.

Although criticized by some for being too large the Type 2400 design devotes a great deal of its

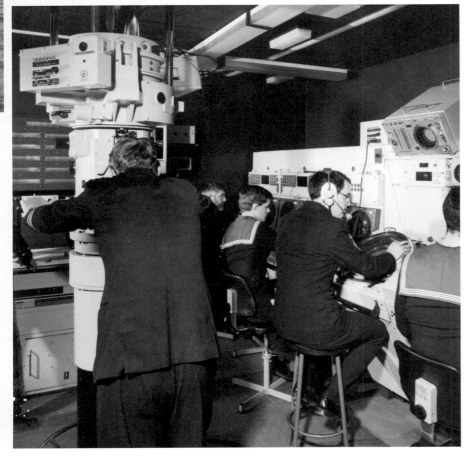

internal volume to weapons and systems. The Naval Staff Requirement called for an offensive capability comparable to an SSN, which dictates a powerful armament and sensor-fit.

The 13 *Oberon* Class boats were an outstanding design, and are still rated as very quiet SSKs. In 1985 the *Opossum* completed a comprehensive modernization which included the provision of a new sonar, Type 2051, and fire-control system. Another nine boats are in the process of getting the same update, giving the Navy a force of 10 boats to serve until the *Upholders* are fully operational.

One of the most controversial cuts proposed by John Nott in 1981 was the rundown of amphibious forces. After considerable vacillation this decision (which would have meant the virtual extinction of the Royal Marines) was reversed in 1986. The Secretary of State for Defence announced that Swan Hunter Shipbuilders would receive a contract to study the feasibility of extending the service life of the LPDs *Fearless* and *Intrepid*, giving time to prepare designs for their successors.

The Royal Navy's critics, including some of its staunchest supporters, often accuse its senior officers of failing to fight the 'Whitehall Battle' as skilfully as its two rivals the Army and the Air Force. There is much truth in this, but since 1982 the Navy has successfully captialized on public sympathy to get approval for the purchase of 15 Goalkeeper CIWS, four *Cornwall* Class and four 'Duke' Class frigates, four *Upholder* Class submarines and numerous systems and pieces of equipment. Despite considerable sniping from its main rival the RAF it had not lost the new EH101 heavyweight ASW helicopter, and it fought off British industrial pressure to stop the purchase of an American anti-ship missile.

However, the future is not as rosy as it might seem. The cost of equipment is spiralling and there is constant pressure on the Navy to cut back. Manpower remains the most expensive asset, and sadly one of the first by-products of parsimony is large-scale departures from the Service.

One of the most scandalous elements of the Nott 'reforms' was a review of training called Slimtrain. After years of heavy investment in short-based training, relying on simulators to give ratings and officers realistic but cost-effective training on the Navy's most complex weapon systems, the cry went up, 'Get them back to sea'. The folly of this can be compared to a policy of training airline pilots on real aircraft, rather than simulators. By 1986 the drawbacks of Slimtrain's more exuberant concepts had been reversed, but not without inflicting serious damage on the Navy's widely admired standards of training.

One of the lessons of Operation Corporate was the apparent success of extemporized conversions of merchant ships. However, in the sober light of day it was realized that 'lash-ups' in an emergency were no substitute for more detailed conversions. To test the concept of an auxiliary Air Support Ship the container ship SS *Astronomer* (taken up from trade in 1982) was given a much fuller conversion in

1983. Advantage was taken of the American ARAPAHO project, and a portable flight deck and pre-fabricated hangar were acquired from the US Navy.

Named as the RFA *Reliant*, the ship was only a qualified success. The grid flight deck was not popular (spanners and screwdrivers tended to fall through the holes) and the pre-fabricated hangar leaked at the joints. In 1986 the ship was put on the disposal list, but the Navy was not willing to abandon such a promising idea. In 1984 another STUFT (Ships Take Up From Trade) veteran of the South Atlantic, the container ship SS *Contender Bezant* was taken up for a much more elaborate conversion.

The role of the new RFA, to be named *Argus*, is that of an Aviation Training Ship (ATS) to replace the 20-year-old RFA *Engadine*. The shipbuilders Harland and Wolff have put in new watertight bulkheads, a full operations room, two lifts and air ordnance magazines. In peacetime the ship's main role will be to take ASW helicopters out to deep-sea excercise areas, saving flying time and wear-and-tear on pilots and airframes. In wartime or emergency she will also be capable of transporting up to 12 Sea Harriers, and, of course, can also function as an auxiliary aircraft carrier.

The true lesson of the Falklands is that big mercantile hulls can be turned into very effective auxiliary warships but they must be given quite elaborate conversions if they are to operate with naval forma-

TOP RIGHT: *The RFA* Olmeda *replenishing the frigate* Alacrity *between Shanghai and Hong Kong in July 1986.*

RIGHT: *Builder's model of the Type 23 'Duke' class, the first of which was launched in June 1987. The ship is exceptionally quiet and has a reduced radar-profile.*

tions. If not, they are far too vulnerable and under-equipped to be risked in battle.

The Royal Fleet Auxiliary's present status as a quasi-mercantile force, operational directed and controlled by the Royal Navy, but manned by the Merchant Navy, is undergoing change to meet today's operating conditions. Its role remains the support of the Royal Navy, providing its fuel, ammunition and stores of all kinds, but the growing likelihood of limited war, or even quasi-war such as the Falklands fighting make it imperative to provide RFAs with heavier defensive armament. That will rob the ships of their exemption for warship status, and current thinking is that the RFA will have to come under full naval control. It is not a popular change but the conditions of the later 1980s make the old ambiguous status an anachronism.

As the Royal Navy approaches the end of the twentieth century it can be proud of its reputation. The Royal Navy's conduct in the two World Wars and the Falklands demonstrated these qualities to the full. Its traditions are respected but above all it is respected for its professionalism and its high standards of training and discipline. As always its peacetime enemies proved more dangerous than its wartime opponents. If the former can be held at bay the Royal Navy will continue to render the nation and its allies the good service it has done for centuries.

Acknowledgements

The Publisher would like to thank Adrian Hodgkins for the design of the book and Ron Watson who compiled the index. We would like to thank the following picture agencies, institutions and individuals for supplying illustrations on the pages noted:

Archiv Gerstenberg: pages 38-9, 42 (bottom), 43 (bottom), 46, 47 (both)
HMS Ark Royal: pages 174 (top), 178 (top), 179, 185 (top), 186 (bottom)
BBC Hulton Picture Library: pages 40 (top), 68 (top)
Berken of Cowes Ltd: pages 24-5, 144-5
Bison Picture Library: pages 14 (top), 34, 80, 128 (top)
British Aerospace Aircraft Group: pages 180-1

Cammell Laird Shipbuilders Ltd: pages 90-1, 92, 93 (top), 94, 95, 96, 98 (both), 99 (both), 100-1, 102, 103 (both), 106-7, 110
Crown Copyright: page 203 (bottom)
Ferranti Computer Systems: page 219 (bottom)
Fleet Photographic Unit, Portsmouth: pages 197 (top), 199 (bottom), 202 (top) 212-3, 216-7
Robert Hunt Library: pages 19, 22, 50, 56, 57
Imperial War Museum: pages 20 (right), 28 (both), 30-1, 32-3, 36, 37, 40 (bottom), 41, 45, 48 (both), 49 (both), 51, 52 (both), 53, 55, 58, 59, 74 (bottom), 108, 116, 118-9 (both), 122, 123, 124, 125 (top), 128 (bottom), 130, 132, 136, 142, 143 (bottom), 148, 149, 150, 153 (both), 154, 156 (top), 167 (top), 193, 194, 196, 197 (bottom)
Mike Lennon: pages 156 (bottom), 201 (bottom)
Marconi Underwater Systems: page 218 (bottom)
Ministry of Defence/Land Forces: page 203 (top)
Ministry of Defence/Navy Department: pages 25 (inset), 157, 176, 177 (top), 184, 186 (top), 187, 209
National Maritime Museum London: pages 6-7, 9, 10 (top), 11, 12-3, 15, 23, 26 (left), 42 (top) 54-5 (main picture & left), 60-1, 62 (both), 63 (both), 64 (both), 65 (both), 66 (both), 68 (bottom), 69 (both), 71, 75 (bottom), 78, 93 (bottom), 125 (bottom), 131, 135 (bottom), 146-7 (main picture)
Newark Public Library Picture Collection: page 8
Anthony Preston Picture Collection: pages 10 (bottom), 14 (both), 16-7, 18, 20 (right), 21, 27, 56, 67 (both), 70, 72-3, 76-7 (both), 79, 81 (both), 82-3 (both), 84-5 (both), 97 (bottom), 104-5, 109, 112, 117 (bottom), 132-3 (main picture & right), 134 (top), 135 (top), 138, 139, 141, 142-3, 146-7 (top), 152, 155, 158, 162-3 (both), 167 (bottom), 168-9, 170-1, 172-3 (both), 174 (bottom), 175, 177 (bottom 2), 178 (bottom), 182-3 (bottom), 188, 189, 192, 195 (both), 199 (top), 200-1, 204-5 (both pictures), 208, 211, 220-21 (both)
C&S Taylor: pages 160-1
TPS/Central Press Agency: pages 121 (bottom), 151
TPS/Keystone: page 114-5
TPS/3 Lions: page 117 (top)
US Navy: pages 43 (top), 86-7, 88-9 (both)
VSEL Barrow-In-Furness: page 218 (top)
Vickers Shipbuilding: page 113
Vosper Ltd, Portsmouth: pages 182-83 (bottom)
Westland Helicopters Ltd: page 214-5Yarrow Shipbuilders: pages 97 (top), 111, 180 (bottom), 181 (bottom), 185 (bottom), 210